THE RELIGIOUS QUEST OF INDIA (SERIES-04)

THE HEART OF JAINISM

THE RELIGIOUS QUEST OF INDIA (SERIES-04)

THE HEART OF JAINISM

By

MRS. SINCLAIR STEVENSON
M.A., SC.D (DUBLIN)

GYAN

Published by

Gyan Publishing House
5, Ansari Road
Daryaganj, New Delhi-110002
Phone: 011-47034999, 9811692060
E-mail: books@gyanbooks.com

Distribution Network
gyanbooks.com
India, USA, Canada, UK, Australia, France

ISBN : 978-81-212-6794-6 (PB)
First Published, 1915

2nd Impression 2023

Printed at: Gyan Press, Delhi.

THE RELIGIOUS QUEST OF INDIA (SERIES-04)
The Heart of Jainism
Author: MRS. SINCLAIR STEVENSON

THE RELIGIOUS QUEST OF INDIA

EDITED BY

J. N. FARQUHAR, M.A.

LITERARY SECRETARY, NATIONAL COUNCIL OF YOUNG MEN'S CHRISTIAN ASSOCIATIONS, INDIA AND CEYLON

AND

H. D. GRISWOLD, M.A., PH.D.

SECRETARY OF THE COUNCIL OF THE AMERICAN PRESBYTERIAN MISSIONS IN INDIA

UNIFORM WITH THIS VOLUME

ALREADY PUBLISHED

INDIAN THEISM, FROM THE VEDIC TO THE MUHAMMADAN PERIOD.	By NICOL MACNICOL, M.A., D.Litt. Pp. xvi + 292. Price 6s. net.

IN PREPARATION

THE RELIGIOUS LITERATURE OF INDIA.	By J. N. FARQUHAR, M.A.
THE RELIGION OF THE ṚIGVEDA.	By H. D. GRISWOLD, M.A., PH.D.
THE VEDĀNTA . . .	By A. G. HOGG, M.A., Christian College, Madras.
HINDU ETHICS . . .	By JOHN MCKENZIE, M.A., Wilson College, Bombay.
BUDDHISM	By K. J. SAUNDERS, M.A., Literary Secretary, National Council of Y.M.C.A., India and Ceylon.
ISLAM IN INDIA . .	By H. A. WALTER, M.A., Literary Secretary, National Council of Y.M.C.A., India and Ceylon.

EDITORIAL PREFACE

THE writers of this series of volumes on the variant forms of religious life in India are governed in their work by two impelling motives.

I. They endeavour to work in the sincere and sympathetic spirit of science. They desire to understand the perplexingly involved developments of thought and life in India and dispassionately to estimate their value. They recognize the futility of any such attempt to understand and evaluate, unless it is grounded in a thorough historical study of the phenomena investigated. In recognizing this fact they do no more than share what is common ground among all modern students of religion of any repute. But they also believe that it is necessary to set the practical side of each system in living relation to the beliefs and the literature, and that, in this regard, the close and direct contact which they have each had with Indian religious life ought to prove a source of valuable light. For, until a clear understanding has been gained of the practical influence exerted by the habits of worship, by the practice of the ascetic, devotional or occult discipline, by the social organization and by the family system, the real impact of the faith upon the life of the individual and the community cannot be estimated; and, without the advantage of extended personal intercourse, a trustworthy account of the religious experience of a community can scarcely be achieved by even the most careful student.

II. They seek to set each form of Indian religion by the side of Christianity in such a way that the relationship may stand out clear. Jesus Christ has become to them the light of all their seeing, and they believe Him destined to be the light of the world. They are persuaded that sooner or later the age-long quest of the Indian spirit for religious truth and power will find in Him at once its goal and a new starting-point, and they will be content if the preparation of this series contributes in the smallest degree to hasten this consummation. If there be readers to whom this motive is unwelcome, they may be reminded that no man approaches the study of a religion without religious convictions, either positive or negative: for both reader and writer, therefore, it is better that these should be explicitly stated at the outset. Moreover, even a complete lack of sympathy with the motive here acknowledged need not diminish a reader's interest in following an honest and careful attempt to bring the religions of India into comparison with the religion which to-day is their only possible rival, and to which they largely owe their present noticeable and significant revival.

It is possible that to some minds there may seem to be a measure of incompatibility between these two motives. The writers, however, feel otherwise. For them the second motive reinforces the first: for they have found that he who would lead others into a new faith must first of all understand the faith that is theirs already,—understand it, moreover, sympathetically, with a mind quick to note not its weaknesses alone but that in it which has enabled it to survive and has given it its power over the hearts of those who profess it.

The duty of the editors of the series is limited to seeing that the volumes are in general harmony with the principles here described. Each writer is alone responsible for the opinions expressed in his volume, whether in regard to Indian religions or to Christianity.

THE RELIGIOUS QUEST OF INDIA

THE HEART OF JAINISM

BY

MRS. SINCLAIR STEVENSON
M.A., Sc.D. (DUBLIN)
OF THE IRISH MISSION IN GUJARĀT
SOMETIME SCHOLAR OF SOMERVILLE COLLEGE, OXFORD
AUTHOR OF 'NOTES ON MODERN JAINISM', 'FIRST STEPS IN GUJARĀTĪ'
'ON SOME PAINTERS OF THE RENAISSANCE', ETC.

1915

Fecisti nos ad te, et inquietum est cor nostrum donec requiescat in te.

(*Conf. Div. Aur. Augustini*, i. 1.)

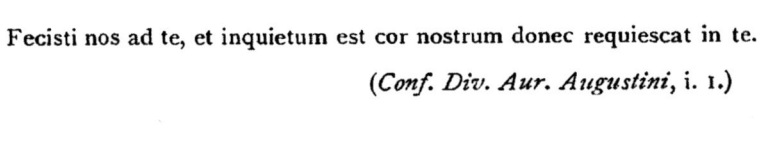

TO MY HUSBAND

WITH

HAPPY MEMORIES

OF

NINE YEARS' COMRADESHIP

IN WORK AND PLAY

PREFATORY NOTE

Amongst the many friends, Indian and English, whose help has made the production of this little book possible, the writer owes a special debt of gratitude to the Rev. G. P. Taylor, M.A., D.D., who years ago first directed her attention to Jainism as an almost untrodden field for research, and who ever since has allowed her to make the fullest use of his unrivalled stores of oriental scholarship; to Mr. J. N. Farquhar, M.A., from whom she has received constant help and suggestion, especially in the compilation of the Historical Summary and the paragraphs on Jaina writers; and to her husband, who, when she was hindered by illness, not only prepared the index, but also undertook, together with Mr. Farquhar, the whole of the proof correcting.

Amongst her Indian friends, the writer would like to thank two Jaina paṇḍits, who successively lectured to her in Rājkot (Kāṭhiāwāḍ) almost daily during a period of seven years, for the patience and lucidity with which they expounded their creed. Each of these gentlemen, the one representing perhaps the more modern, and the other the more conservative, points of view, most kindly re-read the MS. with her.

In her study of Jainism, however, the writer is not only indebted to paṇḍits, but also to nuns in various Apāsarā, to officiants in beautiful Jaina temples, to wandering monks, happy-go-lucky Jaina schoolboys and thoughtful students, as well as to grave Jaina merchants and their delightful wives. Nearly all these informants spoke Gujarātī, but the technical words they used in discussing their faith were sometimes of Gujarātī, sometimes of Māgadhī and sometimes of Sanskrit origin. This 'use', which seems to be one of the idioms of Jainism, the writer has tried to reproduce by transliterating the actual words employed, believing that thus her work would retain more of the character of field-study and have less of the odour of midnight oil than if she had standardized and sanskritized all the terms.

But whatever language they spoke, every one whom the writer asked showed the same readiness to help; indeed almost every fact recorded in this book owes its presence there to the courtesy of some Jaina friend, and every page seems to the writer water-marked with some one's kindness. The difficulty of the task has sometimes seemed overwhelming; but never perhaps does the magnificent old motto *Dominus illuminatio mea* prove a greater inspiration than when one is attempting sympathetically to decipher an alien creed; and to no one does it, together with its sister-saying *Magna est veritas et praevalebit*, ring a happier carillon of hope than to the foreign missionary.

MARGARET STEVENSON.

DUBLIN,
St. Patrick's Day, 1915.

CONTENTS

CHAPTER I

PAGE

INTRODUCTORY 1

The ideal of Indian thought death, not life—Attraction of asceticism—Revolt against Brāhman exclusiveness—Rise of Buddhist and Jaina orders.

CHAPTER II

HISTORICAL SUMMARY 7

The sixth century—Mahāvīra—Order of Pārśvanātha—Sudharma and his successors—The great famine and consequent migration under Bhadrabāhu to Mysore—Sthūlabhadra and the Council of Pāṭaliputra—The Canon of Scriptures—The nudity question—Idolatry—Suhastin—Disruption into Śvetāmbara and Digambara sects—Council of Vallabhi—The Scriptures—Zenith of Jainism—Decline under Mohammedan and Śaiva persecution—Rise of Sthānakavāsī sect—Modern conditions.

CHAPTER III

THE LIFE OF MAHĀVĪRA 21

Birthplace—The fourteen dreams—Birth—Childhood and legends—Initiation—Pārśvanātha's Order—Legends of Mahāvīra's asceticism—Enlightenment—Preaching—Death—Previous incarnations.

CHAPTER IV

MAHĀVĪRA'S PREDECESSORS AND DISCIPLES . . . 48

Pārśvanātha—The Four Vows of Pārśvanātha—The twenty-two earlier Tīrthaṅkara :—Ṛiṣabhadeva—Ajitanātha—Sambhavanātha — Abhinandana — Sumatinātha—Padmaprabhu — Supārśvanātha—Ċandraprabhu—Suvidhinātha—Śītaḷanātha—Śreyāṁsanātha —Vāsupūjya — Vimaḷanātha — Anantanātha — Dharmanātha—Śāntinātha—Kunthunātha—Aranātha—Mallinātha — Munisuvrata — Naminātha — Neminātha — The Followers of Mahāvīra :—Gośāla—Gautama Indrabhūti—Sermon by Mahāvīra—Sudharma.

CONTENTS

CHAPTER V

PAGE

HISTORY OF THE JAINA COMMUNITY 65

CHAPTER VI

INTRODUCTION TO JAINA PHILOSOPHY . . . 89

CHAPTER VII

THE NINE CATEGORIES OF FUNDAMENTAL TRUTHS 94

CONTENTS

CONTENTS

CHAPTER XIII

CHAPTER XIV

CHAPTER XV

CHAPTER XVI

APPENDIX

BIBLIOGRAPHY

Barodia, U. D., *History and Literature of Jainism*, Bombay, 1909.

Benārsi Dāss, Lāla, *Lecture on Jainism*, Agra, 1902.

Bhandarkar, R. G., *Report on the Search for Sanskrit Manuscripts in the Bombay Presidency during the year 1883–4*, Bombay, 1887.

Bombay Gazetteer, vol. ix, part I.

Bühler, J. G., *On the Indian Sect of the Jainas* (translated and edited with an outline of Jaina mythology by J. Burgess), London, 1903.

—— *Ueber das Leben des Jaina-Mönches Hemachandra*, Vienna, 1889.

Colebrooke, H. T., *Miscellaneous Essays*, vol. ii, London, 1873.

Crooke, W., Article on *Indian Religions* in the Imperial Gazetteer of India, vol. i, Oxford, 1909.

De Milloué, *Essai sur la religion des Jains*, Le Muséon, Louvain, 1884.

Encyclopedia of Religion and Ethics (E.R.E.): articles on Jaina topics.

Girnāra Māhātmya (in Gujarātī).

Guérinot, A. A., *Essai de bibliographie jaina*, Paris, 1906.

Hoernle, A. F. R., *Annual Address*, Asiatic Society of Bengal (A.S.B.), Calcutta, 1898.

—— *Uvāsagadasāo*, Calcutta, 1890.

Hopkins, E. W., *The Religions of India*, Boston, 1895.

Jacobi, H., *Sacred Books of the East* (S.B.E.), vols. xxii and xlv.

—— *The Metaphysics and Ethics of the Jainas* (Transactions of the Congress for the History of Religion), Oxford, 1908.

—— *Edition of Hemacandra's Pariśiṣṭa Parvan* (Bibl. Ind.), Calcutta, 1891.

Jaina Dharma Praveśa Pothī Series, Ahmadābād, 1907 (in Gujarātī).

Jaini, Manak Chand, *Life of Mahāvīra*, Allahabad, 1908.

Jhaveri, J. L., *First Principles of Jaina Philosophy*, Bombay, 1912.

Latthe, A. B., *An Introduction to Jainism*, Bombay, 1905.

'Seeker', *Notes on the Sthanakwasi or the non-Idolatrous Shwetambar Jains*, India, 1911.

Shāh, Popatlāl K., *Jaina Dharma Nirūpaṇa* (in Gujarātī).

Smith, Vincent A., *The Early History of India* (third edition), Oxford, 1914.

Stevenson, Rev. J., *Nava Tatva*, London, 1848.

Stevenson, Mrs. Sinclair, *Notes on Modern Jainism*, Oxford, 1910.

Weber, A., *Sacred Literature of the Jainas* (tr.), Indian Antiquary (I.A.), xvii(1888)–xxi (1892).

Jaina Architecture and Archaeology.

Bühler, J. G. *Specimens of Jaina Sculptures from Mathurā*, Epigraphia Indica, i (1892) and ii (1894).

Burgess, J., *Digambara Jaina Iconography*, I. A., xxxii (1903).

Fergusson, J., *History of Indian and Eastern Architecture* (new edition), London, 1910.

Fergusson, J., and J. Burgess, *Cave Temples*, London, 1880.

Guérinot, A. A., *Répertoire d'épigraphie jaina*, Paris, 1908.

Smith, Vincent A., *A History of Fine Art in India and Ceylon*, Oxford, 1911.

CHAPTER I

INTRODUCTORY

The desire of India is to be freed from the cycle of rebirths, and the dread of India is reincarnation. The rest that most of the spiritual seek through their faith is a state of profound and deathlike trance, in which all their powers shall have ceased to move or live, and from which they shall never again be awakened to undergo rebirth in this toilsome and troubled world.

If, therefore, we would try reverently and sympathetically to grasp the inner meaning of an Indian faith, we must put aside all thought of the perfectly developed personality which is our ideal, and of the joy and zest that come from progress made and powers exercised, and, turning our thoughts backwards, face for a while another goal, in which death, not life, is the prize, cessation not development the ideal.

In Indian religions as in ours asceticism has its place, but we must remember the different connotation which that word bears to Indian minds. To the Christian, asceticism is only a means to an end, the eager, glad decision of the athlete to refuse the lower, if it clash with the higher, good. Far different is the Indian ideal, for in India asceticism has been born of fear, fear of future rebirths no less than of present ills. To Indian thinkers asceticism is the beginning in this life of the cessation they crave, and their hope is that thus one by one their powers and talents, with all that leads to and results from action, may drop off, burnt away in the glow of austerity, till only a stump of character remains, from which the soul may easily free itself. The unused gifts shrivel up the quicker if their owner be a professed ascetic, for the more limited the sympathies and the fewer sides of life a mortal touches, the better. All that makes for colour and vividness and joy in life must be sacrificed, and if through voluntary starvation life itself should go, the less risk is there of doing those actions which involve reincarnation.

To men believing thus, the life of the professed ascetic offered irresistible attractions. As such they were cut off from wife and child, and from all the labours and keen joys and sorrows these entail; clothing, food, or shelter need not claim their thought or work; houseless and effortless they might wander at will through a land of hospitality and sunshine.

To understand the creeds of India one must, of course, remember its climate: over a large part of the country, except during the rainy season, when ascetics suspend their wanderings, it is always fine: no drenching rain and (in the greater part of India) no biting frost compel men to provide themselves with houses or fires. The intense heat discourages exertion and robs men of energy, till rest seems the greatest bliss and meditation an alluring duty. And then, as we know only too well, the influence of the climate breeds pessimism eventually in the blithest European or Indian. In the east death and disease come with such tragic swiftness, and famine and pestilence with such horrifying frequency, that the fewer hostages one has given to fortune, the happier is one's lot.[1] To the poor and unaided in ancient India justice was unknown and life and property but ill secured, just as we may see in many native states to this day. All these influences, creed, climate, pessimism and injustice, pressed men more and more towards the pathway of the professed ascetic's life; but the door of this pathway was barred more and more firmly as time went on to every qualification but that of birth.

[1] 'Happy are we, happy live we who call nothing our own; when Mithilā is on fire, nothing is burnt that belongs to me.' *Uttarādhyayana*, *S. B. E.*, xlv, p. 37.

Unless a man had been born a Brāhman,[1] he must remain in all the hurry, sorrow and discontent of the world, until his life's end; but to a Brāhman the way of escape was always open; he must pass through the four Āśrama (or stages), and having been successively a student, a householder, and a hermit, spend the remaining years of his life as a wandering mendicant.

There must have been constant revolts against the exclusiveness that so selfishly barred the door to other castes, and echoes more or less clear of such revolts have come down to us, but only two were really permanent—the revolt of the Buddhists and the revolt of the Jaina. The Buddhists are scarcely found any longer in India proper, but the Jaina exist as an influential and wealthy community of laymen who support a large body of ascetics, the only example of the early mediaeval monastic orders of India which has survived to our day.

Both Buddhist and Jaina orders arose about the same time, the sixth century B.C., a period when the constant wars between various little kingdoms must have made the lot of the common people hideous with suffering and oppression; and a man might well have longed to escape from all fear of rebirth into such a sorrowful world, and have hoped, by renouncing everything that could be taken from him, and by voluntarily stripping himself of all possessions and all emotions, to evade the avaricious fingers of king or fortune.[2]

About this time, too, a wave of religious feeling was making itself felt in various parts of the world, and India has always been peculiarly susceptible to psychic emotions.

[1] Some European scholars doubt this, but all the Jaina the writer has met believe it most strongly; and the aim of this book throughout is to present the Jaina point of view and to reflect current Jaina opinions.

[2] 'At one time, his manifold savings are a large treasure. Then at another time, his heirs divide it, or those who are without a living steal it, or the king takes it away, or it is ruined in some way or other, or it is consumed by the conflagration of the house.' *Ācārāṅga Sūtra*, *S. B. E.*, xxii, p. 20.

The fact of being debarred from entering the ascetic life through the recognized stages and of being treated as in every way inferior was naturally most keenly felt by those in the caste next below the Brāhmans, the clever, critical Kṣatriya,[1] and it is from the ranks of these that the Jaina as well as the Buddhist reformers sprang.

Sacrifice was another occasion of quarrelling between the two castes. The Kṣatriya claimed that in old days they had been allowed to take part with the Brāhmans in the sacrifices from which they were now shut out; but the whole feeling about sacrifice was altering. As the Aryan invaders settled down in India, they grafted on to their original faith much from the darker creeds belonging to the lands and people they conquered, and gradually lost the child-like joy of the earlier Vedic times. The faith of the woodland peoples inspired them with the idea that all things—animals, insects, leaves and clods—were possessed of souls; and this, together with the growing weight of their belief in transmigration, gave them a shrinking horror of taking life in any form, whether in sacrifice[2] or sport, lest the blood of the slain should chain them still more firmly to the wheel of rebirth. So they came to dislike both the creed and the pretensions of their own priests, and the times were indeed ripe for revolt.

The Brāhmans declared that their supremacy and their sacrifices were based on the Vedas, so the authority of the Vedas was denied by the new thinkers. The Brāhmans claimed that the four castes had been created from the mouth, arms, thighs and feet of the Creator, thus ensuring the supremacy of that caste which had issued from the

[1] It seems probable that the atheistic (anti-Brāhmanic) system of philosophy—the Sāṅkhya—also arose amongst the Kṣatriya. Jaina philosophy, as we shall see later, has much in common with this.

[2] 'The binding of animals (to the sacrificial pole), all the Vêdas, and sacrifices, being causes of sin, cannot save the sinner; for his works (or Karman) are very powerful.' *Uttarādhyayana*, *S.B.E.*, xlv, p. 140.

highest portion, i. e. the Brāhmans who came from the god's mouth. So the reformers proceeded to deny the existence of a creator, feeling that, if that creator had existed, not only would he be responsible for the superiority of the Brāhmans but also for all the sorrows that darkened existence.

From the birth-story of their great founder one school of reformers—the Jaina—proved that it was a greater honour to be born of a Kṣatriya than of a Brāhman mother. Indeed all through the Jaina sacred books one comes across traces of this antagonism to Brāhmans and to Brāhmanic practices such as bathing,[1] divination,[2] &c., and one whole chapter, 'The True Sacrifice',[3] is directly written against them.

The Brāhmanic ascetic had to pass through four stages, but once the door of asceticism was forced open by rebels like the Jaina, it was opened as widely as possible, and the postulant was allowed to leap the intervening stages and become a wandering mendicant at once, if he so willed.

Having declared against birth exclusiveness, the Jaina were bound to find some other hall-mark of worth, and for this purpose they laid stress on *karma*. A man's karma[4]—his actions—not his caste, they declared, was of supreme importance, but from this position they have since backslidden, as they themselves lament, and it rests with the Jaina of to-day to free themselves from the shackles of caste which they have allowed to rebind them, and once more to restate this fundamental tenet of their creed.

It must always be remembered that Jainism, though a rebellious daughter, is none the less a daughter of Brāhmanism, many of whose leading beliefs are still held by the

[1] *Sūtrakṛitāṅga*, *S. B. E.*, xlv, p. 294.
[2] Ibid., p. 366.
[3] *Uttarādhyayana*, *S. B. E.*, xlv, p. 136 ff.
[4] 'By one's actions one becomes a Brāhmaṇa or a Kshattriya or a Vaiśya or a Śūdra . . . him who is exempt from all Karman we call a Brāhmaṇa.' *Uttarādhyayana*, *S. B. E.*, xlv, p. 140. See also *Āćārāṅga Sūtra*, *S. B. E.*, xxii, p. 45.

Jaina, while much of their worship exactly resembles Hindu worship, and their *domestic* chaplains, though not their temple officiants, are still Brāhmans; in fact both faiths must be studied if Jainism is to be understood. One might even suggest that one of the easiest approaches to the study of the boundless creed of Hinduism would be through the study of its more clearly defined and less nebulous offspring, Jainism.

CHAPTER II

HISTORICAL SUMMARY

Early Indian history as yet resembles those maps of our grandfathers in which

> Geographers for lack of towns
> Drew elephants on pathless downs.

The genius of the people of India does not lie in historical research : to them metaphysical thought is the chief end of man, and they are content to leave to Western scholars the task of filling in the large gaps of unexplored country in their history. It is the misfortune of Jainism that so much of its life-story falls within these unexplored tracts of time, and, though the Jaina have kept historical records of their own, it is very difficult to correlate these records with known facts in the world's history.

Modern research seems to have proved that this great monastic fraternity arose at the end of the sixth century B.C., and one of its great claims to interest lies in the fact that enshrined in its rules and precepts it has, like some slow moving glacier, brought down to this materialistic century the thoughts of a time when men, ignoring the present, were ready to stake their all on a future life. Originating amongst a people whose trade was war, it has laid greater emphasis on the duty of mercy and the evils of killing than any sect save the Friends ; its founder was an aristocrat, but it has met with greatest acceptance amongst the middle classes ; and though an unworldly faith, whose highest precept it is to discard all wealth as dross, it has nevertheless won its adherents from a class famed throughout India for their love of gain and their reluctance to part with money, and induced these close-fisted merchants to support out of their largesse a large body of religious mendicants. Indeed it would be impossible to imagine any creed or rule of conduct which, prima facie, would seem so little likely to appeal to a constituency of cautious, middle-class bankers and shopkeepers. Yet even to-day Jaina men and women are renouncing everything for the sake of an idea with a heroism that has all the romance of the early Rajput days, when kings and nobles vied with one another to enter the order; and to this wealth of devotion, this still surviving power of renunciation, the religion of the Cross must eventually make a victorious appeal.

It may make for clearness to state quite baldly the few facts which we do know about Jaina history, taking, as it were, a bird's-eye glance over it from a European standpoint, before we look at it from the Jaina point of view.

Mahāvīra, the great hero of the Jaina, was born the second son of a Kṣatriya chieftain, in Magadha (the modern Bihār), then the most powerful state in India. According to Jaina tradition, he was born in 599 and died in 527 B.C.[1] Many modern scholars think these dates are somewhat too early, and are inclined to place his death about the beginning of the fifth century, but absolute certainty is not yet attainable. When he was thirty years of age, he entered a previously established order, that of Pārśvanātha, but left it after twelve months and spent the following eleven years in preaching his Law of Renunciation, albeit with little acceptance. Then came the high tide of success, and during the last thirty years of his life men and women from the lands east of 'the middle country' crowded into his order. His adherents were drawn chiefly from the Kṣatriya aristocracy, with whom he was connected through his mother by ties of kinship. The great ascetic proceeded to organize all his followers into a regular community containing lay as well as monastic members of

[1] Other traditions give 545 and 467.

both sexes; and at his death it contained more than 14,000 monks.

Under Mahāvīra's influence members of two differing opinions had joined the order, those who held with the great leader that the complete abandonment of possessions involved the giving up of all clothing, and also members of another and earlier order, that of Pārśvanātha, who felt that some covering was a necessity and stopped short of this extreme of Renunciation. For long after the founder's death the sections cohered together, and the genius of Mahāvīra in adapting his order to the need of the times was shown in the numbers of harassed men and women who crowded into it, finding in the renunciation of all things—property, affections and emotions—the surest refuge from the trials and changes of this mortal life.

The Jaina sometimes speak of Mahāvīra's order as a protest against caste exclusiveness as such, but some European scholars hold that it was rather a protest of Kṣatriya against Brāhman; and the present practices of the Jaina community would seem to uphold this view, for the modern Jaina is as fast bound as his Hindu brother in the iron fetters of caste.

But, whatever its origin may have been, the order after the death of Mahāvīra continued to flourish under the rule of the great ascetic's disciple, Sudharma, and his successors, as we shall learn from our study of Jaina legends and history.

Unlike Buddhism, Jainism has never spread beyond the borders of India. A religion which, by its very nature, is one of intense individualism, feels little responsibility for another's soul and spends its energy on saving itself, is not likely to spread rapidly or far; yet, as we shall see, Jainism did gradually extend over the whole of India.

In particular it is plain that it found its way into Mysore and the Tamil country at a very early date. We shall study later the literary and artistic results of the predominance of this religion in the south during the early centuries of the Christian era. The following tradition is given by Jaina authorities as the reason for this early transplanting of the faith to such a distance. There is no conclusive evidence of the truth of the narrative, and some modern scholars think it a pure invention; yet it links itself so closely and naturally to later facts, that it is safer to say that it is probably, though not certainly, historic.

Some two centuries after Mahāvīra's death, according to this story, a terrible famine visited Magadha, which had been the scene of his labours. Year after year the monsoon, on which the fertility of the land depends, failed, until at length all the accumulated stores of grain were consumed, and it became apparent that the country had no longer any superfluity, out of which to provide for a large body of mendicants. Accordingly half the community, under the leadership of Bhadrabāhu, moved off towards the south and settled in Mysore; and as the famine lasted for twelve years, they were able to establish their faith in all that region. We are also told that the emigrants were accompanied to Mysore by Ċandragupta, the first Emperor of India, and founder of the Maurya Dynasty, whom the Jaina claim as a co-religionist. They add that he committed religious suicide by self-starvation at Śrāvaṇa Belgolā. If the tradition is trustworthy, the date of the migration must be placed *c.* 298 or 296 B.C., for Bindusāra succeeded Ċandragupta about that time.

This period is perhaps the most important in Jaina history; for not only did it lead to the establishment of Jainism in the south, but it is also the time of the fixing of the earliest canon of Jaina scripture.

Tradition says that all the monks did not migrate to the south; some, under the leadership of Sthūlabhadra, preferred to cling at any risk to the hallowed scenes of their Holy Land. It was perhaps easier for the minority to carry things through than it would have been for the whole unwieldy body; or it may have been that the death of many of their members through famine warned their leaders on how precarious a footing the *memoriter* knowledge of their sacred books stood. However this may be, Sthūlabhadra summoned a council of monks early in the third century B.C. at Pāṭaliputra, the modern Patna, a place historic in the annals of their order and at that time the capital of the Maurya Empire. This council fixed the canon of the Jaina sacred literature, consisting of the eleven Aṅga and the fourteen Pūrva. It seems likely that the books were not committed to writing at this time, but were still preserved in the memories of the monks. The action of the council would thus be limited to settling what treatises were authoritative. Unfortunately, as we shall see later, the sects do not quite agree as to what is meant by the eleven Aṅga and the fourteen Pūrva, so that the work of the famous council of Pāṭaliputra did not carry the weight which Sthūlabhadra hoped it would have done.

During this period not only was Jainism established in the south and the canon of the Scriptures fixed in the north, but also the famous clothes-*versus*-nudity question was raised, never again to be laid. We are told that, when at last the famine was over and the real head of the order, Bhadrabāhu or his successor, could bring some of his travelled mendicants back from the south to the original home of their order, he found that the home-keeping minority had all adopted some form of clothing; and, though the actual schism did not take place until two more centuries had passed, the unity of the order was lost for ever, and any whole-hearted agreement on such a question as the canon of their scriptures was never again possible.

As the Jaina laity had been drawn away from Hinduism by their adhesion to Mahāvīra, they were left without any stated worship. Gradually, however, reverence for their master and for other teachers, historical and mythical, passed into adoration and took the form of a regular cult. Finally, images of these adored personages were set up for worship, and idolatry became one of the chief institutions of orthodox Jainism. The process was precisely parallel to what happened in Buddhism. It is not known when idols were introduced, but it was probably in the second or first century B.C.

The third and second centuries B.C. must have been a period of great activity amongst the Jaina. Under Aśoka the religion is said to have been introduced into Kashmir. Under Suhastin, the great ecclesiastical head of the order in the second century, Jainism received many marks of approbation from Samprati, grandson of Aśoka. Inscriptions show that it was already very powerful in Orissa in the second century and in Mathurā in the north-west in the first century B.C. The history is not known in detail, but it is clear that after the Christian era the faith spread over the whole of the west and rose to great prominence and power in Gujarāt. We have also evidence of its activity in most parts of Southern India during the first millennium of the Christian era.

The next important event in Jaina history is the great schism and the final division into Śvetāmbara (white-clothed) and Digambara (atmosphere-clad, i.e. nude) sects which took place in A.D. 79 or 82. The Jaina have many legends to account for the division taking place when it did; but, whatever the reason, the depth of the cleavage between the two parties is shown by the fact that nowadays every sect adds after its own particular designation the name of one of these two great parties to which it adheres. For instance, the members of the modern non-idolatrous sect, the Sthānakavāsī, call themselves Sthānakavāsī Śvetāmbara, though it would seem to us that in having no idols they differ from the Śvetāmbara far more than the Śvetāmbara differ from the Digambara.

In the meantime the sacred literature of the Jaina was in a thoroughly unsatisfactory state, and was in real danger of being entirely lost. Owing to the conversion or patronage of western kings the centre of Jainism was gradually changing from Bihār to Gujarāt, and so when the great council of A.D. 454[1] came together, it was summoned not in the historic land of Magadha but in the western country won for the Jaina faith by missionary effort. The place chosen was Vallabhi, near Bhāvnagar, and the president of the council was Devarddhi. So far the Śvetāmbara and Sthānakavāsī sects concur, though they do not agree as to the canon of the scriptures then determined. In Kāṭhiāwāḍ at the present time there are at least eleven sub-sects amongst the Sthānakavāsī Jaina and eighty-four amongst the Śvetāmbara, and these hold differing views as to the correct list of books rightly comprised in their canon. Curiously enough they do not seem much to study the sacred texts themselves, but usually content themselves with quoting lists of the names of their books. It will perhaps suffice for our purpose if we note one such list from amongst those that have been given to the writer.

A. *The Eleven Aṅga.*

1. Āċārāṅga Sūtra.
2. Suyagaḍāṅga (Sūtrakṛitāṅga) Sūtra.
3. Thāṇānga (Sthānāṅga) Sūtra.
4. Samavāyāṅga Sūtra.
5. Bhagavatījī or Vivihapannanti.
6. Jñātādharma Kaṭhāṅga.
7. Upāsaka Daśāṅga.
8. Antagaḍa Daśāṅga (Antakṛitāṅga).
9. Anuttarovavāi Dasāṅga (Anuttaropapātika).
10. Praśna Vyākaraṇa.
11. Vipāka Sūtra.

B. *Twelve Upāṅga.*

1. Uvavāi (Aupapātika).
2. Rāyapaseṇī (Rājapraśnīya).
3. Jivābhigama.

[1] Other traditions, however, put the date as late as A.D. 467 or even A.D. 513.

4. Pannavaṇā (Prajñāpanā).
5. Jambūdīvapannati (Jambūdvīpaprajñapti).
6. Ċandapannati (Ċandraprajñapti).
7. Surapannati (Sūryaprajñapti).
8. Nirāvalīā (Nirayāvalī) (according to other lists, Kappīā).
9. Kappavaḍīśayyā (Kalpāvantasikā).
10. Pupphiyā (Puṣpakā).
11. Puppaċulīā (Puṣpaċūlikā).
12. Vanhidaśā.

C. *Six Ċhedagrantha* (or Five Ċhedagrantha).

1. Vyavahāra Sūtra.
2. Bṛihatkalpa (Vṛihatkalpa).
3. Daśāśrutaskandha.
4. Niśītha.
5. Mahāniśītha.[1]
6. Jitakalpa.[2]

Four Mūḷagrantha (according to the Śvetāmbara canon).

1. Daśavaikālika.
2. Uttarādhyayana.
3. Āvaśyaka.
4. Oghaniryuti.

Four Mūḷagrantha (according to the Sthānakavāsī canon).

1. Daśavaikālika.
2. Uttarādhyayana.
3. Nandī Sūtra.
4. Anuyogadvāra.

This completes the Sthānakavāsī canon, but the Śvetāmbara also accept the following :—

Ten Payannā (or Prakirna).

1. Ċausaraṇa (Ċatuḥśaraṇa).
2. Santhārā (Sanstāraka) Payannā.

[1] Sthānakavāsī Jaina do not recognize the Mahāniśītha or the Jitakalpa.

[2] Some Śvetāmbara Jaina do not accept the Jitakalpa, but add another Mūḷagrantha.

3. Tandulaveyālīā (Tandulavaiċārika).
4. Ċandāvijaya (Ċandravedhyaka).
5. Gaṇīvijaya (Gaṇividyā).
6. Devindathuo (Devendrastava).
7. Vīrathuo (Vīrastava).
8. Gaċċhāċāra.
9. Jyotikaraṇḍa (Jyotiṣkaraṇḍaka).
10. Āyuḥpaċċakhāṇa (Āturapratyākhyāna).

In certain other lists the Śvetāmbara canon is made to contain eighty-four books by adding twenty more Payannā, twelve Niryukti, and nine miscellaneous works, including the *Kalpa Sūtra*, which is held in special honour among the Śvetāmbara. Both Śvetāmbara and Sthānakavāsī agree that there were originally twelve Aṅga, but that the twelfth or Dṛiṣṭivāda Aṅga, containing an account of the fourteen Pūrva, has been lost.

What is the relation of the new canon to the old? It is probable that the Aṅga of the later correspond to those of the original canon; but it is also probable that during the centuries they underwent many changes. Jaina tradition acknowledges that all the Pūrva were lost at quite an early date. The other books are doubtless of later origin; yet even they rest on early tradition and probably contain a good deal of early material.

The original canon was not written, but it is not unlikely that individual monks used writing to aid memory long before the second codification. It seems certain that in A.D. 454 the whole canon was reduced to writing, and that a large number of copies were made, so that no monastery of any consequence should be without one.

The Jaina are very proud of the fact that their scriptures were not written in Sanskrit but in 'one of the most important, the best preserved, and the most copious of all the Prākṛit dialects',[1] that of Ardha-Māgadhī; that is to say,

[1] *Imperial Gazetteer of India*, ii, p. 261.

not in the language of the learned but of the common people; and we who have our scriptures and our book of Common Prayer in our mother tongue can understand their pride.

The Śvetāmbara do not, as a rule, allow their scriptures to be read by laymen, or even by nuns, but restrict the study of them to monks. The laity seem to read chiefly a book composed of quotations from their scriptures. The Sthānakavāsī are not so strict, and allow most of their sacred books to be read by the laity, but not the *Ċhedagrantha*, which they say were intended for the professed alone. The most popular of the books amongst the Sthānakavāsī laity are the *Upāsaka Daśāṅga*, the *Āċārāṅga Sūtra*, and the *Daśavaikālika.* To judge by their preaching and lectures the *Kalpa Sūtra* would seem to be the scripture most studied by the Śvetāmbara sādhus.

The Digambara canon differs so entirely from the Śvetāmbara that it does not seem probable that the sect was represented at the great council of A.D. 454.

They call their scriptures their Four Veda, and members of their community at Mount Ābu and at Pālitāṇā gave the writer a list of them in the following order:

1. Prathamānuyoga.
2. Karaṇānuyoga.
3. Ċaraṇānuyoga.
4. Dravyānuyoga.

Professor Jacobi adduces in proof of the antiquity of the Jaina scriptures, amongst other things, the fact that they contain no reference to Greek astrology which was introduced into India in the third or fourth century A.D.

As we have already seen, it seems probable that, though the canon of the scriptures had been fixed in 300 B.C. by the council of Pāṭaliputra, they had not all been committed to writing, but had generally been handed down by word of mouth from teacher to disciple; the result, however, of the council of Vallabhi was the enshrining of the sacred lore in manuscript books. To this day the manuscript scriptures are considered more sacred than those which have been printed—the writer has sometimes seen a little pile of rice placed before a bookcase to do honour to the manuscript scriptures it contained.

The zenith of Jaina prosperity lasted from the council of Vallabhi down to the thirteenth century. Strangely enough the years that witnessed the decline and fall of Buddhism saw the spread both in the west and south of its rival faith, and though Jainism almost vanished from Bihār, the land of its birth, yet in the west it became the court religion. The events of these happy centuries are enshrined, as we shall see, in the legends that are still current amongst the Jaina, and more abiding monuments to this epoch of prosperity remain in the books that were written and the temples erected in the sunshine of royal favour.

The princely names the Jaina best love to recall in this connexion are Maṇḍalika, a king of Surāṣṭra (Kāṭhiāwāḍ) about A.D. 1059, who repaired the temple of Neminātha on Mt. Girnār; Siddharāja Jayasiṁha, a king of Gujarāt (died A.D. 1125), the first patron of Hemaćandra, who often went on pilgrimage to Girnār, and his successor Kumārapāla (A.D. 1125–59) whom the Jaina claim to have been converted to their faith,[1] and who is said to have established Jainism as the state religion.

But the decline of Jainism was close at hand. The Jaina attribute the first destruction of their temples to the hostility of the Brāhmans, especially under Ajayapāla, A.D. 1174–6, but the injuries he inflicted were as nothing to the devastation wrought by the Mohammedans. As the Irish execrate the name of Cromwell, so did the Jaina that of Alā-ud-dīn—'the Bloody'—who conquered Gujarāt A.D. 1297–8.

[1] At any rate he built thirty-two temples to atone for the sins of his teeth!

He razed many of their temples to the ground, massacred their communities and destroyed their libraries. Many of the most beautiful Mohammedan mosques in India have woven into their fabric stones from Jaina shrines which the ruthless conquerors had destroyed.

In the south Jainism had flourished exceedingly after its introduction by Bhadrabāhu, and many of the languages and grammars were largely shaped by the labours of Jaina monks.

In A.D. 640, when the Chinese traveller Hiuen Tsang visited India, he met numbers of monks belonging to the Digambara (naked) sect in the south and admired their beautiful temples. But after his visit a great persecution arose. A Jaina king, Kūna,[1] became converted to Śaivism in the middle of the seventh century and, if we may trust the sculptures at Trivatūr in Arcot, slew with the most horrible severity thousands of his former co-religionists who refused to follow his example. Even if the account of the persecution be exaggerated, there is no doubt that after this time the prosperity of Jainism in the south steadily declined.

To return to the north. The wonder is, not that any temples survived the Mohammedan persecutions, but that Jainism itself was not extinguished in a storm which simply swept Buddhism out of India. The character of Jainism, however, was such as to enable it to throw out tentacles to help it in its hour of need. It had never, like Buddhism, cut itself off from the faith that surrounded it, for it had always employed Brāhmans as its domestic chaplains, who presided at its birth rites and often acted as officiants at its death and marriage ceremonies and temple worship. Then, too, amongst its chief heroes it had found niches for some of the favourites of the Hindu pantheon, Rāma, Kṛiṣṇa and the like. Mahāvīra's genius for organization also stood Jainism in good stead now, for he had made the laity an integral

[1] Vincent Smith, *Early History of India*, third edition, p. 455.

part of the community, whereas in Buddhism they had no part nor lot in the order. So, when storms of persecution swept over the land, Jainism simply took refuge in Hinduism, which opened its capacious bosom to receive it; and to the conquerors it seemed an indistinguishable part of that great system.

The receptivity, however, which Hinduism has always shown towards it is to-day one of the reasons that makes Jainism so difficult to study; for many Jaina, justified by the resemblance in their worship and thought, simply count themselves Hindus and actually so write themselves down in the census returns.

If one effect of the Mohammedan conquest, however, was to drive many of the Jaina into closer union with their fellow idol-worshippers in the face of iconoclasts, another effect was to drive others away from idolatry altogether. No oriental could hear a fellow oriental's passionate outcry against idolatry without doubts as to the righteousness of the practice entering his mind.

Naturally enough it is in Ahmadābād, the city of Gujarāt that was most under Mohammedan influence, that we can first trace the stirring of these doubts. About A.D. 1452 the Loṅkā sect, the first of the non-idolatrous Jaina sects, arose and was followed by the Ḍhuṇḍhīā or Sthānakavāsī sect about A.D. 1653, dates which coincide strikingly with the Lutheran and Puritan movements in Europe.

Jainism has never recovered its temporal power since the days of the Mohammedan conquest; it is no longer in any sense a court religion; nevertheless the influence that it wields in India to-day is enormous. Its great wealth and its position as the religion *par excellence* of money-lenders and bankers makes it, especially in native states, the power behind the throne; and if any one doubt its influence, he need only count up the number of edicts prohibiting the slaying of animals on Jaina sacred days that have recently been issued by the rulers of independent states.

According to the last census the Jaina numbered some 1,248,182, but probably many more are included under Hindus. Their standard of literacy (495 males and 40 females per thousand) is higher than that of any other community save the Pārsīs, and they proudly boast that not in vain in their system are practical ethics wedded to philosophical speculation, for their criminal record is magnificently white.

CHAPTER III

THE LIFE OF MAHĀVĪRA

Birth and Childhood.

We have seen that in the sixth century B.C. the times were ripe for revolt; now, after the event, it is almost easy to prophesy where the revolt was first likely to arise.

The strongest centre of Brāhmanical influence was in the country lying round the modern Delhi—it was the language spoken by the people in this tract of land that was destined to be developed by grammarians into the classical Sanskrit, and it was they who composed much of the old Brāhmanic literature that has come down to us. All this region, Dr. Grierson tells us, was called the 'Midland', but encircling it on east, south, and west was an 'Outland', where the Brāhmanic influence was less strong, and where the thinkers were to be found not in the priestly ranks, but 'among the Kṣatriya class to whose learning and critical acumen witness is borne even in contemporary Brāhmanic writings.'[1] In this Outland near the modern Patna is a town called nowadays Besārh. Birth-place.

Most Indian towns are to-day divided into wards, where the various castes live apart. One must seek the potters in one quarter and the washermen in another, whilst the lowest of all, the despised refuse-removers, live actually outside the city walls.

Some two thousand years ago in Besārh the same divisions existed as would be found to-day; and there, in fact, the priestly (*Brāhman*), the warrior (*Kṣatriya*), and the commercial (*Baniyā*) communities lived so separately that their quarters were sometimes spoken of as though they had been distinct villages, as Vaiśālī, Kuṇḍagrāma, and Vāṇijyagrāma. Strangely enough, it was not in their own but

[1] See art. *Bhakti Mārga* in *E.R.E.*

in the Kṣatriya ward that the man was born who was to be the great hero of the Baniyā, and who was to found amongst these commercial people a religion which, with all its limitations, yet made one of the most emphatic protests the world has ever known against accounting luxury, wealth, or comfort the main things in life. It seems almost paradoxical also that the warrior caste should produce the great apostle of non-killing. He was afterwards known from his exploits as Mahāvīra—the great hero—but his earliest name he derived from his birthplace, being known simply as Vaiśāliya, 'the man of Vaiśālī' (the main ward of the town). The government of such a city or ward seems to have resembled that of a Greek state. 'It was', says Dr. Hoernle,[1] 'an oligarchic republic; its government was vested in a Senate, composed of the heads of the resident Kṣatriya clans, and presided over by an officer who had the title of king and was assisted by a Viceroy and a Commander-in-Chief.' The chief of one of these Kṣatriya clans, the Nāta or Nāya clan, was a man called Siddhārtha, who doubtless attained some eminence in Senate and State, for he eventually married the daughter of this republican king, a Kṣatriya lady named Triśalā.

The fourteen dreams.

This old-world princess longed, as every Indian woman does to-day, to bear her lord a son, and suddenly one night, the legend tells, wonderful dreams came to her as she slept, revealing to her not only that she should bear a son, but also that this son should win everlasting rest and renown.

These dreams of Triśalā's[2] are to-day often graven round the silver treasuries in Jaina temples, and Jaina women love to recall them, for it is given to all the mothers of the great Jaina saints to see them.

i First the happy princess dreamed of a mighty elephant[3]

[1] Hoernle, *J.A.S.B.*, 1898, p. 40.

[2] Many devout laymen and laywomen repeat them every day at their morning devotions.

[3] All mothers of Tīrthaṅkara see first of all this elephant in their dreams, excepting only the mother of Ṛiṣabhadeva, who saw a bull first, hence the child's name.

whose colour was whiter than a cloud, a heap of pearls, the spray of water, or moonbeams, and the sound of whose voice was like thunder.

Then she saw a white bull, whiter than the petals of the ii
lotus, which diffused a glory of light on all around, and this —so one sect of the Jaina, the Digambara, say—foretold the birth of a great religious teacher who should spread the light of knowledge. Another sect, however, the Sthānakavāsī, hold that it showed that he should have strength to bear the yoke of religion, for the yoke that a Jaina ascetic must bear is not light, and no weakling can endure it.

The next dream prophesied that she should bear one iii
who should overcome all his enemies (i. e. his karma, the results of his actions): for she saw a magnificent white lion leap from the sky towards her face; his eyes were like pure lightning, and his tongue came out of his mouth 'like a shoot of beauty'. This further foretold that Mahāvīra should be 'the lion of houseless monks', and so he has the lion as his symbol.

The fourth dream was of the beautiful goddess Śrī or iv
Lakṣmī (the goddess of wealth), whom Triśalā saw floating on the petals of a lotus in the lotus lake on Mount Himavata, with guardian elephants 'anointing' her with water, and this she knew meant that her son should be an 'anointed' king.

Next, a garland[1] of sweet-smelling Mandāra flowers fore- v
told how fragrant the body of the little child should be.

The white moon[2] dispelling the darkness of the wildest vi
wilderness again prophesied a religious preacher.

The radiant sun,[3] red as the beak of a parrot, which vii

[1] The Sthānakavāsī say there were two garlands.

[2] In all the pictures of this moon vision a stag is seen in the centre of the moon. The general belief of all Indians is that there is either a stag or a hare inhabiting the moon. There are a score or more of names for the moon in Sanskrit, and a dozen at least are derived from this belief. The villagers, however, find in the moon an old woman spinning a wheel and a she-goat standing by her.

[3] The Digambara assert that she saw the sun before the dream about the moon.

throttles the cold and 'disperses the evil-doers who stroll about at night, whose thousand rays obscure the lustre of other lights', showed that the child should dispel the darkness of ignorance.

viii The sects do not agree as to what the eighth dream of the princess was about. The Śvetāmbara believe she saw a beautiful banner (an Indra Dhvaja) embroidered with those signs which Hindus and Jaina alike consider specially auspicious, and to whose golden pole[1] was tied a plume of peacock's feathers; while the Digambara affirm that she saw two fishes, which showed the child was to be happy.

ix The ninth dream, the Śvetāmbara say, was a golden pitcher of exquisite beauty, filled with water—or, according to others, with jewels—which was the abode of happy fortune and was wreathed at all seasons with fragrant flowers, portending happiness. The Digambara assert that she saw *two* golden pitchers filled with pure water, to show that the child should be constantly immersed in spiritual meditation.

x The next vision was that of a lotus lake whose flowers 'were licked by bees and mad drones', from which Triśalā knew that her baby would possess all the marks of a perfect being; or, as the Sthānakavāsī say, that the honey of his sermons would be eagerly absorbed by the whole world.

xi The princess then saw the milk ocean, white as the breast of Lakṣmī, tossing its transparent breakers as the wind played over it and the great rivers rushed into it, and this foretold that the child should attain to the perfect knowledge of the Kevalī.

xi a At this point the Digambara, who believe the princess saw not fourteen but sixteen dreams, insert a vision of a throne of diamonds and rubies, which foretold that the coming child should rule over the three worlds.

[1] According to the Tapagaćcha sect the pole was topped by a temple roof.

Her next dream was of a jewel-bedecked celestial abode[1] xii
which shone like the morning sun and which was hung with garlands and pictures of birds and beasts. There the celestial choirs gave concerts, and the place resounded with the din of the drums of the gods which imitated the sound of rain clouds.

Here again the Digambara insert a vision of a great xii a
king of the gods dwelling below the earth. This the
Śvetāmbara do not accept, but both agree about the next xiii
dream, in which Triśalā saw a great vase piled up with jewels. The base of the vase was on the level of the earth, and its height was as the height of Mount Meru, and its brightness illuminated even the sky; it foretold the birth of a child that should possess right knowledge, right intuition, and right conduct.

Her last dream was of a clear fire fed with clarified butter, xiv
whose beautiful flames seemed almost to scorch the firmament, which prophesied that the white-souled child she was to bear should illumine the universe by his wisdom.

All these dreams Triśalā related to Siddhārtha, and the next day the interpreters that he summoned foretold from them the birth of a spiritual conqueror (Jina), lord of the three worlds and the universal emperor of the law.

Some of the more advanced Jaina do not believe that Triśalā actually saw all these dreams,[2] but they hold that before the child's birth both father and mother knew that he would be either a *Ćakravartī* (universal monarch) or a Tīrthaṅkara. Perhaps the legend of the dreams may carry with it this meaning, that at that time there was a universal stirring of desire, and that many were hoping some reformer or religious leader might be born. At any

[1] The Sthānakavāsī believe this abode to have been a huge immovable car as big as a city.

[2] A really orthodox Jaina, however, would deny the title of Jaina altogether to any one who did not hold these and all the other legends mentioned in this book to be literally and historically true, though varying interpretations of them are given.

rate they must have conveyed the welcome assurance that the child at least would safely survive all the dangers that an Indian birth-chamber holds for both mother and babe.

There is another legend about Mahāvīra's birth which is also recorded in the Jaina sacred books, and which possesses some value as showing the intense hatred existing between the Brāhmans and the Kṣatriyas. According to this legend, a Brāhman lady, Devānandā, wife of the Brāhman Ṛiṣabhadatta, living in the Brāhmanical part of the town, saw the Fourteen Auspicious Dreams which foretold the birth of a great saint or Tīrthaṅkara. But Indra,[1] the chief of the gods, saw from his celestial throne what had happened, and knew that the child would be the great Tīrthaṅkara Mahāvīra; so he sent his commander-in-chief in the form of a deer to remove the embryo from Devānandā[2] and to give it to Triśalā, in order that Mahāvīra might not be born in a 'beggarly or Brāhmanical family'. However that may be, the stories go on to show how carefully Triśalā, two thousand years ago, prepared for the joy of motherhood just as a modern woman would, by avoiding all sickness and fatigue and walking in quiet country places, so that she might gain health for body and mind. At last, in the year 599 B.C. of our era, or towards the end of the Duṣama Suṣama period, as the Jaina reckon time, on the thirteenth day of the bright half of the moon in the month Ćaitra, the time came when Triśalā, herself perfectly healthy, gave birth to a perfectly healthy child.

Birth. The thought of India centres largely round marriage and motherhood, and the birth of a manchild then, as now,

[1] The Jaina believe that Indra (or Śakra), the chief of the sixty-four gods of that name, belongs especially to them, but has been stolen from them by the Brāhmans.

[2] It is interesting to compare with this the story of Kṛiṣṇa being removed from the womb of Devakī to that of Rohiṇī, for the Jaina believe Kṛiṣṇa to be one of their own future Tīrthaṅkara.

was the occasion of a very delirium of rejoicing. To-day, in a native state, the birth of an heir is celebrated in very much the same way as it was in Mahāvīra's time. The town is *en fête*, prisoners are released, fines are cancelled, presents are given, and presents (alas !) are exacted.

When the child was three days old, it was shown the sun and the moon (this is not usual now) ; on the sixth day they observed the religious vigil (modern Jaina still worship 'Mother Sixth'), Triśalā bathed on the tenth day, and on the twelfth, after the usual family feast, the boy was named with all pomp and circumstance. In India it is the father's sister who usually names a child, but his parents themselves chose Mahāvīra's name, announcing that 'since the prince was placed in the womb of the Kṣatriyāṇī Triśalā this family's (treasure) of gold, silver, riches, corn, jewels, pearls, shells, precious stones and corals increased; therefore the prince shall be called *Vardhamāna* (i.e. the Increasing[1])'. Mahāvīra was sometimes, as we have seen, called Vaiśāliya from his birthplace; his followers, however, seldom call him by this or by the name his parents gave him, but prefer to use the title they say the gods gave him, that of Mahāvīra, the great hero, or else Jina, the conqueror, though this last is really more used in connexion with the religion (Jainism) he promulgated than with himself. He is also known as Jñātaputra, Nāmaputra,[2] Śāsananāyaka, and Buddha.

It was partly the multitude of his names, partly also the number of legends that loving child-like folk had woven round the cradle of their hero, that long obscured the fact that Mahāvīra was an historical personage. Another reason for doubting his existence lay in the superficial resemblance there is between his life and teaching and that of his contemporary, Buddha. It was assumed that one of the two systems must have sprung from the other,

[1] *Ācārāṅga Sūtra*, *S.B.E.*, xxii, p. 192.
[2] Or Nāyaputra, sometimes Nātaputta.

and it is only through the labours of European scholars like Jacobi, Hoernle, and Bühler that Mahāvīra's historical existence has been proved. It seems strange that Jaina should still be dependent on the labours of scholars of another faith and speech for all they know about their greatest hero!

We have noticed some of the legends that have gathered round Mahāvīra, and it is worth while examining more, since legends help us in a special way to grasp the latent ideals of a faith. We can learn from them what its followers admire and what they despise, and also what qualities they revere sufficiently to link with their leader's name. If we contrast the stories told of Mahāvīra with those told, for instance, of Kṛiṣṇa by Hindus, we shall see at once that the thoughts of these early followers of Jainism moved on a higher, cleaner plane, and this purity of thought is one of the glories of Jainism to-day.

Childhood. Austere though the creed of the Jaina is, there are some amongst them whose habit of mind leads them to interpret even these severe tenets as sternly as possible. This diversity of temperament (which is surely inherent in the human race) manifests itself in the stories told of Mahāvīra's life. The Digambara (who are the straitest sect among the Jaina) always represent their hero as choosing the sterner and less pleasing path: avoiding marriage and going on his way unhindered by any fear of hurting his parents' feelings. The Śvetāmbara sect, on the other hand, believe that, though from his earliest hours Mahāvīra longed to forsake the world and betake himself to a houseless, wandering life, he nevertheless felt he could not do this during his parents' lifetime, lest he should cause them pain. Even before his birth, the legend runs, he decided thus: 'It will not behove me, during the life of my parents, to tear out my hair, and leaving the house to enter the state of houselessness.'[1] So he

[1] *Kalpa Sūtra*, *S.B.E.*, xxii, p. 250.

lived the ordinary life of a happy boy, watched over by the innumerable servants that seem inseparable from Indian life,[1] but enjoying to the full 'the noble five-fold joys and pleasures of sound, touch, taste, colour and smell'.

Both sects delight to tell of his boyish prowess and of how easily he excelled all his companions in strength and physical endurance, as he did in beauty of mind and body. One day, they say, the sons of his father's ministers had come as usual to play with him in the royal gardens, when suddenly a mad elephant charged down on the group of children, who fled hither and thither in their efforts to escape. Mahāvīra, however, quietly went up to the infuriated animal, caught it by its trunk, and climbing up on it, escaped being trodden by its feet by riding on its back!

Another legend tells how, when he was playing with the same children at *āmbalī pīpaḷī* (a sort of 'tick' or 'tig') among the trees, a god appeared and thought to frighten the child by carrying him high up into the sky on his shoulders. Mahāvīra, however, was not in the least alarmed, and, seizing the opportunity to show his superiority over immortals, whacked the god and pulled his hair so hard, that he was only too ready to descend and get rid of his obstreperous burden. The child who had thus defeated one of their number was called Mahāvīra by the other gods—a name mortals were quick to adopt.

According to the Śvetāmbara tradition Mahāvīra married a lady called Yaśodā (belonging to the Kauṇḍinya gotra), and a daughter was born to them named Anujā (Anojjā) or Priyadarśanā. This daughter eventually married a nobleman called Jamāli, who, after becoming one of Mahāvīra's followers and fellow workers, ended by opposing him. Their child (Mahāvīra's granddaughter) had two names, being known both as Śeśavatī and Yaśovatī.

[1] He had five nurses: a wet nurse, a nurse to wash him, one to dress him, one to play with him, and one to carry him.

It was pointed out in the introduction how profoundly some Indians believe that the result of action (karma) ties men to the cycle of rebirth, and that if, through the cessation of life, action and its resultant karma could be ended, so much the less would be the danger of rebirth. This tenet naturally encouraged belief in suicide as a form of prudential insurance! Amongst the recorded deaths by suicide are those of Mahāvīra's parents, who, according to the Śvetāmbara belief, died of voluntary starvation: 'on a bed of kuśa grass they rejected all food, and their bodies dried up by the last mortification of the flesh which is to end in death.'[1] At their death Mahāvīra, who was by now approaching his thirtieth year, felt free to become an ascetic, and asked his elder brother's permission to renounce the world; the brother consented, only stipulating that Mahāvīra should do nothing in the matter for a year, lest people should think they had quarrelled.

The Digambara accounts differ widely from this. According to them, even when only a child of eight, Mahāvīra took the twelve vows[2] which a Jaina layman may take, and that he always longed to renounce the world; other Digambara say that it was in his thirtieth year that, whilst meditating on his 'self', he determined to become a monk, realizing that he would only spend seventy-two years in this incarnation as Mahāvīra. At first his parents were opposed to the idea of their delicately nurtured child undergoing all the hardships that fall to the lot of a houseless mendicant, but at last they consented, and it was during their lifetime that Mahāvīra entered on the spiritual vocation, which in India, as in Europe, has so often proved a suitable career for younger sons.

Modern research would seem to favour the Śvetāmbara belief that Mahāvīra had married, but this the Digambara strenuously deny, for an ascetic who has never married

[1] *Ācārāṅga Sūtra*, *S.B.E.*, xxii, p. 194.
[2] See below, Twelve Vows of a Layman, p. 205.

moves on a higher plane of sanctity than one who has known the joys of wedded life.

Mahāvīra's Initiation.

Jainism, though it denies the existence of a creator and of the three great gods of the Indian Trimūrti, Brahmā, Viṣṇu and Śiva, has never shaken itself free from the belief in many of the minor gods of the Hindu pantheon. It gives these gods, it is true, a very secondary position as servants or tempters of the great Jaina saints, but their existence is accepted as undoubted; accordingly, in the account of Mahāvīra's initiation we shall find many of the old Hindu gods represented as being present.

This initiation, all sects agree, took place when Mahāvīra was about thirty years of age, some time therefore between 570 and 569 B.C. The Nāya clan to which he belonged seem to have supported a body of monks who followed the rule of Pārśvanātha, an ascetic who had lived some two hundred and fifty years before Mahāvīra. It was naturally to this order, probably considered rather irregular by the Brāhmans, that the thoughts of Mahāvīra turned. Its monks had their cells in a park[1] outside the Kṣatriya suburb (Kuṇḍagrāma) of Vaiśālī, and in the centre of this park grew one of those evergreen Aśoka or 'sorrowless' trees, whose leaves are supposed never to know either grief or pain. The Aśoka tree is always associated with Mahāvīra, for the legends say that in his later life an Aśoka tree grew wherever he preached, and it was now under its shade that he made the great renunciation and entered upon that ascetic life, whose austerities were to dry up all the founts of karma and free him from the sorrowful cycle of rebirth.

Mahāvīra had fasted for two-and-a-half days, not even allowing water to cross his lips, and had then given away

[1] The Śvetāmbara call the park Sundavana, the Digambara Sārathi Khaṇḍa.

all his property, which can only have been the ordinary possessions of the cadet of a small House, but which the love of his followers has exaggerated into the wealth of a mighty emperor.[1] Then, followed by a train of gods and men, he was carried in a palanquin to the park and, alighting, took his seat on a five-tiered throne,[2] which was so placed as to face the east. There he stripped himself of all his ornaments and finery, flinging them to the attendant god Vaiśramaṇa, who caught them up as they fell.

Most Hindu mendicants cut or shave off their hair, but a peculiar and most painful custom of the Jaina is that all ascetics, as a proof of their power of endurance, must tear out their hair by the roots. One Jaina writer declares in his English 'Life of Mahāvīra' that 'only those can do it who have no love with their flesh and bones'. It is looked on as a sign that henceforth the monk or nun will take no thought for the body.

As Mahāvīra performed this crowning act of austerity, Indra, the leader and king of the gods, falling down before the feet of the venerable ascetic, caught up the hairs in a diamond cup and took them to the Ocean of Milk. The saint then did obeisance to all liberated spirits, and vowing to do no sinful act, adopted the holy conduct.[3]

The Jaina mark with great precision the five degrees of knowledge that lead to Omniscience. Mahāvīra, they say, was born with the first three, *Mati jñāna*, *Śruta jñāna*,

[1] The Jaina believe that when an ascetic who will eventually develop into a Tīrthaṅkara is about to give away his possessions, the god Indra bestows on him all the wealth that has been buried in forgotten treasure stores, in order that the amount to be given away may be worthy of the giver.

[2] This sort of throne is called a *Pāṇḍuśilā*, and in Jaina temples Mahāvīra's image is generally kept on one.

[3] The *Kalpa Sūtra* gives quite a different account, in which it says that Mahāvīra fasted for two-and-a-half days after all the pomp, and then, 'Quite alone, nobody else being present, he tore out his hair, and leaving the house entered the state of houselessness'. *Kalpa Sūtra*, *S.B.E.*, xxii, p. 259.

and *Avadhi jñāna*. He now gained the fourth kind of knowledge, *Manaḥparyāya jñāna*, by which he knew the thoughts of all sentient beings of five senses in the two-and-a-half continents, and it only remained for him to obtain the fifth degree of knowledge, that of *Kevala jñāna* or Omniscience, which is possessed by the Kevalī alone.

The Digambara, however, do not believe that Mahāvīra obtained the fourth kind of knowledge till some time after his initiation. According to them, he failed to gain it, though he performed meditation for six months, sitting absolutely motionless. At the end of the six months he went to Kulapura; the king of Kulapura, Kulādhipa, came and did him honour, washed his feet with his own hands and, having walked round him three times, offered him rice and milk; these Mahāvīra accepted and took them as his first meal (*pāraṇuṁ*) after a fast of six months. He returned to the forest and wandered about in it performing twelve kinds of penance, but still the knowledge was withheld from him. At last he visited Ujjayinī (Ujjain) and did penance in a cemetery there, when Rudra and his wife in vain tried to interrupt him; it was only after overcoming this temptation and again entering on his forest life of meditation that, according to the Digambara belief, he obtained Manaḥparyāya jñāna. Henceforth Mahāvīra was houseless, and wandered through the land so lost in meditation as to be indifferent to sorrow and joy, pain and pleasure, subsisting only on the alms of the charitable.

Research seems to have established the fact that at first he belonged to the order of Pārśvanātha mentioned above, a body of mendicants leading a more or less regular life, and that in accordance with their custom he wore clothes; but many Jaina will not acknowledge that a Tīrthaṅkara could have belonged to an order even for ever so short a time; they agree, however, that for thirteen months he did wear one cloth.

The legend runs that the god Indra himself gave Mahāvīra the beautiful robe which he wore at his initiation. Before the ceremony the saint had given away all his goods in charity, but a certain Brāhman named Somadatta, being absent at that time, had received nothing. He came and complained, and Mahāvīra was greatly troubled to think that he had nothing left to give him, till he remembered Indra's robe; taking this off, he cut it in two and gave half to the greedy Brāhman. Somadatta was delighted, and showed it off with great pride to a friend of his who was a weaver. The weaver told Somadatta to go back and get the other half and then he would have a robe worth having, which could all be woven into one. The Brāhman was ashamed to actually go and ask for the remaining part, but knowing how completely unconscious of everything that went on around him Mahāvīra was, he walked softly behind the ascetic, and when the robe slipped off (as is the nature of half robes) he stooped, and gently lifting it off the thorns on to which it had fallen, quietly made off with his booty. When Mahāvīra discovered the theft, all he did was to make a parable about it, in which he taught how thorny would be the road of his true disciples in this world, but how priceless would be their value when delivered at last from the thorns that beset them.

Not only was the great ascetic unconscious of the whereabouts of his earthly possessions, he was also absolutely indifferent to pain; for instance, one day he was sitting in meditation outside a village, when some herdsmen, in rough sport, lit a fire between his feet and drove nails into his ears, without the saint being in the least aware of what they were doing.

In India it would be specially easy for abuses to spring up among a body of mendicants; they could gain their food so easily, that a great part of 'the long Indian day' would hang idle on their hands, and our proverb about Satan finding work for idle hands to do has its Gujarātī counterpart: 'A man sitting idle brings ruin to pass.'[1] Many men doubtless had become monks through a constitutional aversion from honest labour, and the climate and leisure, whilst increasing this distaste for work in them, would be apt to create it even in those who had entered the order from the highest motives. Altogether the world-old employer of the unemployed could find fair scope for his mischievous energies amongst them![2] And so before long Mahāvīra found the discipline of Pārśvanātha's monks too lax, and after a year he left them, to wander alone in a state of absolute nudity.

The question of clothes was a crucial one amongst the Jaina. Mahāvīra apparently felt that the complete ascetic must have completely conquered all his emotions, shame amongst others. A true monk would not feel either heat or cold, and so would not need the protection from the weather offered by clothes, and he would be so indifferent to mere appearance as to be unconscious as to whether he wore raiment or not. Being rid of clothes, one is also rid of a lot of other worries too: one needs no box to keep them in, no materials to mend them with, no change of raiment when the first set is dirty or outworn, and, still more important to a Jaina, no water is needed in which to wash them.

On this point Mr. Benārsi Dāss makes some rather interesting remarks in his lecture on Jainism, and throws an astonishingly new light on an old story.

'Jaina monks', he says, 'are naked because Jainism says that as long as one entertains the same idea of nakedness as we do, he cannot obtain salvation. One cannot, according to Jain principles, obtain Mokṣa, as long as he remembers that he is naked. He can only cross over the ocean of the world after he has forgotten that he is naked. . . . As long as a man thinks and knows that he is naked, that there is something like good and evil, he cannot obtain Mokṣa. He must forget it to obtain Nirvāṇa. This is very well illustrated by the well-

[1] नवरो बेठो नखोद् वाळे.

[2] The Brāhmans had tried to avoid some of the more obvious abuses by restricting entrance to the fourth *āśrama* to men of mature years, who had passed through a long course of preparatory discipline.

known story of the expulsion of Adam and Eve from heaven. Adam and Eve were naked and pure. They enjoyed perfect happiness in the garden of Eden. They had no knowledge of good and evil. The devil, their enemy, desired to deprive them of their happiness. He made them eat of the fruit of the tree of the knowledge of good and evil. They at once saw their nakedness. They fell. They were expelled from heaven. It is this knowledge of good and evil, it is this knowledge of nakedness, that deprived them of Eden. The Jains hold the same belief. Our knowledge of good and evil, our knowledge of nakedness, keeps us away from salvation. To obtain it we must forget nakedness. The Jaina Nirgranthas have forgot all knowledge of good and evil. Why should they require clothes to hide their nakedness?'[1]

Sir Monier Williams suggests[2] that the Jaina 'felt that a sense of shame implied sin, so that if there were no sin in the world there would be no shame. Hence they argued rather illogically that to get rid of clothes was to get rid of sin, and every ascetic who aimed at sinlessness was enjoined to walk about naked with the air or sky (*dig*) as his sole covering.'

The Digambara believe that Mahāvīra abandoned clothes at the time of his initiation; the Śvetāmbara, as we have seen, that he abandoned them after thirteen months.

It was whilst Mahāvīra was walking naked and homeless and, as the Digambara believe, keeping absolutely unbroken his vow of silence, that he was joined by Gośāla, a disciple whose story we shall have to study more in detail later. For the present we need only note that Gośāla followed Mahāvīra for six years, but subsequently left him and fell into those grievous sins which so easily beset a mendicant, and to guard against which so many precepts in the Jaina scriptures are directed.

For twelve years Mahāvīra wandered from place to place, never staying for longer than a single night in a village or for more than five nights in a town. The object of this custom may have been to avoid levying too great

[1] *Lecture on Jainism.* Agra, 1902, p. 69.
[2] *Buddhism*, p. 530.

a tax on the hospitality of the people, and also to prevent the ascetic forming close or undesirable friendships, which might tempt him to break either his vow of non-possession of goods or of chastity.[1] The rule was, however, relaxed during the rainy season, when Mahāvīra, like his subsequent followers, made a practice of remaining for four months at the same place, lest he should injure any of the young life that springs so suddenly and abundantly into being, once the monsoon bursts and the rains, on which India's prosperity depends, begin to fall. During these twelve years, we are told, he meditated always on himself, on his Ātmā, and walked sinless and circumspect in thought, word and deed.

'As water does not adhere to a copper vessel, or collyrium to mother of pearl (so sins found no place in him); his course was unobstructed like that of Life; like the firmament he wanted no support; like the wind he knew no obstacles; his heart was pure like the water (of rivers or tanks) in autumn; nothing could soil him like the leaf of a lotus; his senses were well protected like those of a tortoise; he was single and alone like the horn of a rhinoceros; he was free like a bird; he was always like the fabulous bird Bhāruṇḍa, valorous like an elephant, strong like a bull, difficult to attack like a lion, steady and firm like Mount Mandara, deep like the ocean, mild like the moon, refulgent like the sun, pure like excellent gold; like the earth he patiently bore everything; like a well-kindled fire he shone in his splendour.'[2]

Many legends are told of Mahāvīra's absolute absorption in meditation and of his unconsciousness of outward circumstances during these years. One of these stories has a slight resemblance to that of King Alfred and the cakes: Once upon a time the great ascetic sat down to meditate on the outskirts of Kumāragrāma. He crossed his ankles, and, gazing fixedly at the tip of his nose, was soon so immersed in reflection as to be lost to all that went

[1] There is a Gujarātī couplet:
'Water should be allowed to flow that it become not stagnant,
Monks should be allowed to wander that they may be stainless.'
A Sanskrit proverb runs: 'A monk who wanders is worshipped.'

[2] *Kalpa Sūtra*, *S.B.E.*, xxii, pp. 260, 261.

on around him. A busy farmer bustled past and asked this man who was sitting down and apparently doing nothing to look after his bullocks till his return. Mahāvīra neither heard the request nor saw the animals, far less took care of them. On his return the farmer saw the apparently idle man still seated doing nothing, but could get no answer from him as to the whereabouts of his beasts and had to go off in search of them. The bullocks meanwhile, having eaten their fill, returned and lay down to rest beside the gentle saint. The poor owner searched for the beasts the whole night through, and was enraged on returning next morning to find where they were, for it seemed to him a plot to steal the animals; so he seized their halter and began to beat Mahāvīra with it. Fortunately the god Indra knew what was happening and interfered in time to stop such sacrilege; but he begged Mahāvīra to allow him in future to guard him himself, or to appoint some other god to do so. The saint, however, refused any protection, saying that, just as a Tīrthaṅkara must always obtain omniscience by his own unaided efforts, so must he attain Mokṣa unprotected by any one. But the gods had grown nervous lest Mahāvīra should be killed inadvertently, so Indra, without the saint's knowledge, appointed one Siddhārtha (a cousin of Mahāvīra's who had become a god) to protect him.

Enlightenment and Death.

How Mahāvīra attained Omniscience.

We have seen that Mahāvīra was born with three degrees of knowledge and had acquired the fourth. He was now, at the end of his twelve years of wandering and penance, to acquire the fifth degree—*Kevala jñāna* or Omniscience. In the thirteenth year after his renunciation of the world and initiation as an ascetic, Mahāvīra stayed in a place not very far from the Pārasnāth hills called Jṛimbhakagrāma.[1] There was a field there belonging to a farmer

[1] Also called Jṛimbhilā or Jṛimbhikagrāma.

called Samāga[1] which surrounded an old temple, and through this field the river Ṛijupālikā[2] flowed. One afternoon Mahāvīra was seated under the shade of a Sāla tree in this quiet meadow in deepest meditation. Just as before his initiation, so now he had fasted for two-and-a-half days without even touching water, and as he sat there lost in thought, he peacefully attained supreme knowledge. Henceforth he possessed 'complete and full, the unobstructed, unimpeded, infinite and supreme, best knowledge and intuition called Kevala jñāna'. His meditations and austerities had been so profound as to destroy the last of all the karma, the enemies to enlightenment, knowledge and freedom, and henceforth his pathway would be unimpeded. Mahāvīra now added to his titles those of *Jina* (or Conqueror of the Eight Karma, the great enemies), from which Jainism derives its name, *Arhata* (or Being worthy of Veneration), *Arihanta* (or Destroyer of Enemies) and *Aruhanta* or (One who has killed even the roots of karma).

Mahāvīra as a Preacher.

Now,[3] as the conqueror of karma and equipped with supreme knowledge, Mahāvīra began to teach his way, and his first sermon was on the five great vows which we shall study later.

The Jaina declare that Mahāvīra's great message to mankind was that birth is nothing and caste nothing, but karma everything, and on the destruction of karma future happiness depends.

The Brāhmans had laid stress on birth, and had insisted that, however bad a Brāhman were, he would need to do small penance compared with what would be obligatory on even a righteous man of low caste.

Mahāvīra's contemporary Buddha had taught that in desire lay the cause that led to rebirth; that mental

[1] Or Samāka or Sāmaka.

[2] Or Ṛijukula, or Ṛijuvālikā.

[3] If Mahāvīra had preached before he got *Kevala jñāna*, his sermons would have contained some mistakes; now of course they were perfect.

discipline was of supreme importance, and asceticism and austerity of no avail. Mahāvīra, on the contrary, laid the greatest stress on asceticism. In its glow karma could be burnt up, and only through austerities could one become a Tīrthaṅkara.

Mahāvīra's first disciple was Gautama Indrabhūti, who in turn became a Kevalī, and whose story we tell later. After instructing Gautama, Mahāvīra set off on his preaching tours in real earnest, and taught his Rule with great acceptance to all his warrior kinsfolk. Like Buddha, he preached first to the rich and aristocratic, and though his followers to-day are to be found more amongst the middle classes, his earliest supporters seem to have been rulers and petty kings. This may have been because they too disliked Brāhman pretensions and were pleased that one of their own kinsfolk should lead a revolt against them. Mahāvīra's connexions through his mother Triśalā must have been invaluable to him at the beginning of this work; indeed, Dr. Jacobi thinks that the real meaning of the story about the removal of the embryo from one mother to another was to hide the fact that Mahāvīra was really the son of another and far less highly connected wife of the king, and to pretend that he was the son instead of the stepson of Triśalā.[1] This of course the Jaina indignantly deny. The Digambara and Śvetāmbara legends give the names of the different rulers Mahāvīra visited, and tell how Ċetaka, king of Videha, became a patron of the order, and Kuṇika, king of Aṅga, gave him the most cordial welcome, and how, when he travelled as far as Kauśāmbī, he was received with the greatest honour by its king Satānika, who listened with deep interest to his preaching, and eventually entered his order. The Digambara claim that in thirty years he converted to Jainism Magadha, Bihār, Prayāga, Kauśāmbī, Ċampāpurī and many other powerful states in North India. They believe that he did not travel alone,

[1] See Introduction, *S. B. E.*, xxii, p. xxxi.

but that everywhere he went he was accompanied by all the monks and nuns who had entered his order (eventually these amounted to fourteen thousand persons), and that magnificent halls of audience were erected for him to preach in. He preached in a language which they call An-akṣarī, which was unintelligible to the common people, so Gautama acted as his interpreter and translated all he said into Māgadhī.

According to the Digambara again, the place Mahāvīra loved best of all was Rājagṛiha, the capital of Magadha. Its king Śreṇika, with his whole army, had gone out to do honour to the saint on his first entry into the country and had been won over by him. The king asked sixty thousand questions concerning the faith, and all of them being satisfactorily answered by Gautama, he entered the order and became one of the staunchest champions of Jainism.

The Śvetāmbara have recorded the names of the places where Mahāvīra stayed during each rainy season, and they cover a period of forty-one years. First, they say, he went to Asthikagrāma (the village of bones). The name of this village, the commentators declare, was originally Vardhamāna (the Kāṭhiāwāḍ Jaina believe it to have been identical with the modern Waḍhwāṇ); but an evil demon, Yakṣa, collected there an enormous heap of bones belonging to all the people he had killed, and on this heap the inhabitants built a temple, hence the change of name.

Mahāvīra then spent three rainy seasons in Ċampā and Pṛiṣṭiċampā (Bihār). As a prophet he cannot have been without honour in his own country, for he spent twelve monsoons at Vaiśālī and its suburb Vāṇijyagrāma, doubtless recruiting for his order, which, having at its head the brother of their king, naturally held out many attractions to the inhabitants. He was also able to win over all the members of the order of Pārśvanātha to which he had originally belonged. He paid even more visits to Rājagṛiha, where, as the Śvetāmbara and Digambara both agree, he was much beloved, and whose inhabitants prevailed on him to return fourteen times. Another favourite resort, Mithilā, has provided the Jaina ascetics with a proverb: 'If Mithilā burns, what have I to lose?'; and it must have been a place of considerable importance, for Mahāvīra spent six monsoons there, and its kings, as we know from other sources, were men of high standing and culture. The great ascetic spent two rainy seasons in Bhadrikā, and then just for one monsoon he went to Ālabhikā, to Puṇitabhūmi, and to Śrāvastī in turn, and his last monsoon he spent at Pāpā (or Pampā).

It will be noticed how closely these travels of Mahāvīra resemble those of Buddha, and this, and the fact that *they never met*, led to a doubt of Mahāvīra's separate existence. It must have required no small tact to have won over the members of an order to which he had once belonged and afterwards left, but, despite this tact, Mahāvīra seems never to have possessed the personal charm which Buddha had, a charm which even Western people can feel to-day as they read his story; but the Jaina leader certainly possessed a greater power of organization (a gift which seldom goes with charm), and to this faculty we owe the existence of Jainism in India to-day.

The work of Mahāvīra during these years must have closely resembled that of the Dominican or Franciscan monks who (owing how much of their inspiration to him and his compeers we do not know) were to wander over Europe centuries later.

About a year after gaining Omniscience Mahāvīra became a Tīrthaṅkara, one of those who show the true way across the troubled ocean of life. The path Mahāvīra pointed out for others to follow lay in becoming a member of one of the four Tīrtha—a monk, or nun, if possible, otherwise a devout layman or lay woman.

We come now to the closing scene of Mahāvīra's life.

He died in his seventy-second year, some fifty years before his rival and contemporary Buddha.[1] Modern research has shown that the traditional dates for his birth and death,[2] 599 B.C. and 527 B.C., cannot be far wrong. The death of Mahāvīra.

Mahāvīra's last rainy season was spent in Pāpā, the modern Pāvāpurī, a small village in the Patna district which is still held sacred by the Jaina. The king of Pāpā, Hastipāla, was a patron of Mahāvīra's, and, according to some accounts, it was in his 'office of the writers' that the saint died. Sitting in the Samparyaṅka position, he delivered the fifty-five lectures that explain the results of karma and recited the thirty-six unasked questions (i. e. the *Uttarādhyayana Sūtra*), and having finished his great lecture on Marudeva he died all alone, and cut asunder the ties of birth, old age and death.[3]

Legends have gathered as thickly round Mahāvīra's death as round his birth. One tells how nearly all the ruling chiefs of the country had gathered to hear his discourses, and how the saint preached to them with wonderful eloquence for six days; then on the seventh he took his seat upon a diamond throne in the centre of a magnificent hall, which had been specially built for him on the borders of a lake. His hearers had arranged themselves into twelve grades according to their rank, for all were there from the king to the beggar. It was a dark night, but the hall was brilliantly illumined by the supernatural glow that issued from the gods who had come to listen to the illustrious preacher. Mahāvīra preached all night, and towards dawn his hearers fell asleep. The saint knew by his Śukladhyāna that his end was drawing nigh, so he sat reverently with clasped hands and crossed knees (the Samparyaṅka position), and, just as the morning dawned,

[1] Hoernle, *A.S.B.*, p. 42. Buddha's dates are 557–477 B.C.

[2] The word the Jaina prefer to use instead of Death is Mṛityu Mahotsava or Great Death Festival.

[3] *Kalpa Sūtra*, *S.B.E.*, xxii, p. 264 ff.

he attained Nirvāṇa, and the people awakened only to find their lord was dead.

Now at last Mahāvīra was freed; his forty-two years as a monk with all their self-denial and austerities had completely exhausted his karma. He had, unaided, worked out his own salvation, and never again could the accumulated energy of his past actions compel him to be reborn, for all their force was spent. The Jaina say there are two Terrible Ones who dog the soul, like policemen attending a prisoner: one is called Birth and one Death. 'He who is born must die some day or other, and he who is dead must be born in some form or other.' These two Terrible Ones had no longer any power over Mahāvīra, for the chain of karma that bound him to them had been snapped, and never again could the prisoner be sentenced to *life*.

All of Mahāvīra's disciples had been present at his death, save the chief of them, Gautama Indrabhūti. This earliest disciple knew that he could never attain omniscience whilst he was attached to a human being; nevertheless, he could not conquer his love for his master. On the night of Mahāvīra's death he had been sent on some mission, and whilst absent he was able to overcome this last tie of friendship, and having attained Kevala jñāna,[1] he returned to find the master, whom he no longer loved, dead and the people mourning.

The kings who were present on the night that Mahāvīra died instituted an illumination to commemorate him, for they said, 'Since the light of intelligence is gone, let us make an illumination of material matter';[2] and this the Jaina claim to be the origin of the yearly festival of lamps, Divālī, which the Hindus and they alike observe.

Some Digambara give a different version of the saint's

[1] It was only for sixty-four years after Mahāvīra's death that it was possible for any one to obtain Kevala jñāna, but during that time not only Gautama but also Sudharma (on Gautama's death) and Jambū (on Sudharma's death) became omniscient.

[2] *Kalpa Sūtra*, *S. B. E.*, xxii, p. 266.

death, according to which they say that there was neither hall, illumination, nor audience, but that Mahāvīra died quietly and alone, and when he had passed away only his nails and hair were left, all else had dried up and disappeared with his karma. A new body was made from these relics, which was duly cremated with all fitting ceremony.

Mahāvīra's enemies record yet another version—that the saint died in a fit of apoplectic rage. But this hardly accords with the character of the man, nor with his probable physical condition after such prolonged austerities.

Both Digambara and Śvetāmbara Jaina love to visit Pāvāpurī at the feast of Divālī. There are several small temples there belonging to both sects, but the main temple is the one which contains the footprints of Mahāvīra, and a narrow stone bridge leads to this shrine over a lake on which bloom white and red lotus lilies.

Previous incarnations of Mahāvīra.

Mahāvīra, or rather his jīva, the more orthodox Jaina believe, passed through many incarnations previous to his birth as Mahāvīra. Some of the more modern members of the community believe these to be purely legendary, but they illustrate the Jaina view of karma so pictorially as to be worth quoting here.

Once upon a time Mahāvīra was incarnate as a carpenter called Nayasāra, who worked at his trade in the jungle. One day he met there some tired, travel-worn Jaina sādhus, whom he took pity on and fed. They preached to him in return the Jaina creed, with the result that he became a convert. He met his death later through a branch of a tree falling on him, and was reborn as Marīci, the grandson of Ṛiṣabhadeva, the first Tīrthaṅkara.

This was the most famous of his early incarnations, and during it he became a sādhu through listening to a sermon of Ṛiṣabhadeva's. However, he found the life of an ascetic as usually practised very hard, and the hardest part of all was to remember to control speech, word and act, which the Jaina call the three *Daṇḍa*. This difficulty he evaded by an ingenious mechanical pun. The word *Daṇḍa* or stick is the same as the word *Daṇḍa* that connotes the three controls he found it so hard to exercise, so he gathered together three sticks and preached far and wide the comforting doctrine that any ascetic might do what he liked and linger at will on the primrose path of dalliance, provided he carried in his hand three rods. He gained a disciple, Kapila, who preached the doctrine even more vigorously than his master.

Mahāvīra was then reborn a god, and in his next birth was born as a Brāhman, and after that he was born alternately as a god and a Brāhman, with the occasional interlude of being born a king, for countless ages. He was once the famous king Vāsudeva or Tripṛiṣṭa, and during this incarnation he wrought so many evil deeds that he was condemned to spend his next rebirth in hell (Naraka); from there he issued forth in his following incarnation as a lion. When a lion he slew so many people that his evil karma condemned him once more to Naraka for an incarnation; when that was over he became a god, and then a Brāhman, and, alternating between the two, he at last arrived at his twenty-seventh and most famous incarnation as Mahāvīra. During his incarnation as Maričī he had learned [1] that he was to be the twenty-fourth and last Tīrthaṅkara, whereupon he had been so overcome with pride and joy and had shown so much conceit, that he had accumulated a great weight of karma; it was this that very nearly resulted in his being born a Brāhman, but fortunately his karma was exhausted just before his birth in time to admit of his embryo being removed from 'the beggarly Brāhman stock' to the womb of a Kṣatriya lady.

The Jaina women have a story to account for the dis-

[1] King Bharāta had once asked his father Ṛiṣabhadeva who would be among the next Tīrthaṅkara, and Ṛiṣabhadeva had pointed to Maričī who was sitting last in the assembly.

appointment of the poor Brāhman lady Devānandā, which was due, they say, to her evil karma. In a previous incarnation Devānandā and Triśalā had been sisters-in-law, and Devānandā had taken advantage of their intimacy to steal a priceless jewel from Triśalā, and so, by the automatic working of the law of karma, which invariably makes the punishment fit the crime, her jewel of a son was removed from her and given to the woman she had wronged.

CHAPTER IV

MAHĀVĪRA'S PREDECESSORS AND DISCIPLES

Pārś-vanātha.

PĀRŚVANĀTHA, the Tīrthaṅkara who immediately preceded Mahāvīra, may also have been an historical person. Very probably he did something to draw together and improve the discipline of the homeless monks who were outside the pale of Brāhmanism, much as St. Benedict did in Europe. If so, he was the real founder of Jainism, Mahāvīra being only a reformer who carried still further the work that Pārśvanātha had begun.

The Jaina say that Pārśvanātha was born in what is now the city of Benāres about 817 B.C. His father, Aśvasena, was the king of that town, and to his mother, Queen Vāmā, were granted the wonderful dreams which always foretell the birth of a Tīrthaṅkara. Before he was born, his mother, lying in the dark, saw a black serpent crawling about by her side, and so gave her little son the name of Pārśva. All his life Pārśvanātha was connected with snakes, for when he was grown up he was once able to rescue a serpent from grave danger. A Brāhman ascetic was kindling a fire, without noticing whether in so doing he was destroying life or not, when Pārśvanātha happened to pass and drew from the log the Brāhman was lighting a poor terrified snake that had taken up its abode in the wood.

Whilst in the world, Pārśvanātha bore himself with great credit; he was a brave warrior and defeated the Yavana king of Kaliṅga, and he eventually married Prabhāvatī, daughter of Prasannajita, king of Ayodhyā.

At the age of thirty he renounced the world and became an ascetic with the same ceremonies that have been described in the case of Mahāvīra. In order to gain Omniscience he practised austerities for eighty-three days, and during this time an enemy, Kamaṭha, caused a heavy downpour of rain to fall on him, so that these austerities might be made as trying to flesh and blood as possible. Now this enemy was no one else than the Brāhman ascetic whose carelessness in a previous incarnation had so nearly caused the death of the poor snake. But if Pārśvanātha's enemies were active, his grateful friends were no less mindful of him, and the snake, who by now had become the god Dharaṇendra, held a serpent's hood over the ascetic, and sheltered him as with an umbrella; and to this day the saint's symbol is a hooded serpent's head. On the eighty-fourth day Pārśvanātha obtained Kevala jñāna seated under a Dhātaki tree near Benares.

He now became the head of an enormous community, his mother and wife being his first disciples. Followed by these, he preached his doctrines for seventy years, until at last his karma was exhausted, and, an old man of a hundred years, he reached deliverance at last on Mount Sameta Śikhara in Bengal, which was thenceforth known as the Mount of Pārśvanātha.

The four vows of Pārśvanātha.

Pārśvanātha made four vows binding on the members of his community: not to take life, not to lie, not to steal and not to own property. He doubtless felt that the vow of chastity and celibacy was included under the last two heads, but in the two hundred and fifty years that elapsed between his death and the coming of Mahāvīra, abuses became so rife that the latter was forced to add another vow—that of chastity—to those already enumerated. This he did by dividing the vow of property specifically into two, one part relating to women and the other to material possessions. Some Jaina, however, believe that Pārśvanātha's four vows were those of non-killing, non-lying, non-stealing and chastity, that it was the promise to keep nothing as one's own possession that Mahāvīra added to these, and that it was in order to keep this vow that Mahāvīra himself went about naked.

Another reform which they say Mahāvīra introduced was the making confession compulsory instead of optional for monks. All these traditions bear out the idea that Mahāvīra was a reformer rather than a founder of his faith and order, and that the rule of Pārśvanātha had not been found in practice sufficiently stringent.

The Twenty-two Earlier Tīrthaṅkara.

Jainism the oldest religion.

We have begun our survey of Jaina legend with the birth of Mahāvīra, but no Jaina historian would do that. The Jaina firmly believe that theirs is the oldest religion in India, and delight to quote many passages [1] from the Veda which prove to them that Jainism existed before the Veda were written and cannot therefore be an offshoot of Brāhmanism, as most scholars believe. They reject the old theory [2] that Gautama Indrabhūti revolted from Jainism and became the founder of Buddhism, and claim Buddhism as a late offshoot of Jainism, telling the following legend to prove it. During the interval between the days of Pārśvanātha and those of Mahāvīra there lived a certain Jaina monk called Buddha Kīrti, who was well learned in the scriptures. One day he was performing austerities by the side of the river Sarayū in Pālāśa Nagara, and as he sat there he saw a dead fish floating by him. As he watched it, he reflected that there could be no harm in eating the flesh of dead fish, for there was no soul within it. This thought inspired him, the Jaina say, to found a new religion; he left his austerities, assumed red garments, and preached Buddhism.

According to the Jaina, the best way to begin the study of their history is through the stories of the Tīrthaṅkara. We have studied the lives of the two latest Tīrthaṅkara, Pārśvanātha, the twenty-third, and Mahāvīra, the twenty-

[1] See, for instance, *Jain Itihās* series, No. 1, a lecture by Lāla Benārsi Dāss, M.A., Agra, 1902.

[2] They declare that this mistake was never made by Jaina, only by European scholars.

fourth; but the Jaina have legends regarding each one of their predecessors.

1. Ṛiṣabhadeva or Ādinātha.

The first Tīrthaṅkara was born when the world had passed out of its happiest stage and was in the era of Suṣama Duṣama.[1] A Rajput king had a little son born to him, whom his mother called Ṛiṣabhadeva, because in her dream she had seen a bull (*riṣabha*) coming towards her. Ṛiṣabhadeva (also called Ādinātha) taught men seventy-two arts and women sixty-four, for these have only to be skilled in domestic and not in literary and industrial crafts; but his great glory lies in the fact that he first taught men the Jaina faith. He lived for eighty-four lakhs of pūrva of time, of which he spent only one lakh of pūrva as an ascetic. Ṛiṣabhadeva had one hundred sons (amongst whom was the famous king Bharata); their height was five hundred bow-shots. This first Tīrthaṅkara attained mokṣa from Aṣṭāpada (or Kailāsa) in the modern Himālayas.

2. Ajitanātha.

The world grew steadily worse, and in fifty lakhs of crores of sāgara of time the next Tīrthaṅkara, Ajitanātha, was born in Ayodhyā. After his birth all his father's enemies were conquered (*jita*), hence his name, ' the invincible one '. He was born in the period called Duṣama Suṣama, and all the remaining Tīrthaṅkara were born in the same period. His sign, which one sees on all his images in the temples, is an elephant. During his life he himself earned the title of Victorious, for he was so devout an ascetic that he was beaten by none in performing austerities. He attained mokṣa together with a thousand other Sādhus.

3. Sambhavanātha.

After thirty more lakhs of crores of sāgara Sambhavanātha, the third Tīrthaṅkara, was born in Śrāvastī of Rajput parents. The king his father had been distressed to see the way his dominions were ravaged by plague and famine, but when he heard the good news of the boy's birth, he felt there was a chance (*sambhava*) of better times coming, hence the boy's name. He too was able to persuade a thousand

[1] *Otherwise*: Suṣama Duḥṣamā.

ascetics to join his community or *saṅgha*, who eventually all attained mokṣa with him. His emblem is the horse.

4. Abhinandana. The fourth Tīrthaṅkara owes his name to the fact that the god Indra used to come down and worship (*abhinanda*) him in Vanitā, where his parents, Saṁvara and Siddārtha Rāṇī, ruled. He attained mokṣa accompanied by a thousand monks, as indeed did all the first eleven Tīrthaṅkara except Supārśvanātha. Abhinandana has the ape for his sign; he was born ten lakhs of crores of sāgara of time after his predecessor. His height was three hundred and fifty bow-shots.

5. Sumatinātha. The legend about the fifth Tīrthaṅkara, Sumatinātha, is more interesting; he was born in Kaṅkaṇapura, where his father, a Rajput named Megharatha, was king; his mother's name was Sumaṅgaḷā. The child was called Sumatinātha, because even before his birth his mother's intellect (*sumati*) was so sharpened. To prove the queen's ability, a story is told resembling that of the judgement of Solomon. An old Brāhman died, leaving two wives; both women claimed the only son as theirs, and the dispute was taken to the queen to settle, who decreed, as Solomon did (and with similar results), that the living child should be cut in two. This Tīrthaṅkara's sign is sometimes given as a red goose, but others say it is a red partridge. He was born nine lakhs of crores of sāgara after Abhinandana, and his height was three hundred bow-shots.

6. Padmaprabhu. Susīmā, the mother of the sixth Tīrthaṅkara, longed before his birth to sleep on a bed of red lotuses (*padma*), with the result that her son was always the colour of a red lotus, which flower he took for his emblem. His father, Dhara, was the Rajput king of Kauśāmbī. Padmaprabhu was born ninety thousand crores of sāgara of time after his predecessor; his height was two hundred and fifty bow-shots.

7. Supārśvanātha. The father of the next Tīrthaṅkara was the Rajput king of Benares; but his wife suffered from leprosy in both her sides. This dreadful disease was cured before the

child's birth, so he was given the name of *Su* (good) *pārśva* (side). His emblem is the Svastika symbol 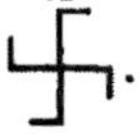. Unlike the other earlier Tīrthaṅkara he attained mokṣa with only five hundred companions. Nine thousand crores of sāgara of time had elapsed since the death of his predecessor, and his height was two hundred bow-shots.

8. Ċandraprabhu.

After a further interval of nine hundred crores of sāgara of time the eighth Tīrthaṅkara was born; his height was one hundred and fifty bow-shots. Before his birth his mother (the wife of the Rajput king of Ċandrapurī) longed to drink the moon (*ċandra*). To assuage her craving, a plate of water was one night handed to her in such a way that the moon was reflected in it; when the child was born, he was found to be as bright and white as the moon, which accordingly became his emblem, and he was called Ċandraprabhu.

9. Suvidhinātha.

Two names are given to the next Tīrthaṅkara. Owing to the peace he brought to a distracted family, all of whose kingly relatives were warring against one another, he is called Suvidhinātha, for on his birth they gave up fighting and took instead to performing their religious duties (*suvidhi*); but as his teeth were so beautiful that they resembled the buds of an exquisite flower (*puṣpa*), he was also called Puṣpadanta. There is a dispute over his emblem: the Śvetāmbara say it is the crocodile, while certain Digambara declare it is the crab. Ninety crores of sāgara elapsed before his birth, and his height was one hundred bow-shots.

10. Śītaḷanātha.

The tenth Tīrthaṅkara had a marvellous power of imparting coolness (*śītaḷatā*) to fevered patients. Before his birth his mother laid her hand on her husband, the Rajput king of Bhaddilapura, and immediately the fever which had defied all the efforts of his physicians left him, and all his life long the saint had a similar power, hence his name, Śītaḷanātha, Lord of Coolness. His sign is the Śrīvatsa svastika 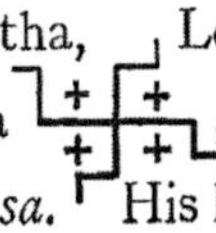, or according to the Digambara, the *Ficus religiosa*. His height was ninety bow-shots, and the interval of time between him and his predecessor was nine crores of sāgara.

11. Śreyāṁsanātha. King Viṣṇudeva, who ruled in Siṁhapurī, possessed a most beautiful throne, but unfortunately an evil spirit took up his abode in it, so that no one dare sit there. His wife, however, so longed to sit on it that she determined to do so at any risk; to every one's astonishment she was quite uninjured, so, when her son was born, he was named Śreyāṁsanātha, the Lord of Good, for already he had enabled his mother to cast out an evil spirit and so do a world of good (*śreyāṁsa*). His sign is the rhinoceros; one crore of sāgara of time had intervened before his birth; and his height was eighty bow-shots.

12. Vāsupūjya. Before the birth of the twelfth Tīrthaṅkara the gods Indra and Vasu used to go and worship the father of the future saint, and as the father's name was Vasupūja and the god Indra used to give him jewels called *vasu*, the child was naturally enough called Vāsupūjya. His sign is the male buffalo, and he passed to mokṣa from his birth-place, Ċampāpurī, accompanied by six hundred Sādhus. Fifty-four sāgara of time had intervened, and his height was seventy arrow-shots.

13. Vimaḷanātha. The sign of the thirteenth Tīrthaṅkara is the boar. He got his name Vimaḷanātha, Lord of Clearness, through the clearness (*vimaḷatā*) of intellect with which he endowed his mother before his birth, and which she displayed in the following manner. A certain man and his wife unwisely stayed in a temple inhabited by a female demon, who, falling in love with the husband, assumed his real wife's form. The miserable man was quite unable to tell which was his true wife, and asked the king of Kampilapura to distinguish between them. It was the queen, however, who solved the difficulty. She knew the long reach that witches and only witches have, and telling the husband to stand a long distance off, challenged the two wives to prove their chastity by touching him. Both

tried their utmost, but, of course, the human wife could not reach so far, whereas the demon wife did and thus showed her real character. Vimaḷanātha had six hundred companions to mokṣa. Thirty sāgara of time had passed before his birth, and his height was sixty bow-shots.

14. Anantanātha.

There was an endless (*ananta*) thread which lay about quite powerless in Ayodhyā; but after the king's wife had given birth to the fourteenth Tīrthaṅkara, it became endued with power to heal diseases; this event, combined with the fact that his mother had seen an endless necklace of pearls, decided the child's name. Anantanātha's birth was divided from his predecessor's death by nine sāgara of time, and his height was fifty bow-shots. His sign is the hawk, or, according to the Digambara, the bear.

15. Dharmanātha.

The fifteenth Tīrthaṅkara was born four sāgara of time after Anantanātha's Nirvāṇa, and his height was only forty-five bow-shots. His parents were the Rajput king and queen of Ratnapurī, and before his birth they exhibited such new zeal in the performance of their religious duties (*dharma*), that the child was given the name of Lord of Religion, Dharmanātha. He attained mokṣa with eight hundred monks. His sign is a thunderbolt.

16. Śāntinātha.

After the nirvāṇa of the ninth Tīrthaṅkara, Suvidhinātha, the Jaina faith disappeared until the birth of the tenth Tīrthaṅkara, who revived it; on his nirvāṇa it disappeared again, but was revived on the birth of the eleventh; and this continued to be the case until the birth of Śāntinātha, the sixteenth Tīrthaṅkara, after which it never disappeared again. The parents of this Tīrthaṅkara ruled in Hastināpura three sāgara of time after Dharmanātha's nirvāṇa. It happened that plague was raging. Before Śāntinātha's birth, however, his mother was able to stay the course of the pestilence by sprinkling the sufferers with water; so when the child was born he was called Śāntinātha, or Lord of Peace (*śānti*). The special interest of this saint lies in the fact that he was the first Tīrthaṅkara to become a ċakravartī,[1] or emperor of the whole of Bhārata (i.e. India). Śāntinātha's height was forty bow-shots, and his emblem is the deer. He attained mokṣa from Mt. Pārśvanātha in Bengal in company with nine hundred Sādhus. With the exception of four,[2] all the Tīrthaṅkara passed to nirvāṇa from this hill.

17. Kunthunātha. After half a palya of time the seventeenth Tīrthaṅkara was born in Gajapurī, where his parents, King Śivarāja and Queen Śrīdevī, reigned. Before his birth his mother saw a heap (*kuntha*) of jewels; during his life people began to show greater kindness to insects (*kunthu*), and the power of his father's enemies was stunted (*kuntha*). Kunthunātha's sign was the goat, and he was thirty-five bow-shots in height. He, like his predecessor, became an emperor, and obtained mokṣa from Pārśvanātha, but accompanied by a thousand companions.

18. Aranātha. Queen Devī, wife of King Sudarśana of Hastināpura, saw a vision of a bank of jewels before the birth of her son, the eighteenth Tīrthaṅkara, who was born a quarter palya of time after Kunthunātha. Aranātha was thirty bow-shots in height, his emblem is the third kind of svastika (the Nandāvartta), he was also an emperor, and he passed to mokṣa from Sameta Śikhara (Mt. Pārśvanātha) with a thousand monks.

19. Mallinātha. The nineteenth Tīrthaṅkara is the most interesting of all, for owing to deceitfulness in a previous life this saint was born as a woman;[3] having, however, done all the twenty things that make an ascetic a Tīrthaṅkara, nothing could prevent his becoming one, but his previous deceitfulness resulted in his becoming a female Tīrthaṅkara. She was born in Mithilā, where her parents, King Kumbera and

[1] There have been twelve of these great rulers, and these with the twenty-four Tīrthaṅkara, nine Baḷadeva, nine Vāsudeva, and nine Prati-vāsudeva make up the sixty-three Great Heroes of the Jaina.

[2] Riṣabhadeva, Vāsupūjya, Neminātha and Mahāvīra.

[3] See p. 121.

Queen Prabhāvatī, ruled. Before her birth her mother longed to wear a garland (*malli*) woven of the flowers of all seasons, and the gods and goddesses themselves brought the flowers to gratify her desire. Mallinātha's symbol is a water-jar, and she also passed to mokṣa from Sameta Śikhara. Her height was twenty-five bow-shots. The Digambara, who deny that any woman can pass to mokṣa without rebirth as a man, deny of course that Mallinātha could have been a woman. Another point of interest is that the time between the Tīrthaṅkara can now be measured by years, and this nineteenth Tīrthaṅkara was born a thousand crores of years after the eighteenth.

20. Munisuvrata. Before the birth of Munisuvrata, his mother, the wife of King Sumitra of Rājagṛiha, kept all the beautiful vows of Jainism (*su vrata*, good vows) as devoutly as if she had been an ordinary woman and not a queen; hence the child's name. His height was twenty bow-shots; he was born fifty-four lakhs of years after the last Tīrthaṅkara. His parents, while Kṣatriya or Rajputs, belonged to the Hari dynasty, whereas all the other Tīrthaṅkara, save the twenty-second, belonged to the Ikṣvāku family. His symbol is the tortoise.

21. Naminātha. The twenty-first Tīrthaṅkara was born in Mathurā after an interval of only six lakhs of years. His father, King Vijya, was engaged in an apparently hopeless warfare with his enemies, but the astrologers declared that if his wife, Queen Viprā, showed her face on the city wall (this was before the time of the zenana system) the enemy would bow down (*nama*) with fear and flee away. This all happened, and the child was named accordingly. Naminātha was fifteen bow-shots in height, his emblem is the blue lotus, and he attained mokṣa from Sameta Śikhara together with a thousand ascetics.

22. Neminātha, or Ariṣṭa Neminātha. The twenty-second Tīrthaṅkara (like the twentieth) is always represented as black; before his birth his mother, the wife of Samudravijaya, king of Saurīpura, saw a wheel (*nemi*) of black jewels (*ariṣṭa*). Kṛiṣṇa and his brother Baḷadeva lived at this time, and were cousins of Neminātha's. This Tīrthaṅkara was ten bow-shots in height, and his sign was the conch shell. Unlike most of the other Tīrthaṅkara, he attained mokṣa from Girnār in Kāṭhiāwāḍ.

The twenty-third and twenty-fourth Tīrthaṅkara are respectively Pārśvanātha and Mahāvīra.

The Followers of Mahāvīra.

Mahāvīra's unruly disciple Gośāla.

The peculiar temptations with which an ascetic's life are beset are illustrated for us in the life of Gośāla, an early antinomian. He seems to have been the head of a body of unclothed anchorites, a section of the Ājīvika monks, and joined forces with Mahāvīra whilst the latter was still practising austerities before the period of his enlightenment. Gośāla, Dr. Hoernle suggests in his exhaustive article on the Ājīvikas,[1] may either have been moved by a desire to learn the tricks of Mahāvīra's trade, or else the strong stern personality of the great ascetic may have had an irresistible attraction for the weaker sensual nature. At any rate, for six years they lived together, but a permanent association was impossible between a man like Mahāvīra and one of Gośāla's tricky, unreliable disposition.

There seems no doubt that they separated owing to some act of unchastity on Gośāla's part, and this had the natural effect of opening Mahāvīra's eyes to the special temptation besetting wandering mendicants. An added element of bitterness would be caused by the disciple venturing to preach before the master felt himself qualified to do so, for whilst Mahāvīra waited twelve years before teaching his Way, Gośāla preached after only six.

It was probably owing to Gośāla's conduct that Mahāvīra

[1] *E. R. E.*, vol. i.

added the vow of chastity to the four vows of Pārśvanātha's order, and all through the Jaina scriptures one seems to find references to this unworthy disciple. 'A wise man should consider that these (heretics) do not live a life of chastity.'[1] 'In the assembly he pronounces holy (words), yet secretly he commits sins; but the wise know him to be a deceiver and great rogue.'[2] A dialogue is given between a disciple of Mahāvīra's, called Ārdraka, and Gośāla, in which Gośāla, like many another impenitent, tries to defend himself by finding fault with his old leader, and takes up an antinomian position: 'according to our Law an ascetic, who lives alone and single, commits no sin if he uses cold water, eats seeds, accepts things prepared for him, and has intercourse with women.'[3]

The references to Gośāla in the Buddhist books, though slighter, bear out the same idea of his character. Dr. Hoernle mentions Buddha's well-known abhorrence of Gośāla, and tells how Buddha classified the ascetic systems differing from his own into those whose members lived in incontinency and those which could only be condemned as unsatisfying—placing Gośāla amongst the former.

Gośāla obtained this his best-known name through having been born in a cowshed, but he is also known by another name, that of Maṅkhali Putra, which the Jaina say was given to him because he was the illegitimate son of a monk. If there were this piteous taint in his blood it would account for his strange dual nature, his strivings, and his failure. After he left Mahāvīra, he and his followers seem to have lived in open defiance of all the laws of ascetic life, expressed or implied, and to have made their head-quarters in the premises of a potter woman in the town of Śrāvastī. There after sixteen years Mahāvīra found him and exposed his real character. Gośāla had previously tried to justify himself by adopting not only

[1] *Sūtra Kṛitāṅga*, *S.B.E.*, xlv, p. 245.
[2] Ibid., xlv, p. 273.
[3] Ibid., xlv, p. 411.

an antinomian position, but also one of absolute fatalism, in which he declared that all things were absolutely fixed and so man was relieved of all moral responsibility. Now he brought forward another doctrine, that of re-animation, by which he explained to Mahāvīra that the old Gośāla who had been a disciple of his was dead, and that he who now animated the body of Gośāla was quite another person; this theory, however, deceived nobody, and Gośāla, discredited in the eyes of the townspeople, fell lower and lower, and at last died as a fool dieth. Just before the end, however, the strange duality of his nature again asserted itself, and, acknowledging that all that Mahāvīra had said against him was true, and that he had left the true faith and preached a false one, he directed his own disciples to drag his body through the town by a rope for people to spit at, and to bury him with every mark of shame.[1] This command they naturally did not carry out, nor would it have been necessary for us so long after his death to have discussed this unhappy man, but for the profound effect his life had on the formulation of Mahavīra's doctrine.

Gośāla is of importance to those of us who are trying to understand Jainism for two reasons: the sin and shame of his life emphasized the need for stringent rules for the order; and the doctrine of absolute fatalism was shown to result in non-moral conduct. Jainism avoids this determinism, as we shall see later, by teaching that, though karma decides all, we ourselves can affect our past karma by our present life.

[1] Some Jaina believe that, because he so sincerely repented before his death, he went not to hell, but to one of the Devaloka, i.e. heavens, and is now, at the time of writing, in the Twelfth Devaloka, from which he will pass in another age to be a Tīrthaṅkara.

Other Disciples.

The Śvetāmbara tell the following story of the conversion of Mahāvīra's earliest and greatest disciple, Gautama Indrabhūti. It happened that once when Mahāvīra went to the city of Apāpā to preach, a rich Brāhman was preparing to offer a great animal sacrifice, and had invited Gautama Indrabhūti and his ten brothers to be present. They heard of the new teacher, and that he was denouncing the animal sacrifice at which they had assisted, and they were very much enraged at his audacity. They therefore determined to oppose him and expose the falseness of his teaching, but felt that they must first learn more of this new doctrine. They listened to Mahāvīra's discourses, and heard the gentle, thoughtful answers he gave to all questioners, till at length, being convinced of the truth of his Way, they cast in their lot with his, and became his chief disciples or Gaṇadhara.[1] Gautama Indrabhūti.

The Digambara give a different account of Gautama's conversion. Indrabhūti was, they say, born of Brāhman parents in a village called Gōvara, his father's name being Vasumati, and his mother's Pṛithvī;[2] he became a very learned paṇḍit and grew extremely vain of his learning. One day, however, an old man appeared and asked him to explain a certain verse to him. Mahāvīra had, the old man said, repeated the śloka to him, but had immediately afterwards become so lost in meditation that he could get no explanation of it from the saint, and yet he felt that he could not live unless he knew the meaning. The verse contained references to *Kāḷa*[3] and *Dravya*, *Pañća Astikāya*, *Tattva* and *Leśyā*,[4] not one of which could Gautama understand, but being too true a scholar to pretend to a knowledge which he did not possess, he sought out Mahāvīra to ask

[1] At this time Ċandana, daughter of Dadhivāhana, king of Ċampā, also entered the order and became the head of the nuns.
[2] *Sanskrit* Pṛithivī. [3] *Sanskrit* Kāla. [4] Often written *Leśā*.

for an explanation. The moment he was in the presence of the great ascetic all his pride in his fancied learning fell from him, and he besought Mahāvīra to teach him. He not only became a convert himself, but took over with him his five hundred pupils and his three[1] brothers.

The Sthānakavāsī tell yet a third story of Gautama's conversion. Indrabhūti was going to assist at a great sacrifice, but, to his surprise, he saw that all the gods, instead of going to the sacrifice, were going to hear an ascetic preach! Gautama asked who the ascetic was, and, going to meet him, was astonished at being called by his own name. He was still more astonished when Mahāvīra proceeded to answer all the unspoken questions and solve all the doubts that had been in his mind about *karma*, *jīva*, *mokṣa*, &c.

All sects believe that, however converted, Gautama by his intense attachment to his master, was for long prevented from attaining Kevala jñāna or Omniscience.

A sermon by Mahāvīra.

The Uttarādhyayana records a sermon entitled *The Leaf of the Tree* which the Jaina say Mahāvīra preached to Gautama to try and help him to reach Kevala jñāna. It is worth while studying it closely,[2] for it tells us much of Mahāvīra's doctrine. Mahāvīra warns Gautama that life will end sometime, even as the withered leaf of a tree must fall to the ground when its days are done; and that its duration is as brief as that of a dew-drop clinging to a blade of grass. Only when the chances of rebirth have resulted in one's being born as a human being can one get rid of the result (*karma*) of past action. How rare is the opportunity; for one's soul might have been imprisoned for aeons in an earth, or a fire, or a wind body; or it might have been clothed with a plant, an insect, or an animal form; one might have been born in heaven or hell as a god

[1] According to other accounts there were only two brothers.

[2] This sermon the Jaina regard as containing the essence of their religion.

or a demon, but only to a human being is the chance of escape open. Even if one happens to be born as a man, one might not be born an Ārya but only an aboriginal or a foreigner (to whom apparently Mahāvīra did not regard the way of escape as open); or if born as an Ārya, one might not be capable or have the opportunity of intelligently hearing and believing the Law; or again, one might not have the strength of will to choose the hard path of asceticism. As Gautama grows old and frail, this priceless opportunity which comes so seldom will gradually pass away from him, so Mahāvīra beseeches him to cast away every sort of attachment that might chain him to rebirth, and, since he has chosen the path of asceticism which leads to deliverance, to press on to the very end. 'You have crossed the great ocean, why do you halt so near the shore? Make haste to get on the other side and reach that world of perfection [nirvāṇa] where there is safety and perfect happiness.'

In the Uttarādhyayana it is recorded that the effect of this sermon was such as to enable Gautama to cut off love and reach perfection,[1] but the Kalpa Sūtra supports the current belief that it was not till the night that Mahāvīra died that this the oldest of his disciples 'cut asunder the tie of friendship which he had for his master, and obtained the highest knowledge and intuition called Kevala'.[2]

Gautama survived Mahāvīra for twelve years, and finally obtained nirvāṇa at Rājagṛiha at the age of ninety-two, having lived fifty years as a monk.

It will be remembered that ten[3] of Indrabhūti's brothers attached themselves to the great ascetic at the same time that he did. They, too, must have been men of strong character, for three[3] of them became heads of communities.

There was another great disciple of Mahāvīra called Sudharma, who also survived him, and to whom we are Sudharma.

[1] *S.B.E.*, xlv, p. 46. [2] Ibid., xxii, p. 265.
[3] The numbers vary in different versions of the story.

indebted for the Jaina scriptures. The Jaina say that Gautama Indrabhūti had become a Kevalī and imparted knowledge which was the result of his own thinking, but Sudharma, not having attained omniscience, could only pass on the teaching of others.[1] He therefore wrote out what he had heard his master say and compiled twelve Aṅga, eleven Upāṅga, and various other works. All that tradition states about Sudharma could be tersely expressed on a tombstone. He was born in a little village called Kollāga, his father was a Brāhman called Dhamila, and his mother's name was Bhaddila. He lived for fifty years as a householder before receiving ordination from Mahāvīra, and then followed him for thirty years. After Mahāvīra's death he became head of the community, and held that position for twelve years, till he too obtained Kevala jñāna, whereupon the headship of the order passed to a disciple of his named Jambū Svāmī. It is said that Sudharma attained mokṣa when a hundred years old.

[1] This must surely be one of the earliest references to the difference between original work and compilation !

CHAPTER V

HISTORY OF THE JAINA COMMUNITY

The Four Tīrtha.

DURING Mahāvīra's lifetime he attracted a great number of disciples, both men and women, and from these grew the four orders of his community: monks, nuns, laymen and laywomen.

Monks.

Chief amongst his followers were fourteen thousand monks (or *muni*) and at the head of these were eleven chief disciples or Gaṇadhara whom Jaina compare to the twelve disciples of our Lord, Gośāla the twelfth corresponding to Judas. Mahāvīra had seen in the case of Gośāla and others the special temptations and dangers which beset ascetics in their wandering life, and he resolved to combat these as well as he could by organization and regulations. He therefore divided his fourteen thousand followers into nine regular schools called *Gaṇa* and placed each school under the headship of one of his chief disciples or Gaṇadhara. The leading Gaṇadhara had five hundred monks under them, but some of the others had only three hundred or two hundred and fifty.

Gautama was at the head of a school of five hundred, and so were his brothers Agnibhūti and Vāyubhūti, his other brother Akampita[1] being at the head of three hundred scholars.

Sudharma was at the head of another school of five hundred monks.

Only two of these eleven Gaṇadhara, Gautama and Sudharma, survived Mahāvīra; the others attained Kevala jñāna and died of voluntary starvation at Rājagṛiha before their master's death.

[1] The Sthānakavāsī Jaina do not believe that Akampita was the brother of Gautama; they think he was only a friend.

All the present Jaina monks are considered to be the spiritual descendants of Sudharma, for the other Gaṇadhara left no disciples.

Nuns. Besides the fourteen thousand monks a great multitude of women followed Mahāvīra, and of these some thirty-six thousand, the Jaina say, actually left the world and became nuns. At their head (at least according to the Śvetāmbara) was Ċandana, a first cousin of Mahāvīra's, or as other accounts have it, his aunt.[1]

In those troublous times acts of oppression and violence must have often occurred, and it was such an act that led to Ċandana's becoming a nun. Once, as a girl, the story runs, Ċandana was walking in an open garden, when a wicked man named Vidyādhara saw her and, fascinated by her beauty, carried her off, meaning to take her to his own home. On his way thither he began to realize how displeasing her presence in his house would be to his wife, so, without troubling to take her back to the garden where he had found her, he abandoned her in a forest. A hillman found her weeping there, took her to Kauśāmbī and sold her to a wealthy merchant named Vṛiṣabhasena, who installed her in his house against his wife's will. The wife grew more and more jealous of her, for Ċandana's beauty increased every day, and ill-treated her in every possible way, clothing her in rags, feeding her on broken meats, and often beating her. Mahāvīra came and preached in Kauśāmbī and poor Ċandana needed but little persuasion to convince her of how evil a place the world was; gladly renouncing it she joined his community and eventually became the head of the nuns.[2]

Laymen. Mahāvīra's third order consisted of laymen; these

[1] Ċandana was the daughter of Ċetaka, king of Vaiśālī; and this Ċetaka was either the brother or the father of Triśalā, Mahāvīra's mother.

[2] The Sthānakavāsī legend differs a good deal. Ċandana according to this was captured in warfare and sold by a soldier into the house where she was ill-treated.

were householders who could not actually renounce the world, but who could and did keep his rule in a modified form, while their alms supported the professed monks. The genius for organization which Mahāvīra possessed is shown in nothing more clearly than in the formation of this and the order of laywomen. These two organizations gave the Jaina a root in India that the Buddhists never obtained, and that root firmly planted amongst the laity enabled Jainism, as we have seen, to withstand the storm that drove Buddhism out of India. The laymen,[1] *Śrāvaka* or Hearers as they were called, numbered during Mahāvīra's lifetime one hundred and fifty-nine thousand men.[2] At the head of their order were Śaṅkhajī and Śatakajī. These Hearers numbered amongst their ranks many nobles of high rank and even kings, who were delighted to thus proclaim their opposition to the priestly pretensions of the Brāhmans; nowadays the Śrāvaka are almost entirely recruited from the mercantile classes.

The fourth and last order consisted of devout laywomen or Śrāvikā, whose household duties prevented their becoming nuns, and who yet served the great ascetic in many ways. They numbered some three hundred and fifty-eight thousand, and at their head were two women Sulasā and Revatī. Sulasā is considered the highest type of the purely domestic woman, the faithful wife or *satī*, and the Gujarātī Jaina women sing the following verse about her in the hymn of praise to the sixteen faithful wives which they chant every morning when they get up: Lay-women.

Sulasā was a really faithful wife, there was no sham about her!
She found no pleasure in worldly delights.
If we saw her face sins would flee away,
If we mention her name our minds are filled with joy.

Revatī is typical of the generous woman who gladly gives alms to ascetics. Once when Mahāvīra was ill (injured

[1] It is interesting to compare with these the Gṛihastha of the Hindus.
[2] The Digambara say 100,000.

through the magic fire the faithless Gośāla had thrown at him) he felt that only one thing would cure him, and that was some of the jam which Revatī made. Much as he longed for it, however, he warned his disciples that they were not to accept it unless Revatī gave it gladly, for it was the very best jam! However, Revatī was so delighted to give it, and pressed it on the monks with such eagerness, that her name has ever since been a synonym for hospitality.

The Great Leaders.[1]

Mahāvīra was during his lifetime the head of all the four orders in his community. After his death Gautama Indrabhūti, according to some authorities,[2] succeeded him and continued to be the spiritual leader[3] for twelve years; he was followed by Sudharma, who held office for another twelve years. Jambū Svāmī, a pupil of Sudharma, succeeded his old master and led the community for twenty-four years; he was the last Jaina to obtain Kevala jñāna, for after him both mokṣa and omniscience were closed to men.[4] At the present time not only omniscience but also the degree of knowledge next below it, Manaḥparyāya jñāna, are lost to mankind.

Jambū Svāmī.

Jambū Svāmī is called 'the celibate', and the following story is told of him. He was the son of a rich merchant in Rājagṛiha, and eight other rich merchants of the same town offered him their daughters in marriage. He (though not only already convinced through Sudharma's teaching of the higher virtue of the unmarried state, but having

[1] The following history is gleaned entirely from Jaina sources and represents what the Jaina say about themselves and their past. It was found impossible to include all the legends, so the selection was left to Jaina paṇḍits who chose those which they considered of crucial importance for the comprehension of their religion. The dates, unless otherwise stated, are those given by the Jaina.

[2] According to others Gautama never held office, having become a Kevalī.

[3] The word the Gujarātī Jaina use for the spiritual headship is पाट *pāṭa*.

[4] This was a sign of the degeneration of the Avasarpiṇī.

actually taken a vow of perpetual celibacy!) offered no resistance to his father and eight would-be fathers-in-law, but married all the eight ladies. After the eight-fold marriage Jambū returned to his father's house, which that very night was attacked by Prabhava, the bandit son of Vindhya, king of Jaipur. The doughty robber had taken the precaution to weave a spell (for he was not only a prince and a robber but also a magician), which ought to have caused all the inhabitants of the merchant's house to fall into a deep sleep; but this aristocratic spell had no effect on Jambū. When Prabhava asked the reason, Jambū explained that, as he was going to enter a spiritual career the next morning, spells had no power over him; Prabhava tried to dissuade him, and apparently their discussion aroused the eight wives of the celibate, for they joined their entreaties with his. Jambū told them many moral tales showing the superior virtues of celibacy; the ladies replied with other stories upholding the honour of the married state, but the palm lay with Jambū, for not only was he, with his parents' consent, initiated next morning by Sudharma, but in a few days Prabhava, the robber, also followed his example and renounced not only his habit of acquiring other people's property, but also his own possessions.

Prabhava. Jambū attained mokṣa according to Jaina authorities in 403 B.C., and was succeeded by Prabhava, the erstwhile prince, robber and magician. It was no longer possible for any one to attain mokṣa, so Prabhava (who died 397 B.C.) was not immediately released from the cycle of rebirth; yet so famous a saint must eventually attain mokṣa, though he would first have to pass through one, three, five, or at most fifteen, rebirths.

It was during this time that the two sects of Osavāla Jaina and Śrīmāla Jaina arose. It is also said that it was now that the image of Mahāvīra was enshrined at Upakeśa Pāṭṭana. This is probably a reference to the first introduction of idol worship into Jainism.

Śayambhava.

Prabhava felt that there was no one amongst the Jaina capable of succeeding him as leader, and being much impressed by the spiritual genius of a staunch Brāhman called Śayambhava, he determined to win him over. He was successful and converted him just after he had offered a great sacrifice. Though he was married, he left his wife to become an ascetic, and the little son Manaka who was shortly after born to her eventually became a Jaina ascetic also, receiving initiation at his father's hands. Śayambhava knew by his supernatural powers that his son would only live a short time, so he wrote a book for him called Daśavaikālika, in which he gave a complete conspectus of the leading Jaina tenets; it is on this book (a monument of a father's love persisting even in the ascetic life) that Śayambhava's claim to fame rests.

He was followed by Yaśobhadra, who died in 319 B.C., and was succeeded by Sambhūtivijaya, who only held sway for two years. The rule of these two was not marked by any outstanding event, but after them we come to one of the great epochs in Jaina history, which began with the leadership of Bhadrabāhu, who succeeded in 317 B.C.

Bhadrabāhu.

The new leader was a scholar, and Jaina credit him with the authorship of the Niryukti or commentaries on the ten canonical books, and of a book on astronomy which is named after him the Bhadrabāhu Saṁhitā. He also wrote what the Śvetāmbara Jaina consider to be their holiest work, the Upasarga Harastotra Kalpa Sūtra.

It was during the headship of Bhadrabāhu and during the reign of Ċandragupta[1] of the Maurya dynasty that a great famine[2] took place, which seems to have been of the most terrible severity. It would of course be very

[1] Ċandragupta (*c.* 322–298 B.C.), grandfather of Aśoka and first paramount sovereign of India. According to Jaina tradition he abdicated in 297 B.C., became a Jaina ascetic, and died twelve years later of voluntary starvation in Śrāvaṇa Belgolā in Mysore.

[2] Dr. Hoernle suggests 310 B.C. as the date of this famine.

difficult for a starving population to support a huge body of mendicants during famine years, and as the monks were homeless and wanderers by profession, it was only sensible that they should wander where food was more plentiful. Now it is probable, as we have seen, that Mahāvīra's community or saṅgha had been formed by the union of two orders of mendicants, one clothed and one naked. This difference, being outward and visible, would be always liable to recur and cause schism, and probably the fusion of the two orders had never been complete, so that the famine sufficed to sever the community along the lines of the old division.

Sthūlabhadra.

Part of the community, numbering, the Jaina say, twelve thousand, went with Bhadrabāhu to the south of India where famine had not penetrated, whilst the other part, also amounting to twelve thousand, remained behind under the leadership of Sthūlabhadra. Sthūlabhadra was the son of Śakaḍāla, who had been prime minister to the ninth Nanda king; on his father's death he was offered the post, but renounced that and all earthly love to become an ascetic.

It was naturally only the more vigorous monks who undertook the long journey to Southern India, and perhaps the older and more infirm ascetics who remained at home had already been allowed to wear some clothing as a concession to their infirmities; the habit of so doing[1] would have been likely now to become general amongst them. Thus one element of division was established amongst the Jaina, that of difference in practice, and it only remained, in order to make the division permanent, that they should have a differing sacred literature. Experience has shown what a unifying force a common sacred literature has on divergent sects, and the converse is also true. For example, it is probably only their refusal to accept the Veda as sacred which has prevented the Jaina from being long ago amalgamated

[1] They seem generally to have worn white garments.

with the Hindus. This element of division was not to be lacking between the two sects of Jaina. Sthūlabhadra was, the Jaina say, keenly alive to the importance of preserving their sacred literature, and he alone had learnt (in Nepāl) the ten Pūrva and (on condition of keeping them secret) the four other Pūrva. In spite of the absence of Bhadrabāhu and his party, he called a council at Pāṭaliputra (modern Patna), which collected the Eleven Aṅga, but found that the Twelfth was missing. This Twelfth Aṅga contained fourteen Pūrva, which Sthūlabhadra was able to supply. When the famine was over, Bhadrabāhu returned; but he and his party refused to accept the work of the council of Patna and declared that the Aṅga and Pūrva were lost; they also declined to wear clothes. Though all this laid a very firm foundation for the schism between the Digambara (sky clothed, i.e. naked) and the Śvetāmbara (white clothed) when it should come, yet the split did not actually arise till A.D. 142, according to Jaina dates, or A.D. 82 according to Dr. Hoernle.

Bhadrabāhu died in 297 B.C. and was succeeded by Sthūlabhadra, who remained the head of the whole community till his death in 252 B.C.

Śrutakevalī. The six spiritual leaders who followed Jambū Svāmī are called Śrutakevalī, because, though the complete omniscience Jambū Svāmī and his predecessors attained was denied to them, they possessed complete knowledge of the scriptures. **Daśapūrvī.** They were followed by the Daśapūrvī, or leaders who knew the ten Pūrva of the Twelfth Aṅga.

The Great Schism.

Two schisms had already taken place during the lifetime of Mahāvīra, and two leaders had left the community. One was headed by Jamāli, son-in-law of Mahāvīra, who denied that a thing is perfected when it is begun (which some Jaina scriptures teach), and was specially annoyed when the doctrine, to his own discomfort, was applied by a disciple to the practical question of bed-making.

The other we have already noted; it was led by Gośāla,[1] and its main tenet was Fatalism.

During the years that immediately followed the death of Sthūlabhadra three more schisms took place, seriously weakening the Jaina church. In 251 B.C. Aṣāḍhā Āćārya headed a schism called Avyakta. Four years later Aśvamitra left the Jaina community and became head of the Kṣaṇikavādī; and in 239 B.C. a Jaina called Gaṅga led a fifth schism.

The great schism had not, however, as yet taken place. It is interesting to remember that Bhadrabāhu had returned from South India to be head over the whole community, even over the refractory part that had taken to clothes; that he, the staunch believer in nakedness, had been followed by Sthūlabhadra, the clothed; and that this man in his turn was followed by a leader who discarded clothing.

Mahāgiri, the next head of the community after Sthūlabhadra's death, is said to have revived 'the ideal practice of nakedness' which had fallen into disuse. During his rule two famous Jaina books are said to have been written: *Tattvārtha Sūtra*, by Umāsvāti, and the *Pannavaṇā Sūtra* (one of the *Upāṅga*), by Śyāmāćārya, who was himself a disciple of Umāsvāti. Mahāgiri's rule is also noteworthy for his endeavours to bring the community back to their primitive faith and practice; he was a real ascetic and recognized that under Sthūlabhadra's sway many abuses had crept into the order. It was doubtless this that had led so many of the community to drift away from it under the leaders of the schisms already mentioned. Mahāgiri was spurred on in his efforts after reform by the memory of a prophecy which foretold that after Sthūlabhadra the monks would become less strenuous in their lives. He was defeated in his aims by the conversion of Samprati, grand-

Mahāgiri.

Samprati.

[1] See p. 58.

son and successor of Aśoka[1] and by the disastrous effects of the royal bounty that thenceforth flowed into the community.

The legend of Samprati's conversion is given as follows by the Śvetāmbara. Suhastin was one of the leading members of the Jaina community under Mahāgiri, and he once met King Samprati in Ujjain (East Mālwā). Now in a previous birth Samprati had been a beggar and had seen Suhastin's disciples carrying sweets. When he asked for some of this confectionery Suhastin said he could only give them on condition of Samprati's becoming his disciple, so he received initiation, took the sweets, ate heartily of them and died. When, as King Samprati, he saw Suhastin again, his former birth came back to his memory, and he again became a convert to Jainism. Samprati tried to spread Jainism by every means in his power, working as hard for Jainism as Aśoka had for Buddhism: he even sent preachers as far as Afghanistan; but unfortunately he quite demoralized the monks with the rich food he showered upon them. Suhastin dared not refuse this food, for, as in his previous birth, the king laid great stress on diet and would have been irreconcilably offended if it and his superabundant alms had been refused. So the old leader of the community, Mahāgiri, saw all his hopes of winning the monks to lives of sterner asceticism overturned; and, finding that remonstrance with Suhastin was of no avail, he separated from him and withdrew to Daśārṇabhadra, where he committed suicide by voluntary starvation.

Suhastin. After Mahāgiri's death Suhastin became *de jure* the leader that he had previously been *de facto*, and the Jaina account him one of their greatest spiritual heads. A strong man was needed, for the community had been much weakened by the three schisms and by the late quarrel between

[1] Aśoka was Emperor of India 273–231 B.C. The Jaina say that he was a Jaina before he was converted to Buddhism.

Mahāgiri and himself; Suhastin therefore set himself to gain new disciples, and owing to his influence many new branches of the order were formed. Perhaps new recruits were received too readily, at any rate it was under him that Avantī Kumāra, whom the Jaina cite as the typical man who found the ascetic life too hard, joined the order. Avantī, the son of a rich man and brought up in luxury, could not bear all the suffering and hardships which fell to his lot as a monk. He dared not return to the world, so, to put an end to a position which he found intolerable, he committed suicide by fasting. His relatives built a magnificent temple on the spot where he died, and the Jaina say that this was the temple of Mahākāla in Ujjain, which is now, however, one of the twelve most famous Śaiva temples in India. Poor Avantī's story is still quoted as a warning not to enter on the mendicant life without counting the cost, and he is known as Avantī Sukumāra—Avantī the delicate.

Susthitasūri.

Suhastin was succeeded by Susthitasūri in 177 B.C. Under him, according to the Jaina, their name of Nirgranthagaćcha was changed to that of Kalikagaćcha in honour of the krores of times the leader repeated the secret mantra taught him by his guru.

Indradinna.

Indradinna, who followed Susthitasūri, is famous, not for anything that he did, but because the great Jaina saint Kalikāćārya flourished under his rule.

Kalikāćārya.

The Jaina tell many stories of Kalikāćārya and the occult powers that his great learning gained him. It was owing to these powers, they believe, that he was able in 61 B.C. to destroy the dynasty of Gardabhila. Kalikāćārya's sister was a nun, and she was once carried off by King Gardabhila. The saint went to a Scythian king and implored his assistance, but the king was afraid of attacking so powerful a sovereign as Gardabhila, especially as he was under the peculiar protection of the goddess Rāsabhī, who was able by the witchery of her singing to make it impossible for any one to approach within fourteen miles of the king.

Kalikāćārya could, however, on his part produce wealth by magic, and by this means he persuaded the Scythian king to come to his aid with an army. They encamped at a safe distance of about fifteen miles from King Gardabhila, and when his protecting goddess began to sing, all the Scythian army shot arrows at her mouth and filled it so full that she was unable to utter a sound. The spell being broken, Gardabhila was easily captured, and Kalikāćārya's sister released. The king Gardabhila was eventually forgiven and set at liberty; he betook himself to a neighbouring forest, where he was finally devoured by a tiger, to the total extinction of his race.

Kalikāćārya is, however, specially remembered through the dispute which continues to this day about the keeping of Pajjusaṇa,[1] some Jaina sects holding that it should begin on the fourth and some on the fifth day of the month Bhādrapada. The difference arose in this way: Kalikāćārya once visited the king of Peṇṭha (in the Dekkan) and asked him to come and listen to the discourses he was going to deliver at Pajjusaṇa. The king said he would have come if it had been any day but the fifth (in those days Pajjusaṇa only lasted for one day), but that being a special festival of Indra which he was bound to keep, he asked the saint to postpone the fast till the sixth. The ascetic, while declaring any postponement impossible, offered to arrange to hold it one day earlier, on the fourth of Bhādrapada. This was accordingly done, and ever since then some sects[2] have begun the fast on the fourth and some on the fifth. The importance they give to this difference reminds one of the old ecclesiastical dispute about the date of Easter.

Siddhasena Divākara.

According to the Jaina a learned ascetic, Siddhasena Divākara, the son of a Brāhman minister, lived about this

[1] Or Paryuṣaṇa, the sacred festival at the close of the Jaina year.

[2] The Tapagaććha observe the fourth, the Sthānakavāsī the fifth day, the Añćalagaććha sometimes the fourth and sometimes the fifth. Occasionally owing to differing astrologers all sects observe the same day as the beginning of the fast.

time at the court of King Vikramāditya.[1] There was another equally learned ascetic called Vṛiddhavādī, and these two were anxious to meet and discover whose learning entitled him to be regarded as the superior of the other. At last they did encounter each other, but unfortunately they met in a jungle where the only judges they could find to decide their cause were ignorant village cowherds. Siddhasena, fresh from the Sanskrit-loving court, began the dispute, but used so many Sanskrit words that the cowherds had no idea what he was talking about, and quickly gave the palm to Vṛiddhavādī who spoke in the simplest language and quoted many a shrewd rural jest and proverb ; so Siddhasena had to accept Vṛiddhavādī as his conqueror and guru. Siddhasena, however, still proud of his Sanskrit, formed the plan of translating all the Jaina scriptures from Māgadhī (a language understood by the common people) into Sanskrit: but his guru showed him the sin it would be thus to place them out of the reach of ordinary folk, and as penance for the very idea he wandered about for twelve years without uttering a word. His importance to Jainism lies evidently in his failure to sanskritize either the language or the scriptures ;[2] but he is also credited with the conversion to Jainism of King Vikramāditya of Ujjain and of Devapāla, king of Kumārapura. He is supposed to have died about 57 B.C.

Two other events are supposed to have happened about this time, the defeat of the Buddhists in a great argument by a famous Jaina controversialist, an ascetic called Ārya

[1] Vikramāditya, according to tradition, was king of Ujjain, and 'the golden age' of Sanskrit literature is said to have coincided with his reign. He is now considered by many scholars to be a purely legendary monarch.

[2] There is said to be always a marked difference between the speech of a Brāhman and a Jaina, since the former use as many Sanskrit words as possible, and the latter, especially the Sthānakavāsī, use the simple vernacular.

Khapuṭa who lived in Broach, and the founding of Śatruñjaya[1] in the state of Pālitāṇā.

Vajrasvāmī.

The next spiritual leader[2] of great importance for our purpose was Vajrasvāmī, the last and greatest of the Daśapūrvī. It was in his time that the sixth schism took place. A Jaina *sādhu* called Rohagupta[3] taught that there are not seven but only three constituent elements of the earth, viz.: Jīva, Ajīva and Nojīva; the schism is accordingly called the Nojīva schism and is believed to have arisen in A.D. 71. A seventh schism, led by Goṣṭa Mahāl, also took place under Vajrasvāmī's rule. The Jaina believe that Vajrasvāmī was able to call up at will a magic carpet which conveyed him and his friends to any distance, and that once by its means he transplanted the whole community from a famine-stricken district to the town of Purī. The more enlightened Jaina say that this carpet really represents some modern mode of locomotion (steam engine, motor car, or aeroplane) the secret of whose construction Vajrasvāmī had anticipated. Vajrasvāmī had a famous disciple, Āryarakṣita, who had originally been a Brāhman and had studied all knowledge at Benares. His mother spurred him on to study the Jaina Pūrva, and whilst doing so he was converted to Jainism and learnt from Vajrasvāmī the whole of the nine-and-a-half Pūrva. He is famous amongst the Jaina for having arranged the Sūtra into four divisions that they might be the more easily understood.

Vajrasena.

The Great Schism.

We now come to the great division of the community. Vajrasvāmī was followed by Vajrasena, and under his leadership the Digambara finally separated from the main community. The new Head had not the personality of his

[1] Śatruñjaya, the Jaina say, was built by a monk who had the power of rising through the air, and by a disciple of his who had the power of creating gold. This fortunate conjunction of talents has resulted in one of the loveliest temple cities in the world.

[2] Indradinna had been followed by Dinnasūri, and he by Siṁhagiri, and then came Vajrasvāmī.

[3] Rohagupta had a disciple called Kaṇāda who was, according to the Jaina, the founder of the famous Vaiśeṣika philosophy.

predecessors, and was probably not strong enough to hold the balance between two contending parties; at any rate the Digambara now hived off. Differing dates are given for the separation: the Śvetāmbara believe it to have taken place in A.D. 142, the Sthānakavāsī in A.D. 83, whilst Dr. Hoernle places the date about A.D. 79 or 82.

The Śvetāmbara declare that the opposition sect was really founded (like many another sect since!) in a fit of temper, and give the following account of how it occurred. A certain Śivabhūti, who had been in the service of the king of Rathavīrapura, decided to become a Jaina ascetic. On the day of his initiation the king gave him a most costly and beautiful blanket as a farewell present. Seeing how over-fond he was of it, his guru advised him to return the gift, but he refused; whereupon, to save him from the snare, the guru during his absence tore the blanket into small pieces. Śivabhūti was so angry when he found what had happened that he declared that if he might not keep his blanket he would keep no covering at all, but would wander naked through the world like the Lord Mahāvīra himself. His first two disciples were Kauṇḍinya and Kattavīra. His sister Uttarā also wanted to follow him, but, seeing that it was impossible for a woman to go about nude, Śivabhūti refused to allow her to join him and declared that no woman could attain mokṣa without rebirth as a man.

The probability is that there had always been two parties in the community: the older and weaker section, who wore clothes and dated from Pārśvanātha's time, and who were called the Sthavira kalpa (the spiritual ancestors of the Śvetāmbara); and the Jina kalpa, or Puritans, who kept the extreme letter of the law as Mahāvīra had done, and who are the forerunners of the Digambara.

The five main tenets of the Digambara in which they oppose the Śvetāmbara views[1] are: that the Tīrthaṇkara

[1] They also differ on many points of ritual and custom.

Differences between Śvetāmbara and Digambara.

must be represented as nude and unadorned, and with downcast eyes; that women cannot obtain mokṣa; that Mahāvīra never married; that once a saint had obtained Kevala jñāna he needed no food, but could sustain life without eating; and finally the great point over which the split occurred, that ascetics must be entirely nude, a decision which condemns the one or two Digambara ascetics now existing to live in the strict seclusion of a forest, somewhat to the relief of the reformers of their sect, who are thus saved from their interference.[1]

Haribhadra Sūri.

There were several spiritual leaders of no great moment who followed Vajrasena,[2] but the next of real importance was the great Haribhadra Sūri. Haribhadra was originally a learned Brāhman and inordinately proud of his knowledge. He was converted to Jainism through hearing a Jaina nun named Yakanī recite a śloka which Haribhadra could not understand; the nun referred him to her guru, but the guru refused to explain it unless the inquirer first received initiation as a Jaina monk, which he accordingly did. Two of Haribhadra's nephews, Haṁsa and Paramahaṁsa, became his disciples, and later on he sent

[1] The Digambara also differ on certain historical details. The following, according to some authorities, is the list of Āċārya who came after Jambū Svāmī; this list carries their records up to A.D. 216. Viṣṇu, Nandimitra, Aparajita, Govardhana and Bhadrabāhu, who all knew the twelve Aṅga. These were followed by Viśākhāċārya, Paustilāċārya, Kṣatriya, Jayasena, Nāgasena, Siddhārtha, Dhṛitisena, Vijaya, Buddhimāna, Gaṇadeva and Dharmasena; all these eleven knew eleven Aṅga and ten Pūrva. Nakṣatra, Jayapāla, Pāṇḍu, Dharmasena and Kaṁsāċārya, who followed, knew only the texts of eleven Aṅga. Then came four men, Śubhadeva, Yaśobhadra, Mahīyaśa and Lokāċārya, who knew only one Aṅga.

[2] His immediate follower was Candrasūri, under whom the name of the community was changed from Koḍīgaċċha to Ċandragaċċha, only to be renamed Vanavāsīgaċċha under the next leader, Sāmantabhadrasūri, owing to that ascetic's love of living in the forest.

Mānadeva was the next Head of the community. He was waited on by four goddesses, and composed many mantras (called *śāntistotra*), against the plague that raged in Tāxilā. He was followed by Mānatuṅga, the author of the Bhaktāmarastotra. This stotra of forty-four verses was so powerful that each verse when repeated could break open a locked door!

them disguised to study Buddhist doctrines in order to refute them on their return. The Buddhist monks, however, were suspicious of the orthodoxy of these new inquirers and drew images of the Tīrthaṅkara on the steps of their monastery to see if they would tread on them. But the two Jaina boys neatly turned the tables by adding the sacred thread[1] to the sketches and so making them representations of Buddha; this done, they trod on them happily enough. Enraged at this insult to their great leader, the Buddhist monks slew the lads. Haribhadra, maddened at their loss, determined to slay all the monks, some 1,444, in boiling oil by means of his occult powers, but was stopped in time by his guru.[2] He repented deeply of his hasty resolve, and to expiate it he wrote no less than 1,444 books on various subjects, some of which remain to this day.

Siddhasūri[3] was the next great head of the community; he was the grandson of a Prime Minister of Śrīmāla (once the capital of Gujarāt) and the cousin of the famous Sanskrit poet Māgha. Siddhasūri's conversion happened on this wise. After his marriage he became a great gambler, and his wife grieved sorely over his absences from home. One night she was sitting up as usual waiting for his return, when her mother-in-law, seeing her weeping, asked her to go to sleep and said she would sit up for her son. When Siddhasūri returned long after midnight, his mother refused to open the door and told him to go and spend the night anywhere he could gain a welcome, for there was no admittance for him there. Deeply hurt, he sought entrance at the only open door he could find, which happened to be that of a Jaina Apāsaro.[4] The sādhus were all sitting on the floor, Siddhasūri.

[1] The Jaina never wear the sacred thread as the Buddhists do. The Brāhmans of course always wear it from their eighth year.

[2] Bhandarkar gives a different account in his *Search after Jaina MSS.*, 1883, p. 141, where it is said that Haribhadra actually killed the monks. This the Jaina indignantly deny.

[3] His date is variously given as A.D. 536 and 539.

[4] The name given to a Jaina meeting-house and monks' lodging.

recalling what they had learnt during the day, and their head, the gargariṣi, as he was called, told him that before he could join their company he must become a sādhu too. Siddhasūri instantly resolved to do so: he obtained his father's permission, though with great difficulty, and was initiated on the following morning.[1] He studied Jainism deeply and became a great scholar, writing a commentary on the Upadeśamālā of Dharmadāsagaṇī. He then wished to study Buddhism and asked the gargariṣi's permission to go to a Buddhist monastery for this purpose. The gargariṣi agreed, though with misgivings, but stipulated that if ever Siddhasūri felt he was being drawn to the Buddhist faith, he should come back and see him at least once before he joined their order. It fell out as the gargariṣi had feared; the Buddhists were so struck with Siddhasūri's learning that they proposed that he should turn Buddhist and become their Āċārya. Remembering his promise, he returned home to see the gargariṣi once again; he was, however, engaged, and asked Siddhasūri to read a certain book, the Lalitavistara by Haribhadrasūri, whilst he waited. As he read it, repentance overtook him; he was again convinced of the soundness of the Jaina faith, sought forgiveness from the gargariṣi, performed the penance imposed and became a sound Jaina. Eventually he rose to the position of Āċārya and strove by every means in his power to spread the faith.

Śīlaguṇasūri.

The biographies of the successive leaders of the community need not detain us, but about two hundred years later there arose a great sādhu named Śīlaguṇasūri, who is famous as the restorer of the Ċāvaḍā dynasty. Once when wandering as a sādhu in the jungle between Waḍhwān and Kaḍīpāṭaṇa he saw a cradle hanging from a tree with a baby in it. By his knowledge of palmistry he at once discovered that this forlorn child would some day be a king. The child's mother appeared and told him that she was the

[1] The Jaina now wish to institute a period of testing and training before a candidate can obtain initiation.

widow of the vanquished king of Gujarāt, Jayaśikhara, and that the child's name was Vanarāja. Śīlaguṇasūri went to the neighbouring city and told the Jaina laymen of his discovery and of his belief that this child would one day be a king, and advised them to bring him up as a Jaina to the advantage of their faith. It all fell out as Śīlaguṇasūri had foretold, and when, grown to manhood after some years of outlawry, Vanarāja defeated his enemies and recovered the crown, he called Śīlaguṇasūri to his court, declared his intention of reigning as a Jaina king, and built the temple of Pañćāsarā Pārasanātha which still stands in Pāṭaṇa.

Bappa-bhaṭṭīsūri.

An Āćārya named Siddhasena once had a dream in which he saw a lion's cub on the roof of a temple; by this sign he knew that whoever should come to him during the following day would be capable of becoming a great sādhu. The next day a clever lad called Bappa appeared, and Siddhasena asked him if he would like to stay in the Apāsaro and study with him. The boy agreed, and the boy's father too was quite content, until he learnt that Siddhasena wished to turn his son into a sādhu. The father's chief objection was that, as the boy was an only son, his own name would die out, but this was overcome by adding the father's name to the son's and calling him Bappabhaṭṭī. Bappabhaṭṭī as a sādhu was most zealous for the faith. Once he saw a boy weeping in a Jaina temple, who told him that he and his mother (one of the wives of the king of Kanauj) had been driven out through the intrigues of a co-wife. Bappabhaṭṭī arranged for the boy's comfort and assured him that he would one day be king of Kanauj. When this happened, the young king called Bappabhaṭṭī to his court and assisted Jainism in every possible way by building temples and Apāsarā. Bappabhaṭṭī declined to stay long in the morally enervating atmosphere of a court, but during his second visit was enabled to save the king from the toils of a nautch girl. Visiting Bengal, Bappabhaṭṭī won over a reigning prince to the Jaina faith. Later he met a Buddhist preacher whom he defeated in a discussion, thereby gaining for himself the magnificent title of *the Lion who defeated the Elephant in argument.* After spreading the faith in many other ways, he died in A.D. 839.

Śīlāṅgā-cārya. Passing over other leaders of less importance, we come to Śīlāṅgāċārya,[1] the dates of whose birth and death are uncertain, but who was alive in A.D. 862. He wrote commentaries on each of the eleven Aṅga, but unfortunately only two of these remain.

Abhaya-devasūri. In A.D. 1031 a boy of sixteen, named Abhayadevasūri, was made head of the community; he wrote commentaries to supply the place of the missing nine commentaries of Śīlaṅgāċārya.

Hemā-ċārya. Some sixty years later was born the famous Hemāċārya[2] or Hemaċandrasūri, who became Head or Āċārya in A.D. 1121. He wrote a comparative grammar of six of the Prākṛits, with which Siddharāja, the reigning king of Gujarāt, was so delighted that he placed it before him on an elephant and took it to his treasury in state. The next king, Kumārapāla, was converted to Jainism through Hemāċārya's influence. This monarch, besides building magnificent temples, endeared himself still more to his Jaina subjects by prohibiting the killing of animals throughout his dominions. Under Kumārapāla Jainism became the state religion of Gujarāt, and its head-quarters were no longer to be found in the district of Bihār its birthplace, but were transferred to the dominions of this Jaina king. Hemāċārya continued his literary labours throughout his long life, and it is said that before his death in A.D. 1184 he had written 35,000,000 śloka on such differing subjects as religion, history and grammar. As Hemāċārya wrote chiefly in Sanskrit, his name is held in high honour by educated Hindus as well as Jaina. No Āċārya since Hemaċandra has ever wielded so great an

[1] Or, Śīlāṅkāċārya.

[2] Dr. Jacobi gives Hemaċandra's dates as A.D. 1088 or 1089–1173, *E.R.E.*, vi. 591.

influence;[1] he is called the 'Omniscient of the Kaliyuga', and with his name we may fitly close our account of the early Heads of the Community.

Epigraphic Corroboration.

In our study of the Jaina tradition with regard to Mahāvīra and his successors we have incidentally touched the outstanding points of Jaina history as accepted to-day by European scholars. Not long ago all statements made by the Jaina about themselves were received with the gravest suspicion, but the inscriptions which have been deciphered at Mathurā and elsewhere so corroborate the Jaina account that it would seem well worth while to collect and collate their annals and legends as material for that Jaina history which, owing to the incompleteness of our knowledge, cannot yet be written in full.

The events on which in the meantime most scholars are agreed, and which are borne out in the Jaina history that we have studied, include the existence of the Pārśvanātha order of monks prior to Mahāvīra; the birth of Mahāvīra somewhere about 599 B.C. and his death about 527 B.C.; and the remarkable spread of Jainism under Suhastin in the third century B.C., which, as Dr. Hoernle [2] points out, is corroborated not only by their own paṭṭāvalīs,[3] but also by an inscription of Khāravela on the Khaṇḍagiri rock near Cuttack, which shows that by the middle of the second century the Jaina had spread as far as Southern Orissa.

There is a still earlier inscription dating from about 242 B.C. referring to the Jaina, the edict of Aśoka, the great Maurya king who lived in the third century B.C., which is cited by Vincent Smith.[4] He says in the second part of the seventh 'pillar' edict which he issued in the twenty-ninth year of his reign:

[1] An English-speaking Jaina has written of him thus: 'He was man pious and profound and wiser even than Shakespeare, and had a memory far surpassing that of Macaulay.'

[2] *J.A.S.B.*, 1898, p. 48.

[3] Lists of the succession of teachers.

[4] *Aśoka* (Rulers of India series), pp. 192, 193.

'My Censors of the Law of Piety are employed on manifold objects of the royal favour affecting both ascetics and householders, and are likewise employed among all denominations. Moreover, I have arranged for their employment in the business of the Church (*saṅgha*) and in the same way I have employed them among the Brāhmans and the Ājīvikas, and among the Jains also are they employed, and, in fact, among all the different denominations.'

This, as Dr. Bühler says, shows that the Jaina occupied a position of no small importance even at that date.

The inscriptions in Mathurā dating from the first and second century A. D. also go to prove the trustworthiness of the Jaina historical traditions enshrined in the Kalpa Sūtra, for they show the same divisions and subdivisions of the Jaina schools, families and branches as the Kalpa Sūtra recorded,[1] and they also mention the Kauṭika[2] division (founded by Susthita) which belonged to the Śvetāmbara sect, thus proving the early date of the schism.

After the schism the next great event in Jaina history was the birth of Hemaċandra, his success in winning over to Jainism Kumārapāla (perhaps in A. D. 1125) and the resulting change of the Jaina head-quarters from Bihār, its birthplace, to Gujarāt, which since that date has been the chief centre of Jaina influence.

The legends, however, throw light for us on much of the intervening time, witnessing as they do to the conflicts between Jainism and its two great rivals, Brāhmanism and Buddhism.

The Later Sects.

Under the rule of Hemaċandra Jainism reached its zenith, and after his time its influence declined. Brāhman opposition grew stronger and stronger, and the Jaina say that their temples were often destroyed. Constant dissensions amongst themselves divided the Jaina community into numberless sects such as the Punamīyāgaċċha, the

[1] J. G. Bühler, *The Indian Sect of the Jainas*, London, 1903, p. 43.
[2] Hoernle, *J. A. S. B.*, 1898, p 50.

Kharataragaćcha, the Añćalagaćcha, the Sārdhapunamīyā-gaćcha, the Āgamikagaćcha and the Tapagaćcha.[1]

Thus weakened, Jainism could ill withstand the Mohammedan deluge which swept over India in the twelfth and thirteenth centuries. Jaina temples were razed to the ground, their sacred books burnt and their monastic communities massacred. Buddhism was simply swept out of India proper altogether by the storm, but, as we have already noticed, Mahāvīra's genius for organization now proved the salvation of his community. Firmly rooted amongst the laity, they were able, once the hurricane was past, to reappear once more and begin to throw out fresh branches.

One trace of their suffering still remains in the way the Jaina guard their sacred books in Treasure Houses (often underground) to which no alien can gain admittance.

Rise of the non-idolatrous sects.

The next outstanding event in Jaina history was the rise of the non-idolatrous sects. The Sthānakavāsī love to point out the similarity of dates between their rise, which was a true Reformation as far as they were concerned, and that of the birth and work of Martin Luther in Europe. They arose not directly from the Śvetāmbara but as reformers of an older reforming sect.

The Loṅkā sect.

Loṅkā Śā was the name of an Aḥmadābād Jaina belonging originally to the Śvetāmbara sect, who employed several clerks to copy the Jaina scriptures. About A.D. 1474 a Śvetāmbara sādhu named Jñānajī asked him to copy several sacred books for him: whilst reading these, Loṅkā Śā was struck with the fact that idol-worship was not once mentioned in them. He pointed this out to Jñānajī and others, and a sharp controversy arose between them as to the lawfulness of idolatry. In the meantime a crowd of pilgrims going to Śatruñjaya arrived in Ahmadābād and were won over to Loṅkā Śā's side, but unfortunately they had no sādhu amongst them. At length

[1] This last is the most important sect. It is ruled by twelve Srīpūjya, the chief of whom has his seat in Jaipur.

a Śvetāmbara layman named Bhāṇajī was convinced and decided to become a sādhu. As there was no guru obtainable, he ordained himself and became the first Āċārya of the Loṅkā sect. The office of Āċārya might almost be said to have become hereditary in his hands; for though, of course, he had no descendants, yet he himself selected from the Loṅkā sādhus the one who should fill the office of Āċārya on his death; his successor did the same, and this custom exists amongst the Loṅkā Jaina down to the present day.

The Sthānakavāsī sect.

Some of the members of the Loṅkā sect disapproved of the lives of their sādhus, declaring that they lived less strictly than Mahāvīra would have wished. A Loṅkā layman, Vīrajī of Surat, received initiation as a sādhu and won great admiration through the strictness of his life. Many from the Loṅkā sect joined this reformer, and they took the name of Sthānakavāsī [1] whilst their enemies called them Ḍhuṇḍhīā.[2]

The present writer had the pleasure of meeting the Āċārya of the Sthānakavāsī sect, a gentleman named Śrī Lālajī, whom his followers hold to be the seventy-eighth Āċārya in direct succession to Mahāvīra. Many sub-sects have arisen amongst the Sthānakavāsī Jaina, and each of these has its own Āċārya, but they all unite in honouring Śrī Lālajī as a true ascetic. Excepting on the crucial point of idol-worship, the Sthānakavāsī differ very little from the Śvetāmbara sect out of which they sprang, often indeed calling themselves Sthānakavāsī Śvetāmbara.

[1] Those who live in Apāsarā (not in temples).
[2] Searchers. This title has grown to be quite an honourable one.

CHAPTER VI

INTRODUCTION TO JAINA PHILOSOPHY

A WELL-KNOWN authority has said that it is doubtful whether Jainism can truthfully claim to have contributed a single new thought of value to the sum of philosophy. However that may be, it is absolutely necessary to follow this intricate system through all those long lists with their divisions and subdivisions in which the Jaina love to classify and arrange their thought, if one would understand how they think of the soul (*jīva*) and the means by which it may free itself from the consequence of action and obtain deliverance; for this is the chief content of Jaina philosophy. A special interest to the student of Jaina thought lies in trying to guess —for as yet we are only in the guessing stage—from whence the Jaina have gleaned their various ideas. The animistic element bulks largely in all Indian thought, and one proof of the antiquity of Jainism is the way in which it has incorporated animistic beliefs into its 'systematic theology'; for, as we shall see when we come to discuss the nine categories, the system is not only animistic but hylozoistic. The Jaina, in common with the Buddhists, seem to have accepted as the ground-work of their belief the philosophy of the Brāhman Sannyāsin. They incorporated into their faith the doctrines of transmigration and karma[1] without putting a special stamp on either; but the doctrine of non-killing (*ahiṁsā*), which they also borrowed, they exalted to a position of primary importance, and they laid an entirely new emphasis on the value of austerity both inward and outward. Like Buddhism and Brāhmanism, Jainism might be defined as a 'way of escape'

[1] Save that whilst the Brāhmans believe that karma acts indirectly through the agency of God, the Jaina hold that it acts automatically.

not from death but from life; but unlike either of them, it hopes to escape not into nothingness nor into absorption, but into a state of being without qualities, emotions, or relations, and removed from the possibility of rebirth. It is interesting to look at Jainism in relation to the six schools of Indian philosophy. In reference to them the Jaina quote the old story of six blind men who each laid their hands on a different part of an elephant and tried to describe the whole animal. The man who held the ear thought the creature resembled a winnowing-fan, the holder of the leg imagined that he was clinging to a big round pillar, and similarly each opinion differed, but the owner who saw the whole explained that each had only a portion of the truth. The six men represent the six schools, and the owner is in their view of course Jainism. The Jaina hold in fact that the six schools of philosophy are part and parcel of one organic whole, and that if one be taken by itself it becomes a false doctrine. One of the great questions amongst the schools is as to whether an effect is the same as its material cause or pre-exists in that cause and is only made manifest by the operation which that cause undergoes (this is the Satkārya doctrine of the Sāṅkhya and the Vedānta); or whether the effect is something new and did not exist before (which is the Asatkārya doctrine held by the Vaiśeṣika). On this point Jainism shows its usual comprehensiveness, and believing that both views were linked together from time without beginning, says that 'an effect pre-exists in the cause in one sense and is a new thing in another. If you look at an effect such as a jar as a mere substance, the substance is the same as in the loose earth of which the jar is made; but if you look at the jar as a modification, it is new and did not exist when the earth was in the condition of loose particles'.[1]

Another burning question is whether or no the soul

[1] Bhandarkar, *Search for Sanskrit Manuscripts in 1883–4*, p. 101.

exists and acts. The Kriyāvāda doctrine teaches that the soul exists, acts, and is affected by acts, and this is held by the Jaina[1] in common with the Vaiśeṣika and Nyāya schools. The opposite doctrine—the Akriyāvāda—that the soul does not exist, or that it does not act, or is not affected by acts, is held, according to the Jaina view, by the Buddhists in common with the Vedānta, Sāṅkhya and Yoga schools, and those who hold this doctrine will be, so the Jaina aver, whirled round in the endless circle of rebirths.

Another great question is as to how the soul becomes fettered. The Sāṅkhya school believe it to be owing to an insentient principle which they call *prakṛiti*; the Vedāntists believe also that it is owing to an insentient principle, but this principle they hold to be *māyā* or *avidyā*; but the Jaina believe the jīva to be bound through the *pudgaḷa*[2] of karma.

Deliverance necessarily differs, according as the fetters differ. The Vedānta school holds that mokṣa is gained by learning to distinguish the true soul (*ātmā*) from the illusion (*māyā*) which fetters it, and the Sāṅkhya similarly strives to know ātmā as separated from prakṛiti, but the Jaina conceive of the spirit as freed through austerities from the karma it had accumulated, and existing in limitless serenity.

The Jaina claim not to be Ekāntavādin, those who look at things from one point of view, but Anekāntavādin, those who look at things from various points of view, and the part of their philosophy of which they are most proud is the Saptabhaṅgī Naya.

Dr. Jacobi[3] thinks that this may have been invented to confute the views of some dangerous opponent, probably the Agnosticism of Sañjaya. (Certainly to fight against it would be as difficult and useless as fighting against a London fog!) The *locus classicus* of its exposition to which all

[1] *S. B. E.*, xlv, p. xxv. [2] See p. 106. [3] *S. B. E.*, xlv, p. xxvii.

Jaina immediately refer you is in Dr. Bhandarkar's *Search for Jaina Manuscripts*,[1] from which they always quote it in full.

Seven modes of assertion.

'You can', the famous passage runs, 'affirm existence of a thing from one point of view (*Syād asti*), deny it from another (*Syān nāsti*); and affirm both existence and non-existence with reference to it at different times (*Syād asti nāsti*). If you should think of affirming both existence and non-existence at the same time from the same point of view, you must say that the thing cannot be so spoken of (*Syād avaktavyaḥ*). Similarly under certain circumstances, the affirmation of existence is not possible (*Syād asti avaktavyaḥ*); of non-existence (*Syān nāsti avaktavyaḥ*); and also of both (*Syād asti nāsti avaktavyaḥ*). What is meant by these seven modes is that a thing should not be considered as existing everywhere, at all times, in all ways, and in the form of everything. It may exist in one place and not in another, and at one time and not at another.'

The example paṇḍits gave the writer to illustrate this important doctrine was that one and the same man is spoken of as father, uncle, father-in-law, son, son-in-law, brother and grandfather.

As an illustration of its use they say:

'Let us suppose that an agnostic denies the existence of soul in all ways. To him the Jaina Syādvāda would answer that as soul is a substance, it exists. Soul exists in itself and its modifications, but it does not exist in other substances such as matter (*pudgala*), &c., and also other substances do not exist in soul. So, from this point of view, soul does not exist. But soul sometimes exists and also does not exist at different times. But the soul cannot be spoken of, if we think of affirming its existence and non-existence, at the same time and from the same point of view. Similarly, under certain conditions, viz. when the state of existence (i.e. astitva) itself cannot be spoken of, i.e. *exists* and *exists and does not exist* cannot be spoken of at the same time, we are unable to affirm that existence is possible, that non-existence is possible, and that both existence and non-existence are possible. Thus Syādvāda teaches the fundamental theory that everything in the universe is related to every other thing. . . . The Jaina school of philosophy coincides, in one respect, with Hegel's idea that being and non-being are identical.'[2]

[1] Bhandarkar, loc. cit., pp. 95 ff.

[2] U. D. Barodia, *History and Literature of Jainism*, Bombay, 1909, p. 119.

But though the Jaina are very proud of this part of their philosophy, they hold it as a thing apart, and it does not seem to permeate their daily thought and life. To them the crucial point is, how may a jīva free itself from its transitory imprisonment, and, following the upward path, attain deliverance at last? The answer to this question they find in the Nine Categories.

CHAPTER VII

THE NINE CATEGORIES OF FUNDAMENTAL TRUTHS

First Category: Jīva.

THE Jaina consider that the foundation of true philosophy consists of nine categories.[1] 'He who truly believes the true teaching of the fundamental truths possesses righteousness,' says the Uttarādhyayana.[2]

All three sects of Jaina, however much they may differ with regard to the eyes and adornments of their idols, or as to whether they should have idols at all, agree as to these principles, though the Digambara number them differently, and by including two of them under other heads make the categories seven instead of nine.

The first of these nine categories (*Nava Tattva*) is always given as *jīva*, a word which is varyingly used to connote life, vitality, soul, or consciousness. When jīva is used as equivalent to 'soul' it differs from the Brāhmanic idea of 'soul', for the Jaina believe that whilst the knowledge possessed by the jīva (or ātmā) may be boundless, the jīva itself is limited; whilst followers of the Sāṅkhya, Nyāya and Vaiśeṣika schools believe the soul to be co-extensive with the universe. Both Brāhmans and Jaina believe, in contradistinction to the Buddhists, that the soul is absolute and permanent, and according to the Jaina it is the jīva which suffers or enjoys the fruits of its deeds, and then, in consequence of the karma it has acquired, goes through the succession of rebirths, and finally, obtaining freedom through the destruction of its karma, soars upwards to mokṣa.

[1] An analysis of the Nine Categories is given in the Appendix.
[2] *S.B.E.*, xlv, p. 154.

A famous śloka of the great Hemāćārya thus describes the characteristics of the jīva:

It performs different kinds of actions, it reaps the fruit of those actions, it circles round returning again; these and none other are the characteristics of the soul.

Jīva has further been described as a conscious substance, capable of development, imperceptible to the senses, an active agent, and as big as the body it animates.[1]

In a most interesting note Dr. Jacobi suggests that the Jaina have arrived 'at their concept of soul, not through the search after the Self, the self-existing unchangeable principle in the ever-changing world of phenomena, but through the perception of *life*. For the most general Jaina term for soul is life (*jīva*), which is identical with self (*āyā*, *ātman*)';[2] and the way in which the category jīva is divided and subdivided, building up from the lesser to the more developed life, certainly bears out Dr. Jacobi's contention; for the Jaina lay stress on Life not Self.

Sometimes jīva itself is considered as a division of Dravya (or substance), its chief characteristic being *ćaitanya* (consciousness).

The powers or Prāṇa possessed by Jīva.

This conscious sentient principle, jīva or ātmā, so long as it feels desire, hatred and other attachments, and is fettered by karma, undergoes continual reincarnations. In each new birth it makes its home in a new form, and there assumes those bodily powers or *prāṇa*[3] which its various actions in previous births have entitled it to possess, for the possession or non-possession of any faculty depends on karma. The most perfectly developed jīva has ten prāṇa and the lowest type must possess at least four. Of these ten prāṇa, five are called Indriya prāṇa, since they relate to the senses. They are the sense of touch

[1] Bhandarkar, *Search for Sanskrit MSS. in 1883-4*, p. 106.

[2] *S.B.E.*, xxii, p. 3.

[3] Much confusion has arisen through not distinguishing the Jaina use of the word *prāṇa* from the Vedāntist, with whom it means breath, and who say that there are five vital prāṇa or breaths.

(*Sparśendriya*) ; the sense of taste (*Rasendriya*) ; the sense of smell (*Ghrāṇendriya*) ; the sense of sight (*Ċakṣurindriya*); the sense of hearing (*Śravaṇendriya*).

There are also three other powers known as Baḷa prāṇa : bodily power (*Kāyabaḷa*), speech (*Vaċanabaḷa*) and mind (*Manabaḷa*). The ninth Prāṇa, Ānapāna prāṇa (or Śvāsoċċhvāsa) gives the powers of respiration; and the tenth prāṇa, Āyu prāṇa, is the possession of the allotted span of life during which the jīva has to sustain a particular bodily form.

The divisions of Jīva into :— i. Two classes.

In order to understand Jīva more fully, the Jaina divide it according to the class of beings in which its past karma may force it for a time to take up its abode. The first division which they make is into Siddha and Saṁsārī. A man's karma may force him to dwell in some being still struggling with all the troubles of this present world, sullied by contact with Ajīva (insentient matter), and having further rebirths to undergo before he can reach mokṣa; or he may have attained deliverance and become a Siddha. The Saṁsārī live in the world, but the Siddha, or perfected ones, who are freed from karma, live in a place called Īṣatprāgbhāra, which consists of pure white gold and has the form of an open umbrella.[1] The beings who dwell there have no visible form, but consist of Life throughout and possess paramount happiness which admits of no comparison.

ii. Three classes.

We have divided Life into two classes: Siddha and Saṁsārī, perfected and unperfected; we may now, the Jaina say, divide Saṁsārī life into three divisions: male, female and neuter.[2]

iii. Four classes.

Or again, we may regard it in four ways, according to the place where it was born. Jīva born in hell are called

[1] Cp. *S. B. E.*, xlv, p. 212.

[2] With the Jaina, however, these words do not seem to bear quite the usual English connotation. Living things are sometimes considered neuter, and non-living things male or female.

Nārakī; those born in a state lower than human and inhabiting the bodies of insects, birds, reptiles, animals, or plants are named *Tiryañċ*; *Manuṣya* are jīva born as human beings; and those who are born as spirits, whether gods or demons,[1] are called *Devatā*. These four possible places of birth are shown in the accompanying Svastika sign, which is constantly seen in Jaina books and temples.

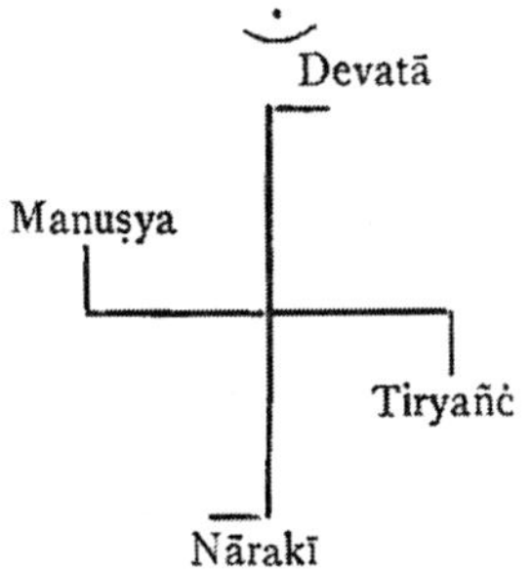

iv. Five classes.

Jīva may be classified in five ways, according to the number of senses it possesses, as Ekendriya, Be-indriya,[2] Tri-indriya, Ċorendriya, and Pañċendriya.[3]

iv (*a*). Ekendriya jīva.

Ekendriya jīva possess only one sense, the sense of touch, but have four prāṇa: touch, body, the power of exhaling and inhaling, and the allotted term of life.

They are subdivided into Pṛithvīkāya, Apakāya, Teukāya, Vāyukāya, and Vanaspatikāya. Things belonging to the earth, such as stones,[4] lumps of clay, salts, chalk, diamonds and other minerals, are called *Pṛithvīkāya* ekendriya. Though ordinary persons are unable to perceive in these the power of suffering, yet a Kevalī can do so, for he sees that they have four prāṇa, including the power of breathing and of touch. The longest span for which a jīva can be

[1] A Vedāntist would not use the word devatā to express an evil spirit, and this has sometimes led to confusion.

[2] *Sanskrit* Dvīndriya, Trīndriya, Ċaturindriya, Pañċindriya.

[3] It is interesting to compare these divisions with those of Gośāla, which they much resemble.

[4] Dr. Jacobi shows how this and the other animistic beliefs of Jainism point to its antiquity. *S. B. E.*, xlv, p. xxxiii.

compelled to inhabit such a lodging is twenty-two thousand years, and the shortest time less than forty-eight moments,[1] but as the jīva's karma is gradually exhausted, it will be reborn into happier conditions.[2] These earth lives are also divided into those which we can see and those which are invisible to the human eye. By ill-treating any earth life we deprive ourselves of our chance of happiness and perfect wisdom.

The Jaina believe that water[3] itself (not, as is so often supposed, the animalculae living in it) is inhabited by Ekendriya jīva called *Apakāya* ekendriya. Apakāya include rain, dew, fog, melted snow, melted hail, &c. The shortest span a jīva can pass in water is a moment,[4] though more usually it will have to wait there for rebirth for at least forty-eight moments; but the longest time its karma can condemn it to this imprisonment is seven thousand years. It is this belief in the power of inflicting pain on water that makes Jaina monks so particular about only taking it when it has been boiled and strained and prevents some of them using it at all for toilet purposes!

A man's karma again may force him to become a *Teukāya* ekendriya, or fire life, and he may have to pass into an ordinary fire, the light of a lamp, a magnet, electricity, a meteor, flintstone sparks, a forest conflagration, or a submarine fire,[5] but one can only be condemned to be a fire life for a period varying from one instant[6] to three

[1] Antarmuhūrtta.

[2] Jaina differ from some other schools of thought in believing that it is possible for the jīva inhabiting a man to be so weighed down by evil karma that it may in its very next rebirth have to pass into an Ekendriya Pṛithvīkāya, or earth life. They also differ, of course, from the Vedāntists, who believe in one all-soul, not in numberless individual souls like these.

[3] Compare 'the heroes (of faith), humbly bent, (should retain their belief in) the illustrious road (to final liberation) and in the world (of water bodies)'. *Ācārāṅga Sūtra, S. B. E.*, xxii, p. 5.

[4] Some Jaina think it is forty-eight moments.

[5] Jaina, like many Hindus, believe that waves are caused by submarine fire in the bed of the ocean.

[6] Samaya.

days (i.e. seventy-two hours). A difference of opinion exists amongst Jaina as to whether one can be condemned to become lightning or not, for it does not seem to be known for certain whether or no Teukāya exists in lightning.[1]

Again, all sorts of wind, such as cyclones, whirlwinds, monsoons, west winds and trade-winds, are thought of as inhabited by what are called *Vāyukāya* ekendriya jīva. It is difficult for us to understand that wind has a body and can be made to suffer pain, but all this is plain to a Kevalī. The period a jīva may spend as wind varies according to his karma from one instant to three thousand years.

All vegetable life, or *Vanaspatikāya*, also possesses but one indriya. These jīva are divided into two classes: *Pratyeka*, or life such as that of a tree (e.g. an orange or mango tree), whose various branches, fruits and leaves possess life derived from it, and *Sādhāraṇa*, the life possessed by potatoes,[2] onions, carrots, figs, &c. Strict Jaina will not eat any of the latter class, for example, potatoes, beet, onions, &c., because more than one jīva has taken up its lodging there; but they will take oranges and mangoes, once they are ripe, for then they are inhabited by only one life. Life as a vegetable[3] may last from one instant to ten thousand years.

Ascending the scale, we come to jīva possessing two senses (or *Be-indriya*), that of taste as well as that of touch, and having six prāṇa: taste, touch, body, the power of exhaling and inhaling, an allotted term of life, and speech. Such are animalculae, worms, things living in shells, leeches, earth-worms. No one can be condemned to be a Be-indriya for longer than twelve years. iv (*b*). Be-indriya.

[1] In the Uttarādhyayana it is expressly stated that fire lives do exist in lightning. *S.B.E.*, xlv, p. 217.

[2] In one potato there are countless bodies, and in each body countless lives exist.

[3] Dr. Jacobi points out that plants and animals, being admitted by all to be living beings, were considered a better support of the hylozoistic theory than wind. *Āćārāṅga Sūtra*, *S.B.E.*, xxii, p. 9.

A strict Jaina abstains from killing anything even in the Ekendriya class, but the actual vow of Ahiṁsā or Non-killing for laymen starts from the Be-indriya class. Monks vow not to kill anything in the Ekendriya class, and hence refuse to touch water, clay, a clod of earth, fire, &c. They cannot of course help breathing air, but to hurt it as little as possible they cover their mouths with a cloth. Monks never snap their fingers, or swing or fan themselves, lest they should injure air. No point in Jainism has been more misunderstood than this, even scholars[1] supposing the mouth-cloth to be worn to prevent the taking of animal life, whereas it is to prevent the taking of air life.

iv (*c*). Tri-indriya.

In the next highest class, *Tri-indriya*, are placed all those beings that in addition to the sense of touch and taste have also the sense of smell, and so possess three indriya and seven prāṇa. In this class are red ants, white ants, black ants, bugs and moths. A Jaina told me that in order to please the insects of this class a devout householder when he finds vermin will often place them on one particular bedstead and then pay some poor person from four to six annas to spend the night on that bedstead! Others, however, deny this. Of course no true Jaina will kill vermin, but will carefully remove it from his body or house to some shady place outside where it can dwell in safety. They say that, far from killing vermin, they are bound to protect it, as it has been created through their lack of cleanliness. No one's karma can force him to pass into this class of being for more than forty-nine days, or for less than an instant of time.

iv (*d*). Ċorendriya.

Beings still higher in the scale are the *Ċorendriya*, those possessed of the four senses of touch, taste, smell and sight; these of course have eight prāṇa. Wasps,

[1] Mr. W. Crooke, for instance, says (*Imperial Gazetteer*, vol. i, p. 416), 'They wear a screen of cloth before their mouths, lest they should unwittingly inhale and destroy animal life.'

scorpions, mosquitoes, gnats, flies, locusts and butterflies should be included under this heading, and also, according to some Jaina, moths, which are, however, often classed as Tri-indriya. Beings cannot be kept in this division for longer than six months without rebirth.

iv (*e*). Pañćendriya.

The extra sense added to the jīva in the next class is that of hearing; and these *Pañćendriya* should therefore, to correspond, be possessed of nine prāṇa. Some, however, have an extra prāṇa added, that of mind, and these are called Saṁjñī pañćendriya, whilst the rest who have only nine are called Asaṁjñī. There are four divisions of the Pañćendriya: hell beings, lower animals, human beings and demigods. Of these the hell beings, human beings and demigods are possessed of intelligence, and so are certain creatures such as cows, buffaloes and other domestic animals; whilst frogs, fish and *disease germs* have no intelligence, for these are all self-created!

Germs which are thus classified in a way that seems strange to us as Pañćendriya are of great importance in Jaina philosophy. When engaging in Pratikramaṇa (or Paḍīkamaṇuṁ), i.e. Confession, Jaina think of the sins they may have committed against any being possessing any indriya and ask forgiveness. At this time they also think of any germs which they may have created by sinning against the laws of sanitation in fourteen specified ways. If through a man's carelessness or insanitary habits germs should have multiplied and infection spread, Mahāvīra declared him to be guilty of a sin as grave as that of murder.

The minimum of time which a being may be sentenced to spend as a hell being or a demigod is ten thousand years, and it may extend to thirty-three sāgaropama. In the case of human beings (including germs, which are ranked as humans!) and lower animals, the period may extend from one instant to three palya of time.

We have already followed the Jaina as they divided

v. Six classes. Jīva, in two, in three, in four, and lastly in five ways. We now come to the six ways in which Jīva may be divided, namely, into Pṛithvīkāya, Apakāya, Teukāya, Vāyukāya, Vanaspatikāya, and Trasakāya. Of these we have studied earth, water, fire, wind and vegetable lives, so it only remains for us to look at *Trasakāya*. The Jaina say that in the class of Trasakāya are included all lives that have the power of motion and which, when swayed by *trāsa* (dread), can try and get out of danger. All lives possessing two or more indriya are included under this heading as Trasakāya or mobile, whilst earth, water, fire, air and vegetable are considered immobile.

vi. Seven classes. Again, Jīva may be classified in seven ways: hell beings (which are all neuter !), male lower animals, female lower animals, male human beings, female human beings, male demigods and female demigods.

vii. Eight classes. This last is perhaps a somewhat artificial classification introduced for the sake of symmetry, but when we come to the next series, where Jīva is divided into eight classes, we touch on one of the most important points in Jaina philosophy, and one which it shares with the followers of Gośāla. The Jaina say Jīva may be divided into eight classes according to the six Leśyā[1] by which it is swayed, and according to whether it is swayed by any emotion or not.[2] These emotions affect the colour of the soul they govern just as a crystal is coloured by the hue of the substance on which it rests.

vii (*a*). Beings in the first class, or *Saleśī*, include all who are yet swayed by any of the three good or three bad emotions.

vii (*b*). *Kṛiṣṇaleśyā* is the worst of the three bad emotions, and it is described as being black as a thunder-cloud, bitter as a Neem tree, smelling like a dead cow, and rougher

[1] Or Leśā.

[2] Jaina divisions are not, unfortunately for the student, mutually exclusive, and even include the whole along with its parts.

than a saw to the touch. Jīva, under the direction of this so graphically described bad temper, accumulate karma by all sorts of cruel and violent acts without stopping to think of the consequences. All the emotions last for differing periods according to whether they influence a god, a hell being, or a man.

In the third division are all those ruled by *Nīlaleśyā.* vii (*c*).
This emotion is less evil than the last, though it is still evil enough; its colour is blue as indigo, its taste more pungent than pepper, it still has the odour of a dead cow about it, and its roughness is as bad as ever. A man under its influence is envious of the good qualities of others; he will not only not perform austerities or acquire knowledge himself, but tries to hinder others from doing so; and he is lazy, gluttonous, and wanting in modesty. Such a man thinks only of his own happiness, and pursuing only his own pleasure is continually beset by evil thoughts and purposes.

The last wicked emotion that may lead men to do evil vii (*d*).
is called *Kāpotaleśyā.* It is grey in colour like a dove, as bitter of flavour as an unripe mango, and of as evil an odour and as rough to touch as its predecessors. A man under its command becomes crooked in thought and deed, he develops into a thief and a liar, loves intrigue, and delights to expose the bad qualities of others whilst concealing his own faults. It is torment to such a person to see others prosperous or wealthy.

There are three good emotions whose scent is like to vii (*e*).
fragrant flowers and whose touch is as soft as butter, and these govern three more classes of beings. The first good emotion, *Tejoleśyā*, is red like the rising sun and sweeter to the taste than ripe mangoes. It removes all evil thoughts from the jīva under its sway as dawn destroys the darkness of night, and all under its influence are bright and happy. Men governed by it are firm in their religion, afraid of sinning, anxious to keep the law, desirous of

getting knowledge, humble and free from curiosity, straightforward and righteous.

vii (*f*). The second good emotion takes its name, *Padmaleśyā*, from the lotus-flower, for jīva beneath its dominion open their hearts to all good things as lotus lilies expand to the sun. Its colour is yellow,[1] and its taste is better than honey. Through its power a man controls anger, pride, deceit and avarice, and gains as a reward a quiet mind, whose thoughts are always calm and collected.

vii (*g*). The last emotion, the *Śuklaleśyā*, is the highest of all; it is as white as pearls, and its taste sweeter than sugar. Love and hatred disappear when a man is under its influence, and he feels in harmony with all nature. Knowledge is now complete, austerity finished and character perfected, for, governed by it, the mind itself becomes a sun and has no stain of evil and, unbarred by karma, the way lies open to mokṣa.

vii (*h*). The eighth class of jīva are called *Aleśī*, for they have done with all feeling and completely stultified everything in their personality which might respond to emotion. Only the Siddha are to be found in this class.

viii. Nine classes. The Jaina divide Jīva again in nine ways: Pṛithvīkāya, Apakāya, Teukāya, Vāyukāya, Vanaspatikāya, Be-indriya, Tri-indriya, Ćorendriya, and Pañćendriya, but all these have already been discussed, and this division is only made for the sake of symmetry.

ix. Ten classes. When Jīva is classified in ten ways, the five old divisions we already know of (Ekendriya, &c.) are used, but each of these is subdivided into two classes, *Paryāptā* and *Aparyāptā*, according as they have or have not all the Paryāpti. There are six of these paryāpti: *āhāra*, the seed of life; *śarīra*, the body; *indriya*, the senses; *śvāsoććhvāsa*, breathing; *bhāṣā*, speech; and *mana*,[2] intellect; and in this order the Jaina believe the jīva develops them as it passes by transmigration from life to life. The

[1] Sthānakavāsī say pink.

[2] *Sanskrit* manas.

resemblance between paryāpti and prāṇa will be noticed. A Jaina sādhu told the writer that the peculiarity of paryāpti consisted in the fact that when a jīva migrated from one life to another, it could obtain these paryāpti in the space of forty-eight minutes. Others, however, say that paryāpti and prāṇa are practically identical. Some jīva have all six paryāpti, some five, and some four; but none can have less than four; if a jīva dies before it attains the number decreed for it, it is classed as Aparyāptā.

x. Eleven classes.

When Jīva is classified in eleven ways, to the first four orders of indriya are added the three subdivisions of pañćendriya (*nārakī*, *tiryañć* and *manuṣya*) which we have already discussed, and then to these are added the four subdivisions of demi-gods, or Deva.[1] Jaina subdivide their gods into Bhavanapati, the lords of the lower parts of the earth, who are often serpents of various kinds; Vyantara, evil spirits such as ghosts, witches, goblins, &c.; Jyotiṣī, who live in 'planets', under which are included sun, moon, and stars; and Vaimānika, or residents of celestial worlds, which are sometimes larger and sometimes smaller than our world.

xi. Twelve classes.

The twelve ways in which Jīva can be looked at are made up of Pṛithvīkāya, Apakāya, Teukāya, Vāyukāya, and Vanaspatikāya (i.e. the five divisions of Ekendriya), Trasakāya (the collective name for the last four indriya), and the subdivision of each of these six classes into Paryāptā and Aparyāptā.

xii. Thirteen classes.

The thirteen ways are similarly artificially formed by dividing the six Leśyā into Paryāptā and Aparyāptā and adding Aleśī.

xiii. Fourteen classes.

In the fourteen-fold division the five orders of Indriya are divided into Paryāptā and Aparyāptā, but Ekendriya are divided into two new classes: *Sūkṣma* ekendriya and

[1] It will be remembered that demi-gods were the fourth subdivision of Pañćendriya.

Bādara ekendriya. In the first of these are lives so minute that they can never be seen, killed, or destroyed, whilst those of the Bādara ekendriya can be killed or destroyed, and can sometimes be perceived. To make up the number to fourteen the two divisions of the fifth class, Saṁjñī and Asaṁjñī, are included.

The Second Category: Ajīva.

The second great Tattva of the Jaina deals with Ajīva (things inanimate), and is in all respects the opposite of Jīva. Until jīva is freed from one particular division (*pudgaḷa*) of ajīva, it is impossible for it to progress towards deliverance. The union of jīva with ajīva is never so absolutely complete as to make their separation impossible.

Ajīva is divided into two main classes: Arūpī (without form) and Rūpī (with form). *Arūpī ajīva* has four great subdivisions: Dharmāstikāya,[1] Adharmāstikāya, Ākāśāstikāya and Kāḷa.[2]

Dharmāstikāya.

Dharmāstikāya helps the jīva associated with pudgaḷa[3] to progress just as (to use their own illustration) water helps on the movements of a fish. It is divided into three classes: Skandha, Deśa, and Pradeśa. The whole power of motion is called *skandha*; a large fraction of it is called *deśa* as long as it is linked with skandha; while *pradeśa* is a small fraction of deśa. The Jaina declare that they had so thoroughly studied the laws of motion that they were cognizant of the law of gravity long before Sir Isaac Newton discovered it.

[1] The ordinary meaning of Dharma and Adharma is of course merit and demerit, or right conduct and unrighteousness, as Dr. Jacobi[a] and Dr. Bhandarkar[b] translate them; but all the Jaina that I have met in India assure me that these two words are here used in a special technical sense which we shall better understand as we discuss these divisions.

[a] Introduction, *S. B. E.*, xlv, p. xxxiv.

[b] Dr. Bhandarkar, *Search for Sanskrit Manuscripts*, p. 96. Dr. Bühler falls into the same trap, *Indian Sect of the Jaina*, p. 9.

[2] *Sans.* Kāla.

[3] Pudgaḷa (*Sans.* pudgala) is roughly translated by Jaina as 'matter'.

Adharmāstikāya the Jaina explain by an illustration of a man walking along a road on a hot day; he sees the shadow of a tree, and the shadow first attracts him to seek its shelter, and then keeps him quietly resting under it. So Adharmāstikāya without any movement on its part first attracts and then keeps motionless the one attracted. It has the same divisions of skandha, deśa, and pradeśa as Dharmāstikāya.

Adharmāstikāya.

The third subdivision of Arūpī Ajīva is *Ākāśāstikāya*, or that which gives space and makes room. If, for example, a lamp is lighted, it is Ākāśāstikāya which gives space for its beams to shine in; if a nail be knocked into a wall, it is Ākāśāstikāya which gives it space to go into the wall. Again, if a lump of sugar is dropped into a cup of water and melts, the Jaina declare that the water remains water and the sugar sugar, but that a hidden power gives the sugar room to melt, and this power is Ākāśāstikāya. As a house affords room for its residents, so Ākāśāstikāya gives space for Ajīva to dwell in. Ākāśāstikāya is also divided into skandha, deśa, and pradeśa, but the skandha of Ākāśāstikāya includes space in the heavens as well as on the earth.

Ākāśāstikāya.

The real nature of *Kāḷa* or time (the fourth division of Arūpī Ajīva) can only, according to the Jaina, be understood by the initiated. To the worldling Kāḷa bears the connotation of 'time',[1] and he divides and subdivides it into seconds, minutes, hours, days, years, &c. But to the initiated Kāḷa is indivisible,[2] and is that which is continually making old things new and new things old.[3] As an illustration, the Jaina quote the fate of a jīva or soul which may be forced by its karma to inhabit the body of a child. The child grows up into a young man, and finally dies in old age, and the jīva is forced to inhabit

Kāḷa.

[1] Or Vyavahārika Kāḷa.
[2] Addhāsamaya.
[3] Dr. Griswold draws attention in this connexion to Bergson's doctrine of Time in his *Creative Evolution*.

afresh the body of another infant. The jīva remains the same, but the power that made its covering body at one time old and then young again is Kāḷa. As Kāḷa in this sense is indivisible, it cannot have the divisions of skandha, deśa, and pradeśa.

All these four divisions of Arūpī ajīva are further subdivided with regard to *Dravya* (substance), *Kṣetra* (place), *Kāḷa* (time), *Bhāva* (nature), and *Guṇa* (qualities). For instance, Dharmāstikāya is considered of one substance; its place is the seven lower worlds, including the worlds of the serpents, this world, and the worlds of the demi-gods; with regard to time, it is without beginning and without end; its nature is without colour, without smell, without taste, imperceptible to touch, and without form; its quality is that it helps motion. Adharmāstikāya when looked at in this way agrees with Dharmāstikāya in every point, excepting that its special quality is to arrest motion. Ākāśāstikāya differs in that it has its place in both Loka and Aloka, and that its quality is to afford space. Kāḷa with regard to place is found in two-and-a-half continents only (i.e. Jambūdvīpa, Dhātakī Khaṇḍa and half of Puṣkara), and its quality is to make old things new and new things old. In this way they make up twenty divisions, and sometimes thirty by skandha, deśa, and pradeśa, out of the four original divisions of Arūpī ajīva, without, however, adding enough new material to make it worth our while to follow out the labyrinth.

Pudgaḷāstikāya.

The *Rūpī* division of Ajīva contains only *Pudgaḷāstikāya*, or matter which possesses colour, smell, taste and form, and is perceptible to touch. Pudgaḷa can be consumed or destroyed, and it may decay or alter its form. Where there is no pudgaḷa present, none of the five primary colours, black, green (or blue), red, white, or yellow, can be present, and so, for instance, a Siddha who is freed from pudgaḷa is freed from colour also. The smells of pudgaḷa, the Jaina say, are of two kinds, pleasing and unpleasing,[1] and a Siddha being free from pudgaḷa is also free from odour.

Pudgaḷa may have any of the five flavours: pungent, bitter, astringent, sour, or sweet. It may be of five shapes: circular, globular, triangular, square, or oblong, i.e. 'stretched out like a log lying on the earth.' A Siddha, of course, is freed from all shape.

There are eight kinds of 'touch' that pudgaḷa may have: it may be light or heavy, hot or cold, rough or smooth, wet or dry; but a Siddha can possess none of these qualities.

Jaina indulge their genius for subdivision by dividing each colour by the two smells, five flavours and eight touches, and then again they divide each smell by the five colours, five tastes and eight touches, and so on, till they get 560 divisions out of pudgaḷa.

Pudgaḷa is also divided into four classes: Skandha, Deśa, Pradeśa, and Paramāṇu (i.e. the smallest particle). Skandha, deśa, and pradeśa are linked together, but paramāṇu is separate and indivisible.

The pudgaḷa enter and leave our bodies incessantly, and are infinitely more numerous than jīva. As we shall see later, the Jaina believe that karma arises out of pudgaḷa.

The Jaina hold that it is through Jīva and these five divisions of Ajīva (Dharmāstikāya, Adharmāstikāya, Ākāśāstikāya, Kāḷa, and Pudgaḷāstikāya) that the universe exists, and that these serve instead of a creator, whose existence they do not acknowledge.

[1] In order that the uninitiated may realize this deep truth, the following legend is told. Once a king crossed a stream wherein a dead dog lay, and to avoid the smell held a cloth across his nose. When he asked his prime minister why he did not do likewise, he replied that he knew his Jaina philosophy, and realized that it was of the nature of pudgaḷa to be sometimes sweet and sometimes evil smelling. Seeing his master unconvinced, he secretly drew water from the very place where the corpse of the dog lay, and, having filtered, iced and spiced it, offered it to the king, who drank it with delight. Afterwards learning its source, he learnt also that the same pudgaḷa may sometimes be of a sweet odour and sometimes of an evil one.

The Third Category: Puṇya.

Nine kinds of Puṇya.

Another of the great Tattva deals with *Puṇya* or merit.[1] The actions which lead to the good karma which bring peace of mind are called puṇya, and there are nine ways of performing these actions.

i. Anna puṇya

If we give food to deserving people who are hungry, weak, destitute of help and needy, we perform *Anna puṇya.* The greatest merit is gained when the food is given to monks or nuns, but these must be Jaina ascetics (not Hindu for instance), and in order to gain the fullest benefit from charity the food must be given in such a way as not to involve hiṁsā.[2] It will be remembered that Mahāvīra in a previous birth, when a woodcutter, gained great puṇya by feeding a party of monks who had lost their way. His reward was that in his next incarnation he became a devatā, and after many many rebirths was incarnate as Mahāvīra. For less illustrious services one may in the next life become a merchant, or a ruler, or gain some other coveted position.

ii. Pāṇa puṇya.

In common with many other religions that have arisen in sultry lands, Jainism teaches that a special reward is attached to giving water to the thirsty (*Pāṇa puṇya*). There is no harm in giving unboiled water to a layman, but boiled water must always be given to an ascetic. The story of Neminātha, the twenty-second Tīrthaṅkara, shows how great the reward is. A king named Śaṅkara and his wife Jaśomatī once showed kindness to some thirsty monks by giving them water in which grapes had been soaked. In their next birth, as a reward, the king was born as Neminātha and his wife as the daughter of a famous king of Soraṭh; in this incarnation, though betrothed, they did not marry, but instead they both became ascetics on the day fixed for their wedding, and eventually obtained mokṣa.

iii. Vastra puṇya.

A great reward is also obtained by giving clothes to the

[1] The Digambara include Puṇya under Āśrava (see p. 139).
[2] i. e. destruction of life.

poor (*Vastra puṇya*) and especially to monks, as the following legend teaches. Once upon a time a rich merchant's wife saw some monks shivering with cold, and made them blankets of cloth of gold out of some magnificent material she had by her. As a recompense she became in her next birth Marudevī, the mother of the first Tīrthaṅkara Ṛiṣabhadeva, and attained mokṣa in the same incarnation.

iv. Layaṇa and v. Śayana puṇya.

Another legend illustrates the reward gained by any one, even a heretic, for building or lending a house to a monk (*Layaṇa puṇya*), or providing seats, beds or bedding (*Śayana puṇya*). A potter named Śakaḍāla, a follower of Gośāla, once saw Mahāvīra enter his village and approach his dwelling. At first he thought of not inviting Gośāla's great opponent into his house, but seeing Mahāvīra's divine qualities, he at length asked him in and gave him lodgings and a bed. (He could not offer food, as a sādhu may not eat at the house where he stays.) In return Mahāvīra taught Śakaḍāla the law and converted him to the true faith, and he became a devoted Śrāvaka in this life and after death a god. Being reincarnated as a man, he became a sādhu and so reached mokṣa.

vi. Mana puṇya.

vii. Śarīra puṇya.

By thinking well of every one and wishing them well we gain *Mana puṇya*, and by exerting ourselves to render them service or to save life we accumulate *Kāya* or *Śarīra puṇya*, as the following history shows. In a certain forest there was a small clearing, and once, when a terrible fire raged in the wood, all the animals rushed to this spot, and it became dangerously overcrowded. Even the mighty elephant had taken refuge there, and as he happened to raise his foot to change his position a hare ran under it. The elephant saw at once that if he put his foot down he would crush the hare, and in that crowded space there was not another place to which the hare could possibly move. So the elephant continued to hold his foot in the air for hours and hours, until at last, worn out, he fell to the ground and died. Immediately he was reincarnated as the son of a mighty king, and in his next birth became an ascetic and attained mokṣa.

viii. Vaćana puṇya.

Merit is also won by speaking without hurting any one's feelings, and so as to influence others towards religion and morality (*Vaćana puṇya*). Kṛiṣṇa, for instance, the favourite Hindu deity, when King of Dvārakā, once heard Neminātha preach. He felt that he himself could not face the hardships of a monk's life, but he urged any of his subjects who could to receive initiation, and promised to look after their families. Some of the people thereupon became monks, and this brought Kṛiṣṇa[1] so much Vaćana puṇya that he is bound eventually to become a Tīrthaṅkara, though he has a lot of karma to work off first.

ix. Namaskāra puṇya.

One may also obtain merit by reverent salutations (*Namaskāra puṇya*). The Jaina say that one first bows to religious men, then one gets to know them, next one decides to follow their example and by so doing one attains mokṣa. The Digambara and Śvetāmbara can obtain merit by bowing reverently to the images in their temples, but the Sthānakavāsī, having only gurus to bow to, show them double reverence and so have been accused of worshipping[2] their gurus, which they indignantly deny, pointing out that they make them no offerings of flowers, fruit, &c. It would be quite impossible to write down even the names of the legends told with the object of illustrating the great rewards gained by doing reverence. In fact the first step to mokṣa is said to be climbed by bowing. We have seen that the god Kṛiṣṇa is to be a Tīrthaṅkara, and the Jaina say that he will take his first step from Pātāla (a lower region), where he now is, towards this high future by doing reverence.

[1] We shall find constant examples of the influence Kṛiṣṇa worship has on the Jaina. Many of them read and love the *Bhagavadgītā* almost as much as the Hindus, though it is not one of their scriptures.

[2] They point out the following mistake in the *Imperial Gazetteer of India* (Oxford, 1907), vol. i, p. 417: 'The Dhondiyas, who worship their gurus', by which they complain that their feelings have been wounded.

The forty-two ways of enjoying the fruit of Puṇya.

We have seen that there are nine chief ways of laying up merit: the Jaina believe that there are forty-two ways in which the reward of this merit can be reaped. If one is very happy in having all that one needs to eat, drink and wear, one knows that one is enjoying *Śātavedanīya*. If one is born in a high family (*Ūñčagotra*); if one has had the joy of being born as a man (*Manuṣya gati*), and not as a beast, god, or hell being; and moreover if one is sure to be born in one's next birth as a man and not a beast (*Manuṣya anupūrvī*), one is experiencing three happy results of puṇya. The last of these results is often likened to the reins that pull an ox on to the right road, so strong is the force inherent in puṇya. If the merit acquired were very powerful, one might be born as a god and so enjoy *Devatā gati*, even becoming Kṛiṣṇa or Indra. To be even a minor god is a stage higher than being born as an ordinary man, and another of the fruits is *Devatā anupūrvī*, which keeps one on the path of becoming a god.

If we have all five senses in this life, it shows that we are enjoying *Pañčendriyapaṇuṁ*, and if we have a large and imposing body instead of a little one like an ant, that is owing to *Audārikaśarīra*. Sometimes puṇya has a magical effect, owing to which one may gain *Vaikreyaśarīra*, or a body like a god's, which can appear and disappear at will, can produce six or four hands, and become mountainous or minute. Certain monks by virtue of their knowledge and of their austerities gain the power of sending out a tiny body from themselves which can go to Mahāvideha and obtain answers to any doubts or spiritual difficulties from the Tīrthaṅkara there.[1] This tiny body is called *Āhārakaśarīra*, and the power of creating it is regarded as one of the most valued fruits of puṇya. Certain other fruits of puṇya (*Audārika aṅgopāṅga*, *Vaikreya aṅgopāṅga*, and *Āhāraka*

[1] Not from the Siddha, who take no interest in anything earthly.

aṅgopāṅga) carry with them the assurance of having the full complement of limbs with these last-mentioned three bodies. It is only through having heat in one's body (*Taijasaśarīra*) that such physical functions as digestion, circulation, &c., can be carried on, and the possession of this heat is one of the fruits of puṇya. Tejoleśyā is inherent in such a body, and so is the power of producing magic fire. Every one possesses a body (*Kārmaṇaśarīra*) round which his various karma accumulate, and without which one could never experience any of the happy fruits of merit; the very possession of this body is owing to puṇya, for every one has amassed merit of some kind.

Several of the rewards result in bodily strength or beauty, such as *Vajraṛiṣabhanārāća saṅghayaṇa*, which ensures one's possessing bones in one's body as hard as iron and as strong as a bull's; *Samaćaturastra saṇṭhāṇa*, that gives a well-proportioned, shapely and elegant body; and *Śubha varṇa*, *Śubha gandha*, *Śubha rasa* and *Śubha sparśa*, which endow one with a good complexion, pleasing bodily odour, good corpuscles in one's blood, and a skin that feels smooth as a peach to the touch. Again, the fruit of puṇya ensures one's being neither too fat nor too lean, but of exactly right weight (*Agurulaghu nāmakarma*), and also makes one so powerful (*Parāghāta nāmakarma*) that one is always victorious. Asthma or consumption are a clear sign that one has committed sin in a previous existence, for merit would have won *Uććhvāsa nāmakarma*, which ensures one's having no impediment in one's breathing.

Jaina also believe that as a result of merit they may be born again as Jyotiṣī devatā, living in the sun for one life and giving off almost unbearable effulgence. This effulgence is a result of *Ātapa nāmakarma.* Others as a reward of merit go to the moon, where it is very cold, and so they give off a cold radiance which is due to *Anuṣṇa nāmakarma.* Even one's method of walking is affected by one's previous actions, and a stately gait (*Śubhavihāyogati*), like that of an elephant, a goose, or a bull, is a much coveted prize for merit.

Another fruit of puṇya (*Nirmāṇa nāmakarma*) leads to one's being born with all one's limbs supple and perfect. Through *Trasa nāmakarma* one is certain to be born as at least a two-sensed being and may be endowed with all the senses. Some lives are microscopic, but if one has acquired *Bādara nāmakarma*, one may rest assured that one will at least have sufficient size to be perceptible to the naked eye. In whatever class of life one is born, provided only one has gained *Paryāpti nāmakarma*, one will be perfect in that class.

Every ailment and every illness is traced back to a fault in a previous birth : thus a rickety child must have committed some sin which prevented its gaining *Sthira nāmakarma*, for that would have given it strong and well-set limbs, fine teeth and a well-knit frame.

It has been already mentioned that Jaina believe that every onion, potato, garlic, carrot, turnip and ground root is the home of innumerable jīva. If a man has acquired *Pratyeka nāmakarma* he cannot be forced to dwell in one of these underground roots, but in whatever body he may be born, he will have that body to himself. There cannot be more than one jīva inhabiting a human body at the same moment, nor more than one in a bird, beast, or insect; it is only underground roots that take in troops of tenement lodgers.

Certain other rewards ensure one's having a handsome body (*Śubha nāmakarma*), at least from the waist up, or being loved by all with whom one comes in contact (*Subhaga nāmakarma*), having a pleasant voice (*Susvara nāmakarma*), gaining respect from all whom one meets (*Ādeya nāmakarma*), or even gaining fame wherever one goes (*Yaśokīrtti nāmakarma*).

Three different results of puṇya decide the term of

life which one will spend as a god (*Devatā āyuṣya*), or a human being (*Manuṣya āyuṣya*), or a lower animal (*Tiryañč āyuṣya*). The greatest and the final reward of puṇya is *Tīrthaṅkara nāmạkarma*, which ensures one at last becoming a Tīrthaṅkara.

The Fourth Category: Pāpa.

The eighteen kinds of Sin.

In order to understand the religion of the Jaina we must try and grasp their idea of sin, for it is a very different conception from the Western, being in fact often ceremonial rather than moral.

i. Jīva hiṁsā.

To take any life seems to the Jaina the most heinous of all crimes and entails the most terrible punishment; yet the central thought of Jainism is not so much saving life as refraining from destroying it. '*Ahiṁsā parama dharma*—Destroy no living creature! Injure no living creature! This is the highest religion!' declared a modern Jaina lecturer, and with almost Irish eloquence he goes on to say: 'I stand before you this noon to speak on a religion whose glory the dumb creatures, the cows, the goats, the sheep, the lambs, the hens, the pigeons, and all other living creatures, the beasts and the birds sing with their mute tongues; the only religion which has for thousands of years past advocated the cause of the silent-tongued animals: the only religion which has denounced slaughter of animals for sacrifice, food, hunting, or any purpose whatever.'[1] 'The foundation principle of the Jaina religion', writes another,[2] 'is to abstain from killing.' They even call their faith the religion of non-killing (*Ahiṁsā dharma*).

To people believing thus, killing (*Hiṁsā*) is the greatest sin and abstaining from killing (*Ahiṁsā*) the most binding moral duty. There is a higher and a lower law for ascetics and for the laity. A monk must strive not to take any life

[1] Lecture by Mr. Lāla Benārsi Dāss, Jain Itihās Society, Agra, 1902, pp. 1 ff.

[2] Popatlāl K. Shāh, *Jaina Dharma Nirūpaṇa*, p. 33.

(insect, vegetable, or animal) that has even one sense, but the laity are only forbidden to take any life possessed of two or more senses. The Jaina make a very interesting distinction between spiritual and actual murder (*Bhāva hiṁsā* and *Dravya hiṁsā*). One sins against Bhāva ahiṁsā by wishing for any one's death or desiring harm to befall them. Not only so, but if one does not continue and complete one's own education, or strive to improve one's own mind, or if one fails to exercise and discipline one's own soul, one commits Bhāva hiṁsā, for one kills by stultification what one might have been.[1] Dravya ahiṁsā (or the forbidding of material killing) is absolutely binding on all Jaina of every sect, and to offend against this is the greatest of all sins. Breaches of the seventh commandment are considered as breaking this law,[2] because more than one jīva are thereby held to be destroyed.

As a man kills a jīva, so will he be killed in hell, and lurid pictures are published to illustrate this tenet; but if any one kills a monk, that monk in the next world is given the privilege of killing his murderer without sinning against Ahiṁsā.

The Jaina say (with how much truth is doubtful) that their ancient rivals the Buddhists were once as careful as they to observe the rule against killing, but when Buddhism spread to different lands, it had to be adapted to the habits of people who declined to give up slaughter. A Jaina friend of the writer once acted most dramatically the way in which he declared Buddhists in Burma who desire to eat fish lift them carefully out of the water, and, having left them on the bank to die, say: 'Lo, here is a poor thing that has died! No sin will accrue to us if we eat it.' They also assert that the Buddhists in Tibet, calculating that sin

[1] This is strangely contradictory of the general aim of the whole system, which is none other than the gradual and complete stultification of character.

[2] In another aspect such offences are regarded by the Jaina as a form of stealing.

accrues equally whether they kill the smallest or the greatest jīva, say: 'Therefore since we must acquire sin, let us kill an elephant,' and so get as much as possible for their money.

In connexion with Ahiṁsā the lecturer whom we have before quoted gives a derivation for the word *Hindu* which is perhaps more ingenious than ingenuous:

'Hindus were not those who originally lived on the banks of the river Indus. Hindus were those from whom *hiṁsā* was away. Let us not misunderstand words. Let us interpret them correctly. It is those men who are the slaves of taste who say that Hindus were those who lived on the banks of the Indus. We, Jaina, call Hindus those from whom *hiṁ* or *hiṁsā* is *du* or *dūr*, i.e. away!'[1]

ii. Asatya or Mṛiṣā-vāda.

Though Hiṁsā is the greatest of crimes, the Jaina also recognize seventeen other sins, and the next worse of these is untruthfulness, *Asatya* or *Mṛiṣāvāda*. They divide the way ordinary folk talk into four classes: they may tell the truth; or they may tell absolute lies; they may occasionally make use of white lies; or their conversation may be a mosaic of truth and lies. Now a Jaina is only allowed to speak in two ways: either he must tell the truth; or, if that be too difficult, he may avail himself of white lies; but he must neither lie, nor speak the half-truth half-lie that is ever the blackest of lies.

The sad story of King Vasu shows the power of absolute candour and the fall that follows any declension from it. Vasu was known as 'the Truth-teller', and his throne was established on veracity; indeed, so strong was the power engendered by his absolute fidelity to truth, that his throne was supported by it alone at a great height from the ground. Two men named Parvata and Nārada came to him to ask him to tell them the exact significance of the word Ajā, for one held it to mean 'grain' and the other 'goat'. The king's paṇḍit had told him that it meant 'grain', but instead of saying this, the king, endeavouring to please both parties, gave the word a double signification, saying

[1] Lāla Benārsi Dāss, loc. cit., p. 75.

it might mean either 'goat' or 'grain'. The result of this deviation from the strict truth was that the king's throne fell to the ground, but if you look in a dictionary you will see the word bears a double meaning to this day!

The rules regarding truthfulness and untruthfulness differ for monks and laity, as we shall see when we come to discuss the twelve vows.

iii. Adattādāna.

Dishonesty (*Adattādāna*) is another class of sin which is forbidden to all Jaina; besides actual theft, this sin includes keeping lost property or treasure trove, smuggling, cheating, taking bribes, and all treason and law breaking. It was explained to the writer that the reason why treason and law breaking were included under this category was that originally they led to much financial profit, and all illegitimate financial profit was stealing; nowadays they are not so advantageous, but they are still strictly prohibited. Under this head is also forbidden all sharp practice in business, together with the misappropriation of trust funds and the use of charitable funds for private gain.

iv. Abrahmačarya.

Another sin that also bears a different connotation for the professed religious and the layman is unchastity (*Abrahmačarya*); for whereas a layman is bound to maintain his own wife in all honour and happiness, it is sin for a sādhu to allow so much as the hem of his garment to touch a woman. When we deal with the vows, we shall notice how much Eastern and Western monasticism have in common on this point.

v. Parigraha.

The Jaina realized how many sins sprang from excessive love of one's own possessions. They taught that if a monk kept one garment or one vessel above the allowed number, or if he even became over attached to one that he lawfully possessed, he committed the sin of *Parigraha*, or covetousness. In the same way the layman was instructed that if he showed uncontrolled grief when one of his cattle died or his money disappeared, he too had given way to greed.

vi. Krodha.

As one studies more closely the Jaina idea of what sin

consists in, one is struck with their profound knowledge of the human heart, a knowledge shared by all faiths which practise confession. Another thing that strikes one is the great stress they lay on anger (*Krodha*) as a source of sin. The merest globe-trotter notices how differently we Westerners look at anger, hardly accounting it a sin, while to an Oriental it seems a most heinous offence. We shall have to return to the subject of anger again and again in our analysis of Jaina thought; here it will suffice to notice that the Jaina hold that anger, though generally unrighteous (*apraśasta*), may also sometimes be righteous (*praśasta*). For instance, it is righteous for a guru to scold a lazy disciple [1] or for a magistrate to speak severely, but it is unrighteous to get angry without a cause, or to add to the ill feeling between two persons.

vii. Māna. The seventh of the eighteen kinds of sin is conceit or

[1] That even when angry with reason a guru must govern his anger the following legend shows. Once a guru had an impertinent disciple, and as the master sat engaged in his evening Paḍīkamaṇuṁ, thinking over his sins of the day, the disciple reminded him that he had walked on and killed a frog, and must perform prāyaścitta for this sin. Now the guru had not killed a frog, the one seen by the young man having been hurt by other passers-by; and feeling that at any rate it was not a novice's part to remind him of it, the guru leapt up from his seat, brush in hand, determined to chastise the cheeky youngster; unfortunately for himself, he rushed against a pillar and dashed his brains out.

The poor guru having died in a fit of anger slipped far down below the human level he had been on, and was reborn not as a man but as a snake, in fact a cobra. He took up his abode in an ant-hill near Waḍhwān and became, sad to say, not only a cobra, but a very bad cobra, who bit everybody who came near him; at last he established a reign of terror, and the road leading past the ant-hill was deserted through fear of him.

At this time Mahāvīra was alive, and his peregrinations happened to bring him to Waḍhwān; despite all his friends' warnings, he determined to remedy this evil; so he went out and sat down on the snake's ant-hill and meditated there. The enraged cobra dashed out and bit him over and over again, but Mahāvīra continued his meditations. Suddenly, as he looked at the master, all his former life came back to the snake's memory, he repented of his wrath, and ever after allowed little boys to chase him and ants to walk over him unmolested, and eventually died in the odour of sanctity. He is now steadily mounting the ladder of higher births.

Māna, and of conceit there are eight forms:[1] pride of caste, of family, of strength, of form, of wealth, of reputation, of learning, and last but not least, the pride of being a landed proprietor.

A great deal of confusion has arisen over the word *Māyā*, which the Jaina use to denote the eighth sin. The Vedāntists of course use the word to mean *illusion*, and a smattering of their philosophy is now so common, that many people loosely read Vedāntism into all Indian philosophy and suppose māyā invariably to have this meaning. The Jaina, however, consider themselves to be nearer to the Sāṅkhya than the Vedānta school of philosophy, and their properly instructed[2] teachers declare that the word generally means intrigue, cheating, attachment, ignorance, wealth, and only occasionally illusion. In the Jaina scriptures it usually connotes intrigue or cheating.

viii. Māyā.

A commercial people are naturally prone to this sin, but the sanction it carries with it is very heavy—a man who cheats in this life may be born *a woman* in the next! Not only commercial but religious cheating may involve this penalty, as the case of Mallinātha, the nineteenth Tīrthaṅkara shows. In a previous life he and five friends delighted to perform their religious duties together, and all six fasted and meditated with the utmost regularity and circumspection. Gradually, however, Mallinātha began to long to outdo

[1] Jaina children are taught to remember these different sorts of conceit in little rhymes much like those of Jane Taylor's which we children of a Western growth learnt in our childhood. Legends too are told showing the result of each of the eight kinds of conceit. As an example of the evil results brought about by pride, hear the sad story of Maričī, the son of Bharata, King of India. Bharata was the son of Ṛiṣabhadeva, the first Tīrthaṅkara, and it was revealed to him that his son should become a Tīrthaṅkara in a future life. Overhearing this, Maričī became very conceited and danced and jumped with joy. As a consequence of showing too much emotion a fetter (*ṭāṅkuṁ*) was formed, and this bound Maričī to become a beggar in his next incarnation, though nothing of course could prevent his eventually becoming a Tīrthaṅkara, which he did as Mahāvīra.

[2] It is a common complaint amongst the Jaina that so many of their gurus are extraordinarily ignorant of their own religion.

them in austerity, and thus get ahead of them on the path to liberation; and so, yielding to temptation, he once added an extra fast to the days they had agreed to observe and kept it on the quiet without telling his colleagues. His friends were deeply grieved when they discovered the deceitful way they had been outdone, but Mallinātha suffered also; for though he had acquired so much merit that it automatically made him a Tīrthaṅkara, the spiritual māyā he had indulged in turned him into a female one.[1]

ix. Lobha. The Jaina have many legends that show the evils of *Lobha* or avarice, the ninth kind of sin. Thus, a great king, Subhūma, lost his kingdom through greed and was drowned in the sea; and it was through avarice again that a certain merchant prince lost all his millions and died without a *pie*. Indeed the proverb *Lobha pāpanuṁ mūḷa*, 'avarice is the root of sin', is current not amongst Jaina only but among all Indians.[2]

Kaṣāya. We now come to an analysis of these four sins (anger, conceit, intrigue and greed), together called *Kaṣāya*, which is of the first importance to our sympathetic understanding of the strength of Jainism. The value of Jaina philosophy lies not only in the fact that it, unlike Hinduism, has correlated ethical teaching with its metaphysical system, but also in the amazing knowledge of human nature which its ethics display. Very often Jaina divide and subdivide a subject in such a way as to throw no fresh light on it, but in the subdivisions of these four faults (which they rightly and profoundly regard as sister sins) they have seized on an essential truth, that the length of time a sin is indulged in affects the nature of the sin; for sins grow worse through long keeping.[3]

[1] Digambara of course do not believe this, as they hold that no woman can ever be a Tīrthaṅkara.

[2] It is interesting to compare with this the Christian saying: 'The love of money is the root of all evil.'

[3] Compare again: 'Let not the sun go down upon your wrath'; for the anger which is kept overnight has grown deadly by the morning.

The worst degree to which any of these four sins may be indulged is called *Anantānubandhī*, when the sin is cherished as long as life lasts, and if there be an offender in the case, he is never forgiven. Whilst under the sway of sin to this degree, it is impossible for a man to grasp any ideas of religion or to give his mind to study.

In the next degree (*Apratyākhyānī*) the sin, though nursed for a year, is confessed at the great annual confession of sin.[1] During the time that a man is under its influence he might possess an intellectual grasp of religious principles, but it would be impossible for him to carry them out into his daily life.

In the third degree (*Pratyākhyānī*) the sin lasts only for four months and is confessed and given up at Ċomāsī[2] (the four-monthly confession), but during those months in which it is indulged, it prevents a man becoming a really holy monk or layman, though outwardly he may keep the vows. For instance, it would not hinder his doing some outward act such as giving up eating potatoes, but it would prevent his really giving up all attachment to the world.

The same four faults are cherished to the least of the four degrees (*Sañjvalana*) when renounced at the evening confession, or at least not carried beyond the fortnightly confession; but during the time a man indulges them to even this degree, though it would be possible for him to become a monk, he could not become the ideal sādhu as depicted in the scriptures, the goal which every true ascetic has set before him, and which he hopes to attain. This point the enlightened and spiritually minded Jaina love to discuss and compare with the Christian ideal of consecration and throwing aside every weight to reach the goal.

The Jaina are past masters in the art of illustration, and it is interesting to notice in their sacred books and in their sermons how many of their allegories are drawn

[1] See p. 259.

[2] *Sanskrit* Ċaturmāsī.

from common objects of the countryside. It makes one realize how largely India is a country of villagers.

Each of the four sins has its own parable. In the case of anger, the least degree is likened to a line drawn on water, which soon passes away; the next to one drawn in the dust, which is stamped out and effaced in a day; the third to a crack in the dried mud at the bottom of an empty village tank, which will not disappear till the yearly rains fill the tank and cover it; and the worst of all to a fissure in a mountain side, which will remain till the end of the world.

To illustrate the four degrees of eonceit, the Jaina take the stages of the growth of a tree, and remind us that the twig is pliable and easily bent again to humility; that the young branch of a tree can bend humbly if a storm force it; and that the wood of the stem may be taught humility (though with difficulty) by being oiled and heated; but coneeit in the worst degree outdoes any simile taken from a tree, being as unbending as a pillar of stone.

Deceit or intrigue again leads to crookedness: in the least degree it can be straightened as one can straighten a bamboo cane; in the seeond degree it is like the crooked track of moisture left in the dust by the dripping from the water carrier's leather bucket; when it grows worse it is as erooked as a ram's horn; and in the worst degree of all it is like the knot in the root of the bamboo, the crookedest thing in the land.

The most subtle perhaps of all the similes is that which deals with greed, and the Jaina illustration of its effects on the soul is of special interest, for this sin is said to change the eolour of the human heart. If avariee be cherished even to the least degree, it will stain the soul yellow like turmeric, but this diseoloration ean easily be washed off; if greed be given way to for a fortnight, the heart will be soiled like earthen cooking-pots whieh ean only be eleansed with great labour; if one eherishes it for four months, its stain grows as difficult to efface as the marks left by the oil of a cart wheel; and in the last degree it can never be washed away in this life, whatever efforts one may make, but is as ineffaceable as the crimson dye.[1]

The result of any of these four sins, if indulged in to the worst degree, is to condemn a man to rebirth in hell; the next worse forces him in his next life to become a bird, a beast, or an insect; if he has not indulged his sin for longer than four months, he may be born as a man; if he had thrown it off within a fortnight from its inception, he might become a god; but if in all his life he had remained free from all wrath, conceit, intrigue and greed, he would become a Siddha without rebirth.

All these four, Krodha, Māna, Māyā and Lobha, are called Kaṣāya, or things which tie one down to this world; they are also called Ċaṇḍāḷa Ċokaḍī, the four vile or outcaste ones, and the following legend is told to show how indulgence in them destroys all true dignity and drags one down to the lowest level. A certain Brāhman, having bathed and worshipped, felt himself polluted by the accidental touch of a sweeper woman, and, being enraged, swore at her. To his astonishment she promptly caught hold of his garments, and the more he swore at her, the more tightly she clung. Mad with rage, the Brāhman rushed to the king demanding redress. The king asked the woman how she had dared to catch hold of a Brāhman, but she replied that the Brāhman had already polluted himself by receiving a Ċaṇḍāḷa into his heart when he became angry, and therefore her touch could no longer pollute him, for he had become her fellow outcaste.

The Jaina sum up their teaching about these four sins by

[1] To Jaina it is of special interest that about a century before this idea had been incorporated into their teaching, the great Hebrew prophet was also reflecting on the discoloration produced on the soul by sin, but declared that there was One who could remove even the crimson stain. 'Come now, and let us reason together, saith the Lord: though your sins be as scarlet, they shall be as white as snow; though they be red like crimson, they shall be as wool.' Isaiah i. 18.

saying that when wrath leaves, forgiveness for others[1] enters; when conceit goes, humility comes; intrigue gives place to simplicity; and when avarice disappears, content reigns.

x. Rāga or Asakti.

The tenth class of sin is even more worth our studying, for it seems to put into our hands the key that unlocks the very heart of Jainism and reveals the loneliness within. All over-fondness (*Rāga* or *Āsakti*) for a person or thing is sin, since it hinders that perfect detachment from the world which is the goal of the whole system.

It is easy to see that in a coarse way an attachment may hinder a monk's progress, but the legend that the Jaina tell to illustrate this obvious fact is worth recording, for it shows how clearly they have realized the strange contradictions in character that may exist in the same person. It is told how Mahāvīra once preached at the court of Śreṇika, King of Magadha, with such power that the heir, Prince Nandiṣeṇa, became converted and, leaving all his splendour, went to live in the woods. There unhappily he fell under the sway of a courtesan, and as he felt he could neither leave her nor give up his belief that Jainism was the true faith, he had resort to that most intricate of all compromises, a bargain with his conscience. He decided to stay with her and also to preach Jainism, though he no longer practised it; he determined as a further sop to his conscience to regularly convert ten people to Jainism every day. He continued to do this for some time, but one day he happened to have only ten people in his audience, and though he converted nine of these, the tenth, a goldsmith, was a very hard nut to crack. The woman wanted her breakfast, but the erstwhile prince was determined to get his tale of ten converts complete. At last the woman called out 'Why on earth don't you convert yourself and so get your ten, and let us have our breakfast?' The taunt went home, and there and then he tore out the

[1] The Jaina pathetically believe that though there is forgiveness for sins against others, there is none for sins against themselves.

hair, which had grown whilst he dallied with sin, and returned to the forest. The Jaina say that such a man, having overcome rāga, would on his death go to svarga.

This was of course an example of wrong love, but the Jaina believe that indulgence in even right affection will hinder one's attaining liberation, as the pathetic story of Mahāvīra's greatest disciple, Gautama, shows. It will be remembered that Gautama could not conquer his personal attachment to the great ascetic, and despite all his endeavours he continued to think of him as '*my* master' and '*my* friend', thus showing that he had allowed himself to become attached by the roots of his personality to another. Only on the night that Mahāvīra died was he able to overcome all *mamatva* or feeling of personal devotion and possession. It had been easy for Gautama to give up all outward possessions of wealth and property, it was agony to him to tear out love from his heart. Devout Jaina are very interested in the contrast between this story and that of the Christian disciple, Thomas, who touched the highest development of the Christian faith when his mamatva became perfected, and he could say to his Master: '*My* Lord and *my* God.'[1]

Our study has now brought us to a most interesting parting of the ways between Jainism on the one hand and both Hinduism and Christianity on the other, for the understanding of which the writer is deeply indebted to both Jaina and Hindu friends, who have taken endless pains to make their view-points clear.

As all personal attachment is burnt up in the glow of asceticism, the true Jaina cannot hold any doctrine of personal devotion (*bhakti*) to a god such as has inspired so much of the most beautiful Hindu literature. Yet there is amongst some modern Jaina a tendency towards giving to Mahāvīra a devotion which almost resembles bhakti; this may be indirectly due to the influence of

[1] St. John xx. 28.

the Bhagavadgītā, which is widely read amongst them, or of the stories they have read of Jesus Christ, for whose person the Jaina, with their eager love of all that is tender and beautiful, have a great reverence. Nevertheless, according to their creed, they do not believe in a Creator, much less in a Father Omnipotent, to whom they might feel such personal devotion. The *state* of godhood is what they fix their thoughts on, a state of passive and passionless beatitude enjoyed by several separate Siddha; and for this state of godhood they are permitted to have an attachment, and it is on their own attainment of this state that they fix their hopes and their ambitions. 'Why should I love a personal god?' a Jaina once said to the writer, 'I hope to become a god myself'. And in one of their sacred books the whole matter is summed up in words terrible in their loneliness: 'Man! Thou art thine own friend; why wishest thou for a friend beyond thyself?'[1]

xi. Dveṣa. The eleventh kind of sin, hatred or envy (*Dveṣa* or *Īrṣyā*), is entirely evil, and the soul that would proceed on the great journey must completely free itself from it. As it often springs from possession, the man who strips himself of all property goes far to rid himself of the sin too, as the following legend shows.

There was once a king named Draviḍa, who on his death divided his property between his elder son, Drāviḍa, and his younger, Vārikhilla, leaving the senior more property than the junior. The younger, however, succeeded by wise management in so increasing his estate that his elder brother grew more and more envious, and finally on some pretext or other a war broke out between the two. During the monsoon there was perforce a truce, and Drāviḍa had leisure to hear a famous non-Jaina ascetic preach on the sin of envy; becoming converted, he went off to the camp of his younger brother to beg forgiveness. The brothers were completely reconciled, and both of them not only

[1] *Āćārāṅga Sūtra*, *S. B. E.*, xxii, p. 33.

renounced envy, but agreed also to renounce their kingdoms, the possession of which had given rise to so great a sin. They became Jaina sādhus and lived at Śatruñjaya, and passing from thence to mokṣa they became Siddha. And still on the full moon day of the month Kārtika, when the faithful go on pilgrimage to Śatruñjaya, they remember the two brothers who gave up all things to free themselves from envy.

Quarrelsomeness or *Kleśa*, the twelfth form of sin, is specially dangerous to family happiness, as we can easily understand, when we remember how many members of a family live under one roof in India. This is believed to be the particular vice to which mothers-in-law are liable, and it is often only owing to the influence of this sin that they complain of their daughter-in-law's cooking! The Jaina scriptures are full of examples of the evils that spring from such quarrelsomeness, showing that it has often not only ruined families but even destroyed kingdoms. xii. Kleśa.

So greatly do the Jaina value the peace of their homes, that the next sin, slander (*Abhyākhyāna*), is also looked at chiefly as a home-wrecking sin. So grievous a crime is it, that nature will work a miracle to discredit it, as illustrated by the following legend. In a certain city a fierce mother-in-law accused her son's wife of unchastity. The poor girl could only protest her innocency, but was quite unable to prove it, till suddenly a great calamity befell the city: the massive gates of the town stuck fast and could not be moved! An astrologer, being called in to help, declared that they could only be opened by a woman so chaste that she could draw water from a well in a sieve and sprinkle with it the obdurate gates. The accused girl seized this chance to prove her innocency, and did it so successfully that her slanderer was confounded and condemned.[1] xiii. Abhyākhyāna.

Paiśunya, or telling stories to discredit any one, is another sin resembling in its guilt that of slander. xiv. Paiśunya.

[1] This story is told in *The Lives of Sixteen Chaste Women*, a famous Jaina classic.

xv. Nindā. It is also a very serious sin to be always eriticizing and finding fault (*Nindā*). The Jaina tell many stories to show that one should look at one's own sins and not at thc sins of others, saying that if one is continually thinking of the faults of others, one's own mind becomes debased and one grows likc thc very sinners one criticizes.

xvi. Rati, Arati. It is natural for an ascetic religion to reekon the laek of self-control in the presence of either joy or sorrow (*Rati Arati*) as a very gravc sin, tending, as it does, not only to injury of health and spirits, but also to excessive attachment to temporal and transitory objects of affeetion.

xvii. Māyā-mṛiṣā. The sevcnteenth form of sin in our list, *Māyāmṛiṣā*, is very far-reaching. It is that speeies of untruthfulness which in ordinary conversation leads to *suggestio falsi*, and whieh in religion leads to hypocrisy. The Jaina love of the eountry-side and thcir shrewd country wit is shown in the fact that the typieal example they quote of thc hypocrite is the stork. This bird, they deelare, stands on the river bank on only one lcg (to pretend he has the least possible eonnexion with the things of earth) and seems to be lost in meditation, but, if a fish appear, he swoops down and kills it, thus committing the sin of hiṁsā, the most heinous of all crimes, whilst professing to be engagcd in devotion.

xviii. Mithyā-darśana Ś?lya. The last of the eighteen sins, *Mithyādarśana Śalya*, embraces those that spring from false faith, such as holding the rcnegade Gośāla, who was nothing but a failure, to be a Tīrthaṅkara, or belicving in a false religion,[1] or taking a man who is a hypocrite for one's guru. There are altogether twenty-five divisions of the sin of false faith, but we need only glanee at one or two of the most important, as throwing an interesting light on the way Jaina regard the religions by whieh they are surrounded. Sueh are *Laukika mithyātva*, or believing in sueh gods as Gaṇeśa or Hanumān, whom the Jaina do not believe to be

[1] All religions outside Jainism are false, but those which do not inculcate compassion are specially unworthy of credence.

gods at all; and *Lokottara mithyātva*, which includes all forms of spiritual bribery, such as the offering of vows to various Jaina saints or gurus for the fulfilment of the worshipper's wishes. Under this it is even forbidden to pray for a child's recovery from sickness! It is also accounted a sin, though a venial one, if a Jaina woman, for instance, promises in the event of a son being granted to her to give a cradle to a temple, or to donate money to a sādhu, or that her husband will feed their caste fellows; for the Jaina say that they should never give alms with any object save that of aiding themselves on the journey to mokṣa, and should be careful not to import into their religion the practices of an alien faith.[1] Two other branches of the sin of false faith are such as might prevent conversion to Jainism: the obstinate holding of a belief, when the holder is convinced it is false (*Abhigrahika mithyātva*); and the resting content in a state of ignorance, when there is an opportunity of striving to learn (*Ajñāna mithyātva*). Other sins included under this head consist in lack of reverence towards sacred things: for instance, he who fails to pay the honour due to a guru or a god is guilty of *Avinaya mithyātva*; and a man who enters a temple wearing his shoes, or chewing betel-nut, or who spits in the temple precincts, is guilty of *Aśātanā mithyātva*. The last of these twenty-five which we need enumerate is *Anabhigrahika mithyātva*,[2] the sin which any Jaina would commit who, for example, became a theosophist, or came to regard all religions as true and all their founders and apostles as equally worthy of reverence and belief.

Such are some of the faults which are included under this sin of false faith, the last on the list of the eighteen kinds of sin. Such a list is in itself enough to justify the claim of the Jaina that the philosophy of their faith is an ethical philosophy; but to Western eyes it seems no

[1] The intelligent Jaina clearly recognize that Hinduism has a very great influence over the religious ideas and practices of the less instructed members of their community.

[2] Otherwise *Anabhi grahitva*.

less remarkable for its omissions than for its inclusions. To judge this list fairly one must remember that it is not an unused piece of lumber stored away in the Jaina statute book, but that the most careless of Jaina test their consciences by it at least once every year, and that the more devout use it every four months and some even every fortnight. It cannot be denied that such lists, together with kindred enactments, have educated the Jaina conscience to some knowledge of what sin is.

The Eighty-two Results of Sin.

Under their fourth principle the Jaina include not only the forms which sin takes, but also the results which follow from it. Jaina have a great admiration for beauty of person and of intellect, and they believe that sin in a previous birth will inevitably produce deformity in mind or body in the next existence.

The five Jñānā-varaṇīya.

They say that there are five ways in which sin can impede knowledge. It may impede the free use of the intellect (*Matijñānāvaraṇīya*). It is true that when a man becomes a Siddha, his soul will have perfect knowledge and will be able to cast aside the mind as no longer needed, but in this life he must use his intellect and his five senses to the full as a means of gaining wisdom. Sin in a previous birth hinders all exercise of the intellect, as dirt clogs the machinery of a watch. Another effect of sin on the intellect is to prevent our gaining any good from hearing or reading the scriptures (*Śrutajñānāvaraṇīya*). Sin also impedes the use of occult powers. Certain Jaina, even after shutting their eyes, know what is going on around them, but the effect of some sins would neutralize this knowledge (*Avadhijñānāvaraṇīya*). By the practice of austerities these occult powers can be so developed that a man can know what is going on in Jambūdvīpa, Dhātakī Khaṇḍa,[1] or half of Puṣkaradvīpa, but previous sin (*Manaḥparyāyajñānā-*

[1] *Or* Kālodadhi Khaṇḍa.

varaṇīya) would spoil these powers, even as another of its results (*Kevalajñānāvaraṇīya*) can prevent any one's attaining omniscience, the highest knowledge of all. Evidently the Jaina have clearly realized that part of the wages of sin is death to the intellectual life.

The five Antarāya.

Sin can also impede our enjoyment of many other things besides intellect. If one is longing to experience the pleasure of giving away, and even has everything ready, sin will prevent one's actually dispensing the alms (*Dānāntarāya*). If a man works hard in business, but never manages to makc a profit, he knows that it is owing to sin (*Lābhāntarāya*). In this case, however, he may hope to overcome the effect of sin, if it had not become ripe enough for punishment, by accumulating merit. There are two ways of enjoying the possession of property: there is the enjoyment a poor man would take in having some great luxury like a motor car, and the enjoyment he has in using such necessaries of life as food and clothing. The fruit of sin will prevent his enjoying either (*Bhogāntarāya* and *Upabhogāntarāya*). The Jaina hold also that sin will prevent a man's rejoicing in his strength, and if they see that some one, though evidently possessing great physical or spiritual powers, has been from his youth up unable to use them (*Vīryāntarāya*), they say at once that he must have committed some sin in his previous birth.

The four Darśanāvaraṇīya.

Sin has a specially evil effect on sight, both physical and spiritual (*Ċakṣudarśanāvaraṇīya*): one effect of sin may be to actually render a man blind, a less gross sin would result in his being short-sighted, and if the sin were only a venial one, its fruit might be only night blindness. Other sins would injure other senses (*Aċakṣudarśanāvaraṇīya*) such as hearing, smelling, tasting and the sense of touch. Then, just as we saw that the degrees of knowledge were impeded as a penalty for sin, so with regard to sight in various degrees: sin prevents any one seeing with the cyes of the soul what people at a distance are doing (*Avadhidarśanāvaraṇīya*), and of course also hinders any one from getting that supernatural vision which is only possessed by the omniscient (*Kevaladarśanāvaraṇīya*). If any sin be very heinous, its fruit may ripen in the very life in which it was committed, so that the sinner may suffer for it before death without having to wait for rebirth, but usually the wages of sin accumulate and only affect a jīva in succeeding lives.

The five Nidrā.

Sin seems to have a specially unfavourable influence on attempts at meditation, for one of the fruits of sin is slumber, that great foe to prayer. All indulgence in sin leads to sleepiness: if the sin had been slight the slumber is light (*Nidrā*), and the sleeper can be awakened easily; but heavier sin brings on heavier slumber (*Nidrānidrā*), from which the awakening is painful. In a worse state sleep comes uninvited to a man as he tries to meditate when he is standing up or sitting down (*Praćalā*); and as a punishment for yet grosser sin it does not wait for movement to cease, but overpowers him even as he is walking along the road (*Ċalā* or *Praćalāpraćalā*). The worst type of slumber (*Styānarddhi* or *Thīṇarddhi*) is the fruit of gross sin, and indues its victims with terrific vigour, so that they possess at least half of the strength of the great Vāsudeva. With this strength they commit in their sleep all sorts of crimes, murders and manslaughters, so that their guilt is increased, and with it is increased also their slumber, hence they are perpetually involved in a hideous circle of crime bringing forth slumber and slumber bringing forth crime, from which there is no relief.

Five unclassified results.

In the long list of eighty-two results of sin one comes after Nidrā to some unclassified results, which we shall deal with more fully elsewhere, such as the being born in a low-caste or poor family (*Nīćagotra*), being born in hell (*Narakagati*), or suffering sorrow on sorrow (*Aśātāvedanīya*), perhaps in hell. As a result of sin, too, the force (*Narakānupūrvī*) is accumulated which will send one to hell, and the time one will have to spend there (*Narakāyu*) is also dependent on our previous sins.

The twenty-five Kaṣāya, including the nine Nokaṣāya.

Next on the long list come the twenty-five Kaṣāya (those sins which result in tying men to the cycle of rebirth). We have discussed[1] sixteen of these under the heads of anger, conceit, intrigue, and greed, and their subdivisions, and must now look at nine minor faults (*Nokaṣāya*) and their results. These sins are such as it is very important for ascetics to avoid, but as they are not in themselves very heinous transgressions, they do not bring such terrible consequences in their train. Nevertheless a sādhu must avoid the sin of laughter (*Hāsya*), for when he made the great renunciation he bade farewell to all enjoyment of merriment. If a sādhu laughs even once, some punishment will follow, and if he persists in the indulgence, it will lead to his rebirth. The next sin is worth remembering, for it brings out most clearly the difference between the Christian ideal of asceticism, as typified, for example, by St. Francis of Assisi or David Livingstone, with their joy in all the beauty and wonder of the world, and the Jaina ideal. A sādhu must not rejoice in beauty (*Rati*[2]) nor in the joyousness of a little child, nor in the sound of exquisite harmony, nor in the glories of art, for a religious has done with all pleasure which is worldly and arises from delight in pudgaḷa. A monk has bidden farewell also to all disgust (*Arati*), and must not feel dismay at the sight of an evil-looking person, or on hearing even the vilest abuse. A sādhu must be free from all fear (*Bhaya*) of men or animals: indeed in their scriptures he is expressly told that, even if he sees a vicious cow coming for him, he is not to leave the road, but with a mind 'not directed to outward things' continue in contemplation.[3] Similarly he must never indulge in grief (*Śoka*) through being deprived of anything, but must remain undisturbed, even if thieves rob him of his last garment. Many legends record how scrupulously good monks have abstained from the next sin,

[1] See pp. 122 ff.
[2] Rati and Arati bear various meanings in Jaina philosophy.
[3] *Ācārāṅga Sūtra*, *S. B. E.*, xxii, p. 147.

that of feeling dismayed when assailed, either by words of hatred or contempt, or by an evil smell (*Dugañčhā*). The remaining three minor faults (*Puruṣaveda, Strīveda, Napuṁsakaveda*) remind us how completely the Jaina ascetic has parted with love and affection, for if he be a true monk, he must form no friendship even with another monk, and similarly no nun may desire the companionship of another nun, or a neuter of a neuter. Though these nine minor faults are sins that the ascetic is specially bound to shun, they also show the things that the layman will do well to avoid, for the over-indulgence in any of them will result in rebirth.

Six results affecting class of jīva.

Sin will further affect the class of beings into which one is born in the next incarnation, for the Jaina draw no barriers between animal and human life, and the result of sin in this life may be to accumulate a force (*Tiryañč anupūrvī*) which will cause one to be reborn on the next occasion as a beast or a bird (*Tiryañč gati*) or as a one-sensed, two-sensed, three-sensed, or four-sensed being (*Ekendriya nāma, Be-indriya nāma, Tri-indriya nāma, Čorendriya nāma*).

Six physical blemishes.

Sin also results in personal ugliness of various kinds. If one sees some one who walks in a very ugly way like a camel or a donkey, one knows at once that it is the result of sin (*Aśubha vihāyogati*); certain ugly diseases (*Upaghāta nāma*), such as boils under the tongue, diseases of the throat, teeth dropping out, or curvature of the spine, are caused by sin. Indians very much admire a complexion of the colour of ripe wheat and dislike a very dark skin; and Jaina believe that complexions are the result of conduct in a past life, and that a really black skin is the fruit of sin (*Aśubha varṇa*). So is an unpleasant bodily smell (*Aśubha gandha*), unpleasant bodily essence (*Aśubha rasa*), and a skin that is unpleasant to the touch (*Aśubha sparśa*). The general result of beliefs of this kind is to dry up sympathy for sufferers from bodily defects.

Sin also results in loss of bodily strength, and to under-

The five Saṅghena.

stand this we must try and grasp a new idea of anatomy. The Jaina believe that sinews are wrapped round the bones of the human frame like a bandage, and that on the tightness of this wrapping the strength of the body depends. Sin has affected this bandage in five particular ways: firstly (*Ṛiṣabhanārāća saṅgheṇa*), owing to the general depravity of the age, the peg that fastened the bandage tightly to the human frame and prevented its getting unwound has dropped out, and got permanently lost, so that there is no security against loss of bodily strength. As the world has grown steadily wickeder, the bandage has passed through successive stages of becoming loose (*Nārāća saṅgheṇa*) and so greatly weakening the body; dropping half off (*Ardhanārāća saṅgheṇa*); slipping right off (*Kīlikā saṅgheṇa*), so as to leave only the two little nails that fastened the bones before they were bandaged; until at last we reach the present epoch, when not only has the bandage entirely disappeared (*Sevārtta saṅgheṇa*), but also the nails that held the bones, and so the human frame, having lost the strength the bandage formerly gave, as well as the cohesion due to the nails, now only keeps together in a weakened condition 'owing to sockets, &c.'!

The five Saṁsthāna.

Sin also results in various deformities in the human body. A good figure is held to be a reward of past merit, and the various failures to reach the perfect physical standard are the fruits of sin. As the upper portion of a banyan tree is famous for its beauty, whilst nearer the ground it looks ugly enough, so it often happens that, though the head and trunk of a man are perfectly formed, his legs are short and spindly; this failure of upper and lower to correspond (*Nyagrodha-parimaṇḍaḷa saṁsthāna*) is the fruit of sin. So is the reverse (*Sādi saṁsthāna*), when the head and trunk are miserably thin and badly developed, while the legs are strong and vigorous. Or the head and legs may be normal, but the torso ill-formed (*Kubjaka saṁsthāna*). The result of sin may be to make a man a dwarf (*Vāmana saṁsthāna*); and still grosser sin may result in the malformation of every limb and every feature (*Huṇḍa saṁsthāna*).

The Sthāvara Daśaka.

Pursuing our way down the long list we come next to a rather heterogeneous group of ten results of sin. Certain sins condemn the soul that commits them to be born in the next life in the class of motionless beings (*Sthāvara*), or perhaps to be so tiny as to be invisible and unable to move (*Sūkṣma*). Other sins prevent a soul acquiring the full number of powers and senses that belong to the class in which it is born (*Aparyāpti*). A still more dreaded result of sin forces a soul to take up its abode in a body already inhabited by numberless other souls (*Sādhāraṇa*). Jaina, as we have seen, believe that thousands of lives lodge in every single potato, onion, artichoke and beet; and so they never eat any tuber, root, or bulb, lest they should take not one but thousands of lives by so doing. No punishment is more feared by the Jaina than that the jīva, instead of having some shelter (human, animal, or vegetable) to itself, may have to lodge along with myriads of others in an overcrowded dwelling. Again, as the result of sin, the body that the jīva inhabits may be complete in every respect, but the limbs may be unstable (*Asthira*): a shaky hand, a palsied head and loose teeth are all put down to sin in a past life. Sin may make a man unlucky and his name so inauspicious (*Aśubha*) that people do not like to mention it early in the morning, lest misfortune pursue them all day; or it may make a man a failure (*Durbhaga*), so that everything he touches goes wrong. The voice, too, may be affected (*Dusvara*), so that it becomes unpleasing to the listener and lacks all harmony: a donkey's bray, the hooting of an owl and the cracked voice of a man all bear witness to sin in a previous life. Though the sound of a voice may be all right, the effect of sin may be to take away all authority from it (*Anādeya*): when a man's commands are disobeyed, his warnings disregarded, and his words disbelieved, it is plain that he must have sinned deeply in his last birth. One notices, too, that however hard some men strive, disgrace instead of fame seems to be their lot (*Ayaśa*); this also is the result of sin.

The last of the eighty-two fruits of sin (*Mithyātva mohanīya*) is the most terrible of all, for it deprives a man of the power of believing in the truth. He is forced by it to believe in a false instead of in a true god; in an evil guru and not in a good one; and in a false creed instead of the true faith. Mithyātva mohanīya.

The Fifth Category: Āśrava.

Karma (the accumulated result of action) is one of the central ideas of the Jaina faith, and the fifth principle of Jaina philosophy deals with the way karma is acquired by the human soul. Just as water flows into a boat through a hole in it, so karma according to the Jaina flows into the soul through Āśrava and impedes its progress. No soul can attain to mokṣa till it has worked off all its karma, auspicious and inauspicious (*Śubha* and *Aśubha*). There are forty-two chief channels or Āśrava through which karma enters a jīva; and of these, seventeen are regarded as major. The forty-two Āśrava.

The easiest way for karma to enter is through the senses: so the five indriya must be guarded; otherwise, through the ear for example (*Kāna āśrava*) pleasant sounds may be heard and so gloated over and indulged in that a man would find it impossible to live without them, and eventually through his delight in these siren sounds forget all duty and be lost to all progress in the upward path. Or once more through the lust of the eye (*Ānkha āśrava*) he may be so entangled by the beauty of women or art as to be hindered from any progress, and so evil would flow into his soul. Again the delight in sweet odours (*Nāka āśrava*), as of flowers, perfumes, or scent, may make him forget his duties. Similarly taste (*Jībha āśrava*) may become a hindrance to him, for he may waste time and money in purchasing delicacies, and even eat things forbidden to the devout. The Jaina lay great stress on the importance of controlling the The seventeen major Āśrava. The Five Senses.

sense of taste, for if that be disciplined, all the other senses can also, they say, be kept in restraint, whereas gluttony affects sight, hearing, smell and the sense of touch. The sense of touch, too, must be carefully controlled (*Sparśa āśrava*), or the love of touching smooth things, for example, may become such a snare that the toucher may be lulled into unconsciousness through the pleasure of it.

The four Kaṣāya.

Karma may enter through the four emotions (*Kaṣāya*)[1] whose exercise ties the soul to the cycle of rebirth, for if anger be indulged (*Krodha āśrava*), it burns the soul of him who gives way to it, as well as the soul of the person he may injure, and so both are harmed. Conceit and pride (*Māna āśrava*) are a terrible foe to progress and open the door to all sorts of karma, besides they are the deadly enemy of courtesy, by which merit is obtained. Deceit and intrigue (*Māyā āśrava*) lead to many kinds of falseness in word and deed, and thus much evil karma is accumulated; and lastly avarice (*Lobha āśrava*) leads first to cheating and then to actual thieving, and is opposed to self-sacrifice and self-restraint.

The Jaina say that these four evil emotions must be checked on the principle of cultivating the corresponding virtue. Thus the angry man must exercise forgiveness, the proud man humility, the deceitful frankness, and the avaricious contentment; but how this is to be done is not explained.

The five Avrata.

Again, through not taking the five great vows evil karma may flow in in five ways (*Pañća Avrata*). If a man fails to go to a guru and, standing in front of him, to promise with folded hands that he will not kill, this simple omission to promise, without any commission, will lead to the acquisition of karma; for the Jaina hold that without the stiffening of resolution that comes through taking the vow one is more liable to do wrong; this liability leads to instability of mind, through which some karma enters. Of course more karma

[1] See pp. 122 ff.

would enter if one should go further and act contrary to the spirit of the vow. Similarly karma is acquired by failing to take, or offending against, the spirit of the vow against lying, thieving, coveting and acting unchastely.

The three Yoga.

Karma will also flow into any soul which has allowed either mind, speech, or body to become too entangled with a material object. If the mind is taken up with meditation on a Tīrthaṅkara or on a Siddha, the influence is good, and a favourable channel (*Śubha āśrava*) is opened up, through which, instead of karma, merit (puṇya) flows into the soul; but if the mind is occupied with an evil thought (e.g. if such and such a merchant dies, I shall get his wealth), a bad channel is opened, and through this bad channel (*Aśubha āśrava*) evil karma enters. In the same way there is a śubha and aśubha āśrava of speech: by repeating the name of Siddha or the Pañča Parameśvara merit is acquired, but by evil or abusive speaking bad karma enters the soul. Finally, if one saves life, for example, by bodily exertion, it is śubha āśrava, whilst killing is, of course, aśubha āśrava.

The twenty-five minor Āśrava.

Besides these seventeen major channels or āśrava, there are twenty-five minor ways by which karma is acquired, all of them connected with action. If one is not careful about the movements of one's body, an injury may be inflicted on some person or thing (*Kāyikī āśrava*) and evil karma acquired, and the same thing may happen through the careless use of weapons (*Adhikaraṇikī*), or through hatred (*Pradveṣikī*), or intentionally (*Paritāpanikī*), or some prāṇa (*Prāṇātipātikī*) may be injured. Again, by beginning to build a house or to till a field some insect life may be hurt (*Ārambhikī*), or by gathering together great stores of grain, cattle, or wealth covetousness may arise (*Pārigrahikī*) and give birth to karma. One might do some one an injury through deceit (*Māyāpratyayikī*), or acquire evil karma by acting contrary to the dictates of Mahāvīra and obeying the commands of some false faith (*Mithyādarśanapratyayikī*). Through omitting to take a vow to go to a certain place (e.g.

to America) one might go there, and when there acquire evil karma, or, in the same way through omitting to take a vow against eating certain things one is liable to eat them and so acquire karma (*Apratyākhyānikī*). By looking at some object with excessive love or hatred, one makes a channel for karma to enter (*Dṛiṣṭiki*), and by touching other objects one produces the same effect (*Spṛiṣṭikī*). Another interesting belief of the Jaina under this head is that sin committed in a previous existence forms a channel through which, in this life, karma may be more easily acquired (*Prātityakī*). The Jaina, who in all sorts of ways show their realization of the dangers of wealth, believe that if the possessor of many goods be much praised for possessing them and thus give way to conceit, he opens the way for evil karma to accrue (*Sāmantopanipātikī*).

Machinery is guilty of destroying so much insect life, that Jaina should only use it with the greatest caution, for a man, even if he be an employé working at the express command of a rajah whom he is bound to obey, does not therefore rid himself of his personal responsibility, but acquires evil karma through every life he takes (*Naiśastrikī*).[1] The employer, however, is also responsible, and if a servant in obedience to his master's order so acts as to injure any jīva, his guilt is shared by his master, who will also have acquired evil karma (*Svahastikī*). There is an expressive Gujarātī adjective 'doḍhaḍāhyuṁ' applied to people who are too wise by half; when folk suffer from this in religious matters and know more than Mahāvīra taught, they open the way for karma to flow in (*Ājñāpanikī*). Defamation also leads to karma, and if a man unjustly speaks ill of another, he has thereby opened the door to evil karma (*Vaidāraṇikī*). The caustic wit of the Jaina shows in the next item on the list, for they teach that if a man pretends to be listening to a sermon with great interest and all the time his wits are wool-gathering, he has

[1] Or *Naisṛiṣṭikī*.

formed a new channel (*Anābhogikī*) for karma. They also aim a shrewd blow at all reformers and such-like troublesome folk by declaring that a very dangerous way of opening new inlets for karma is to act in any way against the prejudices, usages, or beliefs that one knows one's fellow caste-men to hold in this world, or that one believes they will hold in the next! (*Anavakāṅkṣāpratyayikī*). In the same way karma accrues if one acts against rule, or fails to control one's speech, body, mind, or movements (*Prayogikī*). There is a difference of opinion as to the next item on the list (*Sāmudāyikī*). Some paṇḍits hold that it refers to the channels an individual may open by acting in such a way that all the eight karma simultaneously flow in. Others believe it denotes the channels a crowd of people may open at the same moment, as, for instance, if a number of persons go to see a man hanged and all hope that the hangman will not keep them waiting about, but will get the execution over as quickly as possible; when this occurs every single member of the crowd who feels this desire has opened a passage for bad karma. When people act under the influence of deceit or covetousness, they open a way for karma (*Premikī*), and so they do when swayed by anger (*Dveṣikī*). In fact, karma, either good or bad, must accrue so long as one has a body; even a Kevalī (who, knowing all sin, tries to avoid it), so long as he is in the flesh, is forced into some action, and every action good or bad produces karma (*Īryāpathikī*). So long as there is any karma remaining, either good or evil, one cannot reach mokṣa. The logical outcome of this belief one sees, for example, in the action of Mahāvīra's parents, who, trying to avoid all action, lest karma (the result of action) should keep them from liberation, abstained even from the taking of food, and so, prompted by the highest motives, died of starvation. Only by dying can a Jaina help acquiring karma, and karma, either good or bad, ties them inexorably to the weary cycle of rebirth. Here, again, we touch one of the great contrasts between the teaching of Mahāvīra, who, good and great as he was, taught a system, the logical outcome of which is death, and that of the Founder of Christianity, who came that His followers might have life, and have it abundantly.[1]

The Sixth Category: Saṁvara.

We now come to the sixth principle of Jaina philosophy, which is the converse of the fifth, the way, namely, in which the inflow of karma into the soul can be impeded. The karma that has already been acquired can be dissipated and so liberation attained, if only no new karma accrue: 'As a large tank, when its supply of water has been stopped, gradually dries up by the consumption of the water and by evaporation, so the Karman of a monk, which he acquired in millions of births, is annihilated by austerities, if there is no influx of bad karman.'[2]

The fifty-seven ways of impeding karma.

The Jaina themselves consider this principle of Saṁvara of supreme importance, and it contains matter that is more often quoted by them than anything else. Long and wearisome as we shall find the lists it contains of the fifty-seven ways of impeding karma, yet they are worth our study, for, having already learnt what the Jaina mean by sin, we shall now learn what they mean by holiness.

The five Samiti.

The first five ways of arresting the inflow of karma refer to outward behaviour. A man who would be holy must observe the greatest care whenever he walks anywhere not to injure any living thing (*Īryā samiti*). This rule is, of course, specially binding on all monks and nuns, for the Jaina have a comfortably lower standard for the laity. Ascetics must enter and leave their monasteries with the greatest care, lest they step on any insect; they must, wherever possible, avoid field-paths and keep to highways, where an animal or an insect can be more easily seen and avoided; they must walk miles round rather than cross

[1] St. John x. 10. [2] *S.B.E.*, xlv, p. 174.

a green patch of ground wherein there are likely to be many living things ; and they must carefully examine the ground a vāma's length ahead (i.e. the distance of outstretched arms) before treading on it. A sādhu to keep this rule must, curiously enough, never cross the open sea,[1] though he may cross a creek. In order that a layman may keep this rule, he must strive always to act so as to give trouble to no living thing whilst he is walking, sitting, or sleeping.

To arrest the inflow of karma one must also guard the words of one's mouth (*Bhāṣā samiti*): one must always speak kindly, never by word inflict pain on any one, and in every way strive not to sin through speech. The Jaina believe in auricular confession; and if, for instance, a man has eaten a potato but means never to do so again, he will confess his sin secretly to a sādhu, and the sādhu (if he is certain that the penitent means never to offend again) will inflict a certain penance according to the rules laid down in the Vyavahāra Sūtra, Niśītha, or Bṛihatkalpa. Should the sādhu, however, break the seal of confession and repeat what has been told him, he will have failed in Bhāṣā samiti and be guilty of great sin. Under this rule one must also guard against frightening any one by speech, making a mock of any one, or preaching false doctrine.

Circumspection must also be exercised about all matters connected with eating (*Eṣaṇā samiti*). A sādhu is only allowed to use fourteen kinds of things all told, inclusive of wearing apparel, food and drink. He has to beg for everything he eats, but even then his food is limited, for in order to guard against karma he must be careful only to take such food as is allowed to him, e.g. he must not take food underneath which a fire is burning. If it is raining,

[1] It was this interpretation of the rule which prevented any sādhu from accepting the invitation to speak at the Parliament of Religions in America, or from even deputing any one to go. The difficulty was solved by the lay community—the saṅgha—sending a layman.

a monk must not go out from the Apāsaro (monks' rest-house) to beg for food; and, as no layman may take food to the Apāsaro, it often happens that during the rainy season the sādhus get really hungry in their endeavours to avoid acquiring karma. Again, a monk must not take food if he thinks that by so doing he will leave the donor's household in straits; in fact there are altogether forty-two faults which a sādhu must avoid committing when he begs for or receives food. A layman is simply bound to refrain from committing sin in order to obtain food. Under this rule again all intoxicants[1] are forbidden to monks and laymen, and so are meat, butter and honey.

In order to stop the inflow of karma a sādhu must also be careful to possess only five cloths (*Ādānanikṣepaṇā samiti*), and when these are presented to him he must take them with the greatest care, gently removing anything that may be on them, lest in the very receiving of them he injure any insect life. If he borrows a stool (for he may not *own* one) he must dust it carefully and then sweep the ground free from any insects before he sets it down. In the same way a householder should arrest the possible inflow of karma by carefully dusting all his books and vessels with a *poñjaṇī*, the small brush used by the laity, which is a smaller edition of the brush a sādhu may never part from. A layman must also scrupulously sweep his hearth and the wood he is going to burn, and be very careful that the room he is going to keep his water-vessels in is thoroughly swept. The result of these rules (as any one who has had the privilege of friendship with Jaina ladies will testify) is to keep a Jaina house exquisitely clean and fresh.

The careful disposal of rubbish and refuse is another way of preventing karma being acquired (*Parithāpanikā samiti*[2] or *Utsarga samiti*). If a sādhu after begging food

[1] So particular are the old-fashioned Jaina not to touch intoxicants, that one reason they give for refusing to take European medicine is that it might contain alcohol.

[2] Otherwise, *Pratisthāpana samiti*.

find that there is insect life in it, he must neither use it, nor throw it carelessly away, but carefully deposit it where it can neither do nor suffer harm. A monk must never keep either food or water overnight, but must carefully dispose of anything that remains over from the last meal in some convenient place. Monks must try when out begging only to accept as much food as they actually need, for if they have often to throw away things, karma is acquired. All other refuse of every kind must be carefully disposed of by both laity and monks in desert places where nothing can be injured by it.

The three Gupti.

Of equal importance with the five rules for outward behaviour are the rules for the controlling of mind, speech and body, and the Jaina speak of the eight rules together as 'the essence of their creed which a sage should thoroughly put into practice; such a wise man will soon get beyond the Circle of Births',[1] and again as comprehending the whole of the teaching of the Jaina and of their sacred books.[2]

In order that karma may be arrested, the mind must be controlled (*Manogupti*) in three ways: one must not indulge in uncontrolled grief, anger, joy, or anxiety (*Asatkalpanāviyogī*); neither must one show any partiality, but must think alike of rich and poor, realizing that in both there is a soul, and one must fix one's mind on doing kindnesses and obeying the tenets of religion (*Samatābhāvinī*); and above all (*Ātmārāmatā*) one must think steadily, not of external things, but of one's own soul and of the saints who have attained omniscience.

Speech can be specially controlled (*Vaćanagupti*) in two ways: either by observing a vow of silence (*Maunāvalambi*) for a certain number of days, or (*Vākniyami*) by speaking as little as possible, and when it is absolutely necessary to speak, holding a piece of cloth (mumatī) in front of one's mouth in order not to injure the jīva of the air.

The movements of the body must also be controlled (*Kāyagupti*) if the acquisition of karma is to be arrested:

[1] *Uttarādhyayana*, *S.B.E.*, xlv, p. 136. [2] Loc. cit., p. 130.

a human being must be careful to control his movements according to the rules laid down in the scriptures (*Yathāsūtraćeṣṭāniyami*), and at last, when he becomes a saint omniscient, must maintain his limbs in that state of absolute immobility (*Ćeṣṭānivṛitti*) possible only to a Kevalī.

There is the same difference in standard as to the way a monk and a layman must observe the gupti that we have noticed in all the Jaina rules, and the following example may illustrate it. If a sādhu and a layman meet a shooting party, and the sportsmen ask where the deer they are trying to shoot has gone, the monk must keep silence, for he may neither aid in the taking of life nor lie, but the ordinary man may point in a wrong direction or give an untrue reply, for, in order to save life, a layman may tell an untruth. The keeping of the gupti is supposed to protect a sādhu from all temptation; and the scriptures say that if a monk possesses the three gupti, his peace of mind cannot be disturbed even by well-adorned goddesses.[1]

The twenty-two Parīṣaha.

Since the inflow of karma can also be checked by enduring hardship, the laity should endeavour to sustain certain hardships, but the ascetic was expressly commanded by Mahāvīra himself[2] to endure 'the twenty-two troubles' (*Parīṣaha*[3]) that are likely to beset him in his life as a wandering mendicant.

A monk must accordingly be prepared to endure the trial of hunger (*Kṣudhā parīṣaha*), if he cannot obtain food blamelessly and without committing one of the forty-two faults, even though he were to grow as emaciated as the joint of a crow's leg. However thirsty (*Tṛiṣā p.*) he may be, he must never take unboiled water lest he should destroy some life. However cold a monk may feel, he must endure it (*Śīta p.*), without wishing that the sun would rise, that a fire were lighted, or that he had more clothes; nor must an ascetic

[1] *Uttarādhyayana*, *S. B. E.*, xlv, p. 186.
[2] *Uttarādhyayana*, *S. B. E.*, xlv, p. 9.
[3] Or *Parisaha*.

ever warm himself at a fire, or light a fire. In the same way he must endure heat (*Uṣṇa p.*), without fanning himself, going to a river side to cool himself, or longing to pour cold water over his body. If when a monk is meditating, a mosquito or a hornet sting him (*Daṁśa p.*), he must not brush it away nor be irritated by it, but must remain undisturbed, and by self-control conquer his internal foe, as an elephant at the head of the battle kills the enemy.[1] A monk must also endure anything in the way of clothing (*Vastra p.*[2]), being content either to be without it or to receive dirty, old and torn garments. He must also be absolutely indifferent to the sort of lodgings (*Arati p.*) he may be given in the different villages. To the Jaina, woman was always the temptress, never the helpmate, and the ascetic is warned to renounce all liking for women's society (*Strī p.*), remembering that they are 'a slough'. An ascetic is bound also cheerfully to keep the rules about changing his lodging (*Ċaryā p.*): he must never stay longer in a village nowadays than a month in fine weather, or four months in the rainy season, but the shorter time he stops the better (if possible only one night), lest he should grow fond of any one and form a friendship however innocent.

All monks must perform their meditation either sitting or standing, keeping the eyes and limbs absolutely immovable. The more disagreeable a place one chooses to meditate in the better, so the holiest monks choose the most unpleasant spots (*Naiṣidhikī p.*[3]). Every Indian believes that the place where corpses are burned is haunted by all sorts of hideous evil spirits, so that by going to meditate in such a spot, or in a jungle haunted by tigers or lions, a monk very effectually endures hardness, and shows his indifference to fear by remaining immovable even when attacked by evil spirits or wild beasts! If a monk be benighted on his peregrinations, he must gladly endure such hardships

[1] *Uttarādhyayana*, *S. B. E.*, xlv, p. 11.
[2] Or *Aċela p.*
[3] Or *Naiṣedhikī p.*

(*Śayyā p.*) as sleeping in the open air or under a tree, without even a plank for a bed; and in the same way, if no one lends him a bed in a town, he must sleep contentedly without it, knowing that he is thus arresting karma. Karma is also checked by calmly enduring taunts and reproaches (*Ākrośa p.*) and not taking cruel or rankling words to heart.

The Jaina say that, before the 'Pax Britannica' ruled in India, there was constant quarrelling between members of the various religions, and the followers of Śaṅkarāćārya in particular persecuted them; this often led to fights, but the Jaina sādhus were urged to receive even beatings philosophically, being assured that such endurance (*Vadha p.*) would hinder the accumulation of karma; and to help them they were told to reflect, when struck, that after all it might have been worse, for they had not lost their lives. It sometimes happens that a rich man's son or even a prince becomes a Jaina sādhu; and it is specially unpleasant for a man of such social position to go round begging, for 'the hand (of the giver) is not always kindly stretched out to a monk when he is on his begging tour',[1] but by enduring this (*Yāñćā p.*) he retards karma. Sometimes too a monk is met with a blank refusal, or for fear of committing any of the forty-two faults has himself to refuse food offered to him; he must bear this (*Alābha p.*) calmly, thinking that though he get nothing to-day, he may perhaps get something to-morrow.

Illness (*Roga p.*) affords a monk a chance of checking the growth of karma, if he endure it patiently as punishment for past sin (we have already seen that Jaina look on all illness as punishment for sin in a previous existence) and neither desires medical attendance, nor cries out that he is dying or dead, but continues to think of the welfare of his soul, neither acting himself nor causing others to act. The jungle grass in India is so full of thorns and prickles that the Jaina scriptures truly say that if a naked ascetic lies on the grass he will certainly be badly scratched; in the

[1] *Uttarādhyayana, S. B. E.*, xlv, p. 13.

sun the pain of the scratches will grow insupportable, but the ascetic who cheerfully endures this pain (*Tṛiṇasparśa p.*) knows that he is impeding karma. If a monk is given water that has been previously boiled, he is allowed to sponge his body or wash his clothes with it, but he may never bathe or wash his clothes in a running stream; when an ascetic feels dirty and sticky and hot, he must never allow his mind to rest on the delicious joy and refreshment of a bathe, but is told, on the contrary, that by enduring the horror of feeling dirty in his body (*Mela p.*) he is benefiting his soul (!), and practising 'the noble excellent Law, he should carry the filth on his body till he expires'.[1]

It is a perilous moment for a monk when he is praised; but if he can listen with absolute indifference (*Satkāra p.*), he has obstructed the inflow of karma; and, vice versa, he must also carefully perform the easier task of hearing himself blamed unmoved. Even without being actually praised by others, a man may become puffed up through realizing the extent of his own learning and accomplishments: such feelings must be sternly repressed (*Prajñā p.*) if karma is to be checked. To other monks there comes the opposite temptation to be cast down at the thought of their own ignorance (*Ajñāna p.*), but this also must be endured with indifference. Finally, when enduring hardships or studying other religions, a monk must never allow a doubt as to the value of asceticism or the truth of his own religion to enter his mind, but must be willing to endure martyrdom rather than change his faith (*Samyaktva p.*).

The ten Duties of Monks.

An ascetic can also stop the inflow of karma by faithfully observing his ten great duties, which in a lesser degree are binding on the laity also. The first of these duties is forgiveness (*Kṣamā*): every day and every moment of the day a monk must learn to control his anger, and instead of giving way to wrath practise the difficult duty of forgiveness. Monks are constantly reminded of how Mahāvīra

[1] *Uttarādhyayana*, *S.B.E.*, xlv, p. 14.

forgave his enemies, and, instead of getting angry and so letting karma flow into his soul, even preached to a wicked cobra which bit him.

Every day, too, a monk must strive to control the arrogance which rises in his soul, for that would open the door to endless karma, and instead he must cultivate the humility (*Mārdava*) which subdues pride. This duty the Jaina illustrate by the story of the two sons of the first Tīrthaṅkara Ṛiṣabhadeva, which they entitle 'O Brother, come down from the Elephant of Pride'. Ṛiṣabhadeva's younger son, so the legend runs, became a sādhu, and some time afterwards the elder son, Bāhubaḷa, followed his example and became an ascetic too, renouncing, as he thought, everything to do so, but he found that there was one thing he could not renounce, and that was pride in his seniority of birth, so that he could not bow down to his younger brother, who was, of course, his senior in the religious life. For days poor Bāhubaḷa struggled in vain alone in the forest to overcome his pride, till at last his father became aware of the spiritual conflict he was going through, and sent his daughter to help her brother. She spoke so beautifully of the glory of humility, that it enabled him to conquer his pride; and so, becoming humble enough to receive help from a woman, he also became humble enough to do reverence to his younger brother and thus check the entry of karma, which would otherwise have annulled all the merit he had gained through being an ascetic, besides binding him for centuries to the cycle of rebirth.

Again, by separating himself from every sort of intrigue or deceit, in speech or action, and cultivating that simplicity (*Ārjava*) which is opposed to cunning, a monk or a layman can prevent the entry of karma. He must be careful, however, not only not to tell a direct lie, but also never to indulge in speech that could bear two meanings.

A sādhu must keep himself free from all greed (*Nirlobhatā*), possessing nothing but the oldest clothes, and retaining no metal;[1] if he borrow so much as a needle, he must return it ere nightfall, lest, any door being left open through which avarice might enter, karma should enter with it. The Jaina love to tell the story of Kapila, a layman who through fear of greed became a sādhu. Kapila had been left an orphan, and his friends, seeing his poverty, advised him to go to the court of a certain king whose custom it was to give a boṇī (morning gift) of two māsā to the first beggar he met. On his arrival at court Kapila took good care to be the first petitioner the king should see, but when he was offered the customary two coins, he explained to the rājah that he was really very poor, and that as a māso[2] was a very small weight, two would not go far. The king told him to sit down and think what gift would satisfy him, and he would give it him, so Kapila sat down in the pleasant garden and began to think. He asked himself if two or four or even eight māsā would content him, but his greed steadily growing, he saw that even half the kingdom would not satisfy him, for he would still desire the other half. It frightened him to think what karma he might accumulate if avarice, when given way to, grew at this terrible rate. He saw that greed and selfishness are one, and the root of all the evil in the world, and he realized that for him there was no safety save in the religious life, for a sādhu is forced to check the very beginning of avarice.

All monks and laymen must also practise fasting and austerities (*Tapa*[3]), for by so doing they combat desire, one of the great ways through which karma enters. We shall have to examine the twelve ways in which austerities are to be practised when we are studying the eighth principle, Nirjarā.[4]

A monk is also bound to subdue and control his mind,

[1] The writer has known of two sādhus who evaded this rule by keeping their fortune not in coin but in notes tied about their person!

[2] A weight of gold equivalent to $\frac{1}{30}$ of an ounce.

[3] Sanskrit *Tapas*.

[4] See p. 163.

his body and his speech (*Saṁyama*), lest through any act, thought, or word karma should be acquired, and in particular he should guard against taking life in any way.

An ascetic must be careful to speak the truth (*Satya*), lest any deviation from it should give rise to karma, but he is bound to speak the truth lovingly and in such a way as to hurt no one's feelings.

There is a manifold duty of purity and cleanliness (*Śauča*[1]) binding on all monks, for an ascetic must keep himself free from all suspicion of dishonesty or thieving, and oppose to this the constant giving of alms, and he must also keep his body pure and his soul free from all dark thoughts.

An ascetic must also remember never to look on anything as his own (*Akiṁčinatva*): he must regard no person as related to him, and no thing as his property.

A monk must strictly observe the duty of celibacy and chastity (*Brahmačarya*) in nine specified ways, which are called the Nava Vāḍa or Nine Ramparts, and which we need not trouble to detail. In a passage which throws a most interesting light on an old-world Indian household long before the birth of Christ, one of the Jaina sacred books, the Sūtrakṛitāṅga, describes the fate that awaits a monk who breaks the law, marries and settles down.[2] It recites how he will have to fetch and carry for his wife, bringing her lip-salve, ribbons, combs, looking-glasses, &c.; and how, if a son be born, he will have to hold the baby or hand it to its mother. 'Thus some supporters of their sons have to carry burdens like camels. Getting up in the night they lull the baby asleep like nurses. . . . This has been done by many men who for the sake of pleasures have stooped so low; they become the equals of slaves, animals, servants, beasts of burden—mere nobodies.'

The five Čāritra.

The inflow of karma is also arrested by observing the Five Rules of Conduct or Čāritra, which are specially binding on monks and nuns, but should also be observed by the laity.

[1] Instead of Śauča some sects substitute Tyāga, or the renunciation of palatable food, nice furniture and a comfortable house, and Antaratyāga, the renunciation of black thoughts.

[2] *S. B. E.*, xlv, pp. 276 ff.

The first rule (*Sāmāyika ćāritra*) entails two things: the giving up of all evil conduct, and the turning to good actions such as meditation. Both Sthānakavāsī and Śvetāmbara ascetics are supposed to give themselves up to meditation continually, and a layman must do it twice a day. A Digambara layman must meditate four times: morning, noon, evening and midnight. In order to carry out the rule perfectly, both laity and monks must endeavour to keep their minds in a state of equanimity, and to look on all mankind with indifference.

The duty of repentance (*Ċhedopasthāpanīya ćāritra*) is also binding on all who would arrest the growth of karma. If a monk sins, he must confess to his own guru and do the penance inflicted, which will be designed to fit the crime: for instance, if a young monk, feeling hungry, has eaten some of the alms given to him without first showing the food to the senior monk in the Apāsaro, he may be ordered to fast for two days, or to fast from the particular grain he took for four days; if, however, a monk has committed one of the great sins which infringe the five vows, for example given way to unchastity or dishonesty, he would have to take the great vows again, meekly standing in front of a guru. This retaking of the vows is called Navī dikṣā or re-ordination, for it is the actual taking of the vows, and not the accompanying ceremonies, which is regarded as the essential part of initiation. If a layman, on the other hand, sins in some gross way, he would after confession and penance have to retake, not all the twelve vows, but only the one which he has broken.

The third duty (*Parihāraviśuddha ćāritra*) is variously interpreted by the different sects. The Sthānakavāsī and Śvetāmbara believe it to be carried out when nine monks at the order of their superior go out together to perform austerities or tapa for eighteen months. (Of the nine monks six will do tapa for six months, and the remaining three will serve them; for the next six months the three servers will perform their austerities together with three of the original six, and be served by the three remaining; and for the last six months in the same way another six will do tapa and three serve.) The Digambara on the other hand regard the duty as performed simply by being careful not to injure any jīva whilst moving about.

It is not very clear why the fourth rule (*Sūkṣmasamparāya ćāritra*) should have separate enumeration here, for we shall come across it again when we are considering the fourteen steps towards liberation.[1] The rule emphasizes the importance of being bound to the world as loosely as possible, and of casting out the very last root of passion after the tumult caused by it has died away. If a man has done this, he has reached the tenth step in his upward progress.

By the time a man has reached the last stages of this upward road, he will have lost all attachment to the world, and think only of his soul; so that he will automatically keep the last (*Yathākhyāta ćāritra*) of the Five Rules of Conduct.

The twelve Bhāvanā or Anuprekṣā.

Finally the layman or the monk can arrest the inflow of karma by keeping the Twelve Great Reflections or Bhāvanā always in mind.

First, one must constantly remember that all things in this world, ourselves, our bodies, our wives and our children, are transient (*Anitya bhāvanā*), and that nothing is permanent save Dharma (religion) and the soul that has faith in dharma. Once upon a time, so the Jaina illustrate the truth of this reflection, a beggar having eaten an unusually good meal spread his miserable bedding under a tree, placed his waterpot beside him and, putting a stone under his head, fell asleep. He dreamed that he was a king with three wives to admire him, servants to wait on him and slaves to fan him. He awoke to find that all his wealth and all his grandeur had vanished, and that only his torn bedding and his waterpot remained: even so in this life we must expect everything we care for to pass away.

Another thing that a Jaina is bound constantly to remem-

[1] See p. 189.

ber is that there is no shelter for him (*Aśaraṇa bhāvanā*). In this world of misery, disease, old age and death, neither wife, friends, nor guru can afford us protection; only by the practice of dharma can we escape from the cycle of rebirth. To illustrate the truth of this reflection the following story is told. There once lived in India the son of a wealthy landowner, who was so handsome that his father, his mother and his wife all adored him. Suddenly the young man was stricken with an excruciating disease of the eyes, and though his parents and his wife strove to lighten the pain, they were powerless. Gradually the youth realized that, as no one could shelter him from disease, so no one could be his refuge from death, and the reflection induced him to promise to withdraw from the world, if religion could cure him. His eyes were immediately healed, and he went as an ascetic to live in a distant forest. The king of that country happened to pass, and was astounded to find so goodly a youth living the life of a monk, and thought he must have withdrawn from the world in consequence of some injustice or oppression. He therefore offered to take up his cause, remedy any wrong that had been done to him, and protect and shelter him against future injustice. But the ascetic showed the king how impossible it was to find any shelter in this world from oppression or from disease and death, and how the only true refuge was to be found in voluntarily forsaking all that one had, and following a law whose goal was death; on one who had taken up such a life no injury could be inflicted. The king, listening to this moving discourse, realized that in this world he could not even protect his own royal self, and so he too became an ascetic,[1] and by so doing stopped up all the channels through which he could be wounded or through which karma could flow.

By never forgetting that the cycle of rebirth is endless, and that one may be reborn as a bird, or beast, or

[1] Other Jaina deny that the king became an ascetic, and say he was merely convinced of the truth of this bhāvanā.

denizen of hell (*Saṁsāra bhāvanā*), the wise will be stirred up to try and stop the inflow of karma in this life, the only opportunity a man may have for so doing.

We must also remember that we came unaccompanied into the world, that we shall go out of it unaccompanied, and that unaccompanied we shall have to endure the expiation of our karma (*Ekatva bhāvanā*). A king named Nami was led to understand this reflection in the following manner. He once fell very ill, and his queens called in a physician, who ordered him to be rubbed with sandal wood. Each queen, terrified of being widowed, seized a piece of wood and rubbed some part of the king's body. As they rubbed, their many bangles jingled, and the august patient, who was not only ill, but also irritable, exclaimed against the din. Instantly each of the ladies tore off all her bangles save one (to have taken *all* off would have been unlucky, since it would have looked like anticipating widowhood) and the rubbing proceeded in silence. The king asked what they had done, and when they explained to him that each of them was now only wearing *one* bracelet, the true meaning of the bhāvanā he had heard so often dawned on him. Exclaiming that he was born alone and must die alone, he renounced the world and his wives, and proceeding to the forest, received initiation as a monk, and died in a few years.

Again, karma is impeded by remembering that in reality the soul is separate from the body (*Anyatva bhāvanā*), though through ignorance we think of it as attached thereto, for a soul cannot actually be united to body or wealth, wife or child. As an illustration of the importance of this reflection the Jaina tell the following legend. Once upon a time the great King Bharata, the son of Ṛiṣabhadeva, was seated on his throne, magnificently arrayed in all his jewels, when he noticed that the ring he had been wearing on his little finger had slipped off. He thought how ugly the finger looked without it, but reflected that the finger had never possessed the ring, the contact with which had been purely fortuitous. Amused at the idea, he removed the rings from each finger, and noticing how bare each looked when stripped of all adventitious decoration, he became so strongly convinced of the truth of this reflection, that the inflow of karma was arrested, he became at once omniscient, and as in a few more years all his acquired karma also disappeared, he eventually became a Siddha.

The object of another reflection (*Aśauča bhāvanā*) is to lead us to despise our bodies. To do this we must constantly remember that the body is compact of filth, and has such dirty habits that even our souls become soiled by contact with it. If we forget this reflection and become proud of our bodies, great misfortune will befall us, as the following story proves. A certain prince called Sanatkumāra was so handsome that his beauty was discussed in the assembly of the gods, two of whom were sent down in the guise of Brāhmans to discover if he were really as beautiful as he was described. Unfortunately this visit of the gods gave rise to such pride in the heart of the prince, that karma flowed rapidly into his soul; and, as a result of this karma, ill health (which, as we have seen, is always traceable to karma) beset the prince, until at last he had no less than sixteen diseases. However, he patiently endured the karma his conceit had given rise to, gradually worked it off, received initiation as a sādhu, and finally became a Siddha.

The seventh reflection (*Āśrava bhāvanā*) reminds us that in the worldly life karma is constantly flowing in through the various channels which our actions, passions and senses, if uncontrolled, leave open to it, and that all our sufferings come as a result of this karma. How much we may suffer, if we ourselves open the channels, we may learn from the story of King Puṇḍarika. There were once two brothers, both of whom ruled as kings, but the elder brother, Puṇḍarika, realized that this world was merely a junction of canals through which karma was continually flowing, and so decided to renounce his throne and become an ascetic. He received initiation, but gradually found that the life of an ascetic was too hard for him, and eventually persuaded his younger brother, Kuṇḍarika, to give up the kingdom in his favour. Becoming once more a king, Puṇḍarika, instead of being happy, found it only too true that the world is a dreadful place for acquiring karma; and during his life he accumulated so much, that he is still, by undergoing countless rebirths, trying to expiate it.

One must also reflect on and determine to adopt means (such as the taking of vows) which will impede the inflow of karma, and this reflection (*Saṁvara bhāvanā*) is illustrated by the history of the younger brother in the last story. Kuṇḍarika was delighted when his elder brother took his crown, for now, he thought, he would have a chance of arresting the inflow of karma; so, meditating on this reflection, he renounced the world, took the vows of an ascetic, and soon gained mokṣa, leaving his unfortunate elder brother still tied to the cycle of rebirth.

Again, one must remember that by performing austerities one can expiate karma (*Nirjarā bhāvanā*).

One must also reflect on the world (*Loka bhāvanā*), remembering that it was created by no one, and that the elements it contains are in a sense permanent. By thinking of the various worlds under the form of a man, one will understand that at his feet is hell, his body is formed by men who will have to undergo fresh births, the head is Devaloka, and at the top of the head are the Siddha, those who will never again pass through rebirth.

To arrest the inflow of karma one must also remember (*Bodhibīja* or *Bodhidurlabha bhāvanā*) that everything is easy to acquire in this world save the three jewels: Right faith, Right knowledge and Right conduct, which can only be acquired by a human being. In the long cycle of rebirth it seldom happens that a jīva obtains human birth. Reflecting thus, one must determine to use this opportunity to the fullest, and, taking the first step in the pathway of religion, continue on the upward course.

Finally, one must remember (*Dharma bhāvanā*) that the highest religion is to kill nothing and to injure nothing, but to keep the three jewels, and to follow thankfully the law of the Jaina. So doing, one will be able to cross the troubled ocean of the world, be freed from the cycle of rebirth and attain mokṣa.

These twelve [1] reflections are considered so important by the Jaina that one finds them referred to in some form or other in every book on Jainism, and it is recorded of them in one of the sacred books, the *Sūtrakṛitāṅga*, that 'He whose soul is purified by meditating on those reflections is compared to a ship in water; like a ship reaching the shore he gets beyond misery'.[2]

The Seventh Category: Bandha.

The seventh principle of Jaina philosophy deals with the bondage of the soul to karma: this is caused by the union of the soul with pudgaḷa,[3] and the difficulty of understanding it lies in the fact that the word *pudgaḷa* is simply untranslatable. English-speaking Jaina usually render it by the word *matter*, but that is unsatisfactory. Perhaps the safest way to get at the meaning is to quote some of the illustrations the Jaina themselves use. 'Now the principle of Bandha or bondage', says a Digambara Jaina, Mr. Latthe, 'is defined as the mutual entrance into each other's spheres of the soul and the Karman. When the soul is attacked by the passions like anger and love, it takes on the Pudgal [material] particles fit for the bondage of the Karmas, just as a heated iron ball takes up water-particles in which it is immersed. This is the bondage of the Karmas.' [4]

Another favourite illustration is taken from spilling oil. If oil is spilled on a cloth, dust will easily adhere. The

[1] They are sometimes classified into the nine first reflections and the three additional reflections.

[2] *S. B. E.*, xlv, p. 330.

[3] Or *pudgala*.

[4] A. B. Latthe, M.A., *An Introduction to Jainism*, Bombay, 1905, pp. 9 ff.

cloth represents our jīva or ātmā (soul), the oil represents our passions, transgressions and activities (*Kaṣāya*, *Pramāda*, *Avrata*, *Yoga*) by which karma is acquired, and the dust represents pudgaḷa. They say also that karma represents a book of which pudgaḷa are the leaves.

The four kinds of Bondage.

However difficult this is to understand, their teaching about the actual bondage is quite clear. They classify it in four ways: according to its nature, its duration, its intensity, and its mass.

Man creates his own karma according to his own character (*Prakṛiti*): if we are by nature bitter and sharp, we shall have to endure bitter karma; if, on the other hand, we are sweet and pleasant, though we may accumulate karma, yet it will be sweet and pleasant.

Karma can also be classified according to the time it takes to expiate (*Sthiti*): some will take a thousand years, some only a decade, and some can be worked out in a day.

The intensity of karma (*Anubhāga*) also differs: it is much heavier at some times than at others; for instance, if two boys are playing ball and one hits a cow and repents, but the other when he hits the cow is rather proud of so good a shot, then the first boy will have far less heavy karma to expiate than the second.

Some karma has attracted more pudgaḷa, some less; so the Jaina also divide karma according to its thickness and thinness (*Pradeśa*).

To illustrate these four classifications the Jaina take a lāḍu[1] as an example. Some lāḍus, they say, are such as to cure coughs and rheumatism (!), and this shows their nature; others can be distinguished according to the time they keep good; others by whether they have melted butter in them or not; and others are thick or thin according to the amount of flour with which they have been made.

We shall have to study karma more in detail later on, when bondage to it will be further considered.

[1] A lāḍu is a large round sweetmeat, about the size of a tennis ball, made of wheat, sugar, ghī and spices, of which the Gujarātī is inordinately fond.

The Eighth Category: Nirjarā.[1]

In spite of all precautions karma does accumulate, and one of the great categories of the Jaina faith deals with its destruction. This can only be accomplished gradually, and the Jaina compare the way in which water slowly drains out of a porous jar with the tedious way in which our accumulated karma may be dried up. One of the chief ways of reducing the sum of our karma is by burning it up in the glow of austerities; and these austerities are of two kinds, exterior or bodily (*Bāhya*), and interior or spiritual (*Ābhyantara*), all of which, though binding on the ascetics, are also beneficial to the laity.

The six exterior austerities.

i. Anaśana.

The first bodily austerity is fasting (*Anaśana*). One may take a vow to fast for a fixed period (*Itvara*), such as for a day, or for thirty days, or one may take a vow to fast for the rest of one's life (*Yāvatkathika*). Of course the latter vow is the more beneficial and destroys far more accumulated karma, so when a monk is very ill, and knows that he is going to die, he takes this vow. If he has taken the first vow, he may eat nothing, but may drink water or whey, but the second vow excludes water or any liquid as well as all food. This of course amounts very often to suicide by starvation, and it still takes place far more frequently than Europeans realize. For instance in Aḥmadābād, as lately as 1912, a sādhu named Ċhaganalālajī took this vow, though in perfect health, and died after forty-one days' fasting;[2] and the following year in Rājkot a nun named Jīvībāi, having first seriously weakened herself by prolonged fasting, took this vow and died after two or three days. To take this vow and die on a bed of Kuśa grass is called Santhāro; and though in this age of Dusama[3] it is impossible for those who do so to go straight to mokṣa, as they would formerly have done, yet

[1] In order to avoid confusion it should be noted that the Vedāntists use a similar word in a totally different sense to denote God, the Nirjara or undecaying one.

[2] One of the writer's paṇḍits went fifty miles to do *darśana* to this suffering man, the very sight of him conferring merit and nirjarā.

[3] *Sanskrit* Duḥṣamā.

they pass to Devaloka, and may hope, if their previous karma was good and their faith in the Jaina creed strong, to pass to mokṣa after fifteen more incarnations.

ii. Uṇodarī. If any one fears to face a complete fast, he may yet lessen his karma by partially fasting (*Uṇodarī*). He may vow, for instance, to take a mouthful less every day, and so gradually decrease the quantity he eats. The Jaina consider this to be very beneficial to the health of the body as well as of the soul.

iii. Vṛittisaṅkṣepa. There is another vow of fasting, or rather of limiting the food that one eats (*Vṛittisaṅkṣepa*), which may be taken in four different ways. If a monk or layman has been in the habit of consuming twenty different kinds of food, he may promise to limit his choice to, say, fifteen (*Dravya*). Or he may limit the number of places from which he will obtain food (*Kṣetra*), a sādhu vowing, for instance, that he would only beg in one particular street, and a layman[1] that he would only eat food in Rājkot and Aḥmadābād, and so when travelling between those places refusing food at the junctions en route. Again, one may promise that one will restrict one's food by time (*Kāḷa*), a sādhu, for example, eating only the food begged before noon, or a layman promising not to take another meal after his midday one. Or the vow might deal with posture (*Bhāva*), a monk promising only to receive food that is given to him by some one who is standing upright, and a layman deciding only to eat what his wife offers him in a certain position.

iv. Rasatyāga. An ascetic usually vows when ordained to abstain all his life, save when ill, from melted butter, milk, sugar, molasses, or any other food that specially delights him (*Rasatyāga*). He does this lest he should grow fat and sleep too much,[2] and his interest in religion grow dim. A layman often promises to abstain for a particular day from the special food he most enjoys.

v. Kāyakleśa. Jaina believe that they may also reduce their karma

[1] Many laymen vow to eat only in their own houses.
[2] There is a Gujarātī proverb: 'He who eats much will sleep much.'

by bodily austerity (*Kāyakleśa*), such as sitting to do meditation in summer on heated stones in the full glare of the sun, or in winter in the coldest places that can be found, without wearing sufficient clothing. There is one such austerity which is peculiar to Jaina ascetics, *Loča*, or pulling out the hair by the roots. It is said to be most profitable, as showing to the ascetic how hard a life he will have to undergo, and at the same time proving to others that he has strength of mind enough to endure it. If the sādhu is ill, the following words are quoted to him: *Ločevā muṇḍevā kattevā*, i.e. if the pulling out of the hair cannot be endured, hair cutting or shaving may be employed.[1]

vi. Saṁlīnatā.

There is another austerity which might almost be described as the avoidance of temptation by control (*Saṁlīnatā*) in four ways: first by governing the senses (*Indriya saṁlīnatā*) and not allowing the eyes, for instance, to look at anything beyond a certain distance; then by controlling anger, deceit, pride and greed (*Kaṣāya saṁlīnatā*); or by refraining as much as possible from the exercise of intellect, speech, or body (*Yoga saṁlīnatā*), sitting silent, for instance, in a cramped position; and lastly, by being very careful where one goes to stay, and previously ascertaining that no woman lives near (*Viviktačaryā*).

The six interior austerities.

Karma is also dried up by the right use of six interior or spiritual austerities.

i. Prāyaśčitta.

The first of these, confession and penance (*Prāyaśčitta*), is binding on both ascetics and laity. The ascetic must confess to the chief guru, and the layman to whatever sādhu he chooses; and they must perform the penances allotted to them, according to the rules laid down in the sacred books. Also every morning and every evening when they engage in Paḍīkamaṇuṁ[2] they must confess their faults generally in the following Māgadhī formula: *Miččhāmi dukkaḍaṁ*,[3]

[1] Dr. Jacobi (*S. B. E.*, xxii, p. 308, note 1) says he is not aware that removing the hair is resorted to in the case of nuns, but the writer knows as a fact that it is regularly done.

[2] Sanskrit *Pratikramaṇa*. [3] Sanskrit *Mithyāme duṣkṛitam*.

'May my sin be forgiven.' Greater faults a layman will confess privately to a sādhu at intervals of two or four months, or whenever he specially feels the need of confession, and will perform the penance given to him. A sādhu should confess a grave sin at once, for if he should wait even till the time of Paḍīkamaṇuṁ some karma will have accumulated, and more still if he should wait for the big fortnightly Pakkhī Paḍīkamaṇuṁ. The accumulation of karma will be worse if he does not confess till the quarterly Ċomāsi (Ċaturmāsī) Paḍīkamaṇuṁ, and his last chance comes at the annual Saṁvatsarī Paḍīkamaṇuṁ. If he misses that and continues with his sin unconfessed, though to all outward seeming an ascetic, he has ceased to be a true sādhu, and if he dies, he will slip far down the ladder of birth (*Adhogati*). Similarly, if a layman should nurse the sin of anger unconfessed and unrepented of, despite all the opportunities these various services give, he would undoubtedly pass to hell on his death.

ii. Vinaya. Another interior austerity on which the Jaina lay great stress is reverence (*Vinaya*), for this, duly paid, destroys a great accumulation of karma. Both laity and ascetics should show respect to all who are their superiors in knowledge (*Jñāna vinaya*); in faith (*Darśana vinaya*); and in character (*Ċāritra vinaya*). They must keep their minds (*Mana vinaya*) in an attitude of humility towards their superiors; and do them honour by politeness when speaking to them (*Vaċana vinaya*); and by salutation and bodily service (*Kāya vinaya*); and should observe all the old customs of reverence prescribed in the religious books (*Kalpa vinaya*) to be performed either in the house or in the monasteries. Under this last heading is included all the reverence a wife should show her husband.[1] On rising in the morning

[1] A great many Indian gentlemen were being almost unconsciously influenced by the chivalrous way in which they saw Englishmen treat ladies, when the crude militant 'suffragette' movement arose. It is impossible to over-estimate the evil that this movement did to the cause

a Jaina woman prostrates herself at her husband's feet and worships him. (The sentencc in the English wedding service where the *husband* says to the wife 'With my body I thee worship' comes as a terrible shock to an old-fashioned Jaina gentleman!) During the day the wife prepares her husband's meal and only eats when he has finished; and in the evening, when he comes home tired, she massages him.

Karma may also be worked off by another 'austerity' (*Vaiyāvaċċa*), service rendered to ascctics, or to the poor, the helpless and the suffering, by giving them food, water, shelter, or clothing. All the friends of the Jaina desire to see them taking their proper share in the uplift of India, and perhaps one might suggest that this belief of theirs in the reflex benefit of helping others provides them with a powerful text from which to preach the duty of social service. **iii. Vaiyāvaċċa.**

Study is another interior austerity (*Svādhyāya*). The Jaina lay great emphasis on the duty of studying their doctrines and their scriptures by reading, catechizing, repetition, meditation and preaching, but they declare that there is no duty that their laity and especially their college graduates more neglect. Rich Śvetāmbara laymen often pay a paṇḍit to teach their sādhus during the long intervals of the day when, having finished their begging round and having nothing else to do, they spend their time in idleness; but they complain bitterly that the ascetics are generally too lazy to learn. A Sthānakavāsī monk may not study with a paid paṇḍit, only with one who gives his services freely; but they also show little desire to learn. The whole question, however, of the education of their monks is now occupying the attention of the educated laymen of both **iv. Svādhyāya.**

of women in the East; for every foolish act of militancy was chronicled in the papers, and men who were formerly anxious to educate their wives grew afraid to do so. Perhaps the Western women in their selfishness scarcely realized the solidarity of the modern world. One might almost say that every window they broke in England shattered the prospect of some Indian woman gaining a wider outlook on life; and every time they chained themselves up, they riveted the fetters more firmly on their suffering Oriental sisters.

sects, and, together with caste, is regarded as one of the burning questions of the day.

v. Dhyāna. Karma is also destroyed by meditation (*Dhyāna*), which the Jaina consider to be another austerity; but it must be remembered that there are also two evil ways of meditating: one, grieving too much for the dead (*Ārta dhyāna*), wailing and beating one's breast in grief for them; and the other, remembering with anger any personal injuries one may have sustained and brooding over them (*Raudra dhyāna*); by doing either of these things one only accumulates karma instead of destroying it. There are, however, two good ways of meditation: the first is thinking on religious subjects in accordance with the precepts laid down in the sacred books (*Dharma dhyāna*); and the second (which can only be performed after Dharma dhyāna) is the purest and highest meditation of all (*Śukla dhyāna*), when, freed from all earthly thought and cares, the soul meditates on the fact that it itself is on the way to become a Siddha.

vi. Utsarga. The last discipline (*Utsarga*) consists in showing and feeling absolute indifference to the body and its needs. Only ascetics as a rule practise this in its furthest development (*Pādopagamana santhāro*), which leads to death. The sādhu climbs some sacred hill such as Pārasnātha, Girnār, or Śatruñjaya; and there, in order to do nothing that may lead to karma, he does absolutely nothing at all, but awaits death without moving hand or foot, head or body. The influence of a negative religion is then worked out to its irresistible conclusion, and with all the sorrows and ills of the world waiting to be relieved, the soldier deserts his post in order to free his own soul from suffering.

It is strange that a religious system which begins with the most minute regulations against the taking of the lowest insect life should end by encouraging human suicide.

The Ninth Category: Mokṣa.

When the ātmā is freed from all bondage to karma and has passed for ever beyond the possibility of rebirth, it is said to have attained mokṣa or complete deliverance. The old-fashioned Jaina believe mokṣa to be a place situated above the head of the figure that represents Devaloka;[1] while some of the more enlightened describe it as a state or condition of freedom.

A being who has attained mokṣa is called a Siddha or perfected one, and only a human being can directly become a Siddha. 'The space occupied by each of the perfect is boundless', says the Nava Tattva,[2] 'and increases according to any one's desire.[3] The term in which they remain in this state is also infinite. Their parts are innumerable. There is no returning again to a worldly state, and no interruption to their bliss.'

The Jaina definition of a Siddha is a being 'without caste, unaffected by smell, without the sense of taste, without feeling, without form, without hunger, without pain, with-sorrow, without joy, without birth, without old age, without death, without body, without karma, enjoying an endless and unbroken calm'.

Some Jaina say that no one who is born a neuter can ever reach mokṣa; and the Digambara declare that no woman can ever reach mokṣa without first undergoing rebirth as a man.

The Śvetāmbara, whilst holding that it is possible for a woman to become a Siddha, nevertheless declare that very few women indeed have ever had sufficient strength of mind or body adequately to study the faith,[4] or endure the hard life of an ascetic. But while not more than ten

[1] See p. 160. [2] J. Stevenson, *Nava Tatva*, London, 1848, p. 127.

[3] Some Jaina, however, deny that the space can be increased.

[4] That the mere study of the Jaina faith is considered an adequate qualification for Siddhahood may be illustrated by the fact that the present writer has been assured by more than one Jaina that she was bound ultimately to become a Siddha, whether she would or no, simply because she had devoted seven years to the study of this religion.

neuters or twenty women in the old days used to attain perfection, one hundred and eight males used to do so; for the Jaina seem to think men more religious than women. All the twenty-four Tīrthaṅkara, ending with Mahāvīra, have obtained mokṣa and become Siddha, though it is still by the name of Tīrthaṅkara that the people love to speak of them.

In the country of Mahāvideha there are at present about one hundred and sixty Tīrthaṅkara, as well as many Kevalī, who will ultimately proceed to mokṣa. No one in the present age can proceed to mokṣa from Bharatakṣetra, which includes modern India.

There are fifteen different kinds of Siddha: those who have been Arihanta and have become Siddha are called *Jina Siddha*; those who, without even having been Arihanta themselves, have yet been the disciples of Arihanta are called *Ajina Siddha*.

A *Tīrtha Siddha* is one who has been previously a Tīrthaṅkara, and to be considered a Tīrthaṅkara a man must have been an ascetic, have preached, and have founded a community or Tīrtha consisting of at least four people (a monk and a nun, a layman and a laywoman). If a man die before he has preached or founded a community, he will nevertheless become a Siddha if he has had the requisite history behind him (for such a history automatically compels one to become a Siddha), but he will be called *Atīrtha Siddha*: for instance, the mother of Ṛiṣabhadeva became a Siddha, but an Atīrtha Siddha, for at the time that she attained mokṣa no community had been founded.

Though the recognized path to Siddhahood is by becoming an ascetic, a householder of eminent holiness might nevertheless on his death pass straight to mokṣa, as King Bharata did, without ever having been an ascetic; such a jīva is called a *Gṛihaliṅga Siddha.* It is the glory of Jainism that, whatever its present practice, its doctrines steadfastly declare that conduct is greater than caste. It is possible for a non-Jaina who exhibits perfect holiness in his life to pass to mokṣa and become an *Anyaliṅga Siddha*: for instancc, the famous ascetic, Valkalaćīri, who never professed the Jaina creed, bccame a Siddha of this class. Those who follow the usual path and find deliverance by way of asceticism are called *Svaliṅga Siddha.*

The dwellers in mokṣa are also classified according to their previous sex into *Pūlliṅga Siddha*, who were formerly men; *Strīliṅga Siddha*, who were women, and *Napuṁsakaliṅga Siddha*, who during their past life were neuters.

Again they are divided according to the influences that led them to become Siddha. If it was their own gurus who influenced them, they became *Buddhabohī Siddha*; if it was some particular thing, *Pratyekabuddha Siddha*; and if it was of their own notion without any outside influence, *Svayambuddha Siddha.* They are also classified according to whether they proceeded to mokṣa by themselves, as *Eka Siddha*; whereas, if in the samc samaya one hundrcd and eight went together, they are called *Aneka Siddha.*

The Siddha, though they are the highest class of jīva, are never worshipped, although thc Tīrthaṅkara are. When one asks the reason why the same Being should be worshipped in his unperfected and not in his perfected state, even the non-idolatrous Jaina give as the reason that the jīva who has reached Siddhahood has no longer a body, and that it is impossible to worship or pray to a bodiless soul. The answer is intensely suggestive, bearing witness as it does to the materialistic influence of idol-worship on all sects of the Jaina. Jaina are, thercfore, vcry intcrested in the entirely opposite idea that is expressed in our Lord's saying that God is a spirit, and they that worship Him must worship in spirit and truth.[1]

It is illuminating also to contrast the Jaina idea of heaven with that of the Hindus: both use the same words, such as mokṣa and nirvāṇa, and both think of thc highest state as attained by those who have completely stultified their personality, and who are not perfected charactcrs but

[1] St. John iv. 24.

perfectly characterless beings[1] who touch life on as few points as possible; both also agree that souls who have attained mokṣa can never again be reborn; but the great ideal of the Hindus, absorption into the Supreme, is alien to Jaina thought. The Jaina Siddha through all eternity will maintain their separate entity.[2]

Though the Christian idea of heaven is so foreign to them, the Jaina through their quick sympathy with idealism are deeply interested in it as the thought of a fuller life, in which a man, with all his powers perfectly developed, his ideals realized, and his will absolutely attuned to the divine will, moves without let or hindrance to fulfil God's plan for him. They note a further resemblance in the Christian śloka where the promise is given to him that overcometh (Jina) that he shall go out thence no more.[3]

They feel themselves less in sympathy, however, with the Buddhists, who seem to them to use their common word Nirvāṇa as connoting extinction not only *of desire* (with which the Jaina would agree) but also *of the soul* itself, which they would indignantly deny.

With Mokṣa, the ninth principle, the category ends. Tedious as it is, its study is essential to the real understanding of Jainism, whose scriptures declare: 'He who is acquainted with these nine principles, and lays hold of them by faith, is perfect in knowledge. He who is ignorant of them cannot be perfect in knowledge. The words and doctrine of all the Jain Lords is here, and nowhere else to be found; therefore, he whose mind is instructed in these, possesses true and stable knowledge. He who has had this knowledge impressed on his mind for only an hour, is detained only by half the mental and bodily attraction that he was before.'[4]

[1] Cp. Rev. H. Haigh, *Some Leading Ideas of Hinduism*, London, 1903, p. 129.

[2] Another great difference we have already incidentally mentioned. In the Jaina mokṣa there is no thought of escape from māyā, for the Jaina have no conception of māyā in the Hindu sense.

[3] Rev. iii. 12.

[4] J. Stevenson, *Nava Tatva*, p. 128

CHAPTER VIII

KARMA AND THE PATH TO LIBERATION

In our survey of the Nine Fundamental Categories of the Jaina faith we saw that the thought of karma—the energy accumulated by action—underlay them all, that five of them were concerned entirely with either the acquisition, prevention, impeding, or destruction of karma, and two others dealt with bondage to it or freedom from it. That seven out of the nine principles should be thus apportioned shows the enormous importance Jaina, in common with all other Indians, attach to karma. For them it is the key that solves all the riddles of this unintelligible world. Is a man born a cripple? It is owing to his karma. Are Indian immigrants badly treated in South Africa and made to live in special locations? It is owing to the evil karma they themselves acquired when they oppressed the outcasts, and compelled them to live apart from their fellow men.

If a man plead that he personally never thus ill-treated his brother, the doctrine of Transmigration, the undivorceable spouse of karma, is brought in, and he is assured that he must have done so in some previous existence. Nothing is more extraordinary in Indian thought than the way in which the unproved doctrine of karma has been universally accepted as an axiom.

The root of the word karma is, the Jaina tells us, the verb kṛi (*to do*), and they believe it to be the result of actions springing from four sources.

The four sources of karma.

The first source of karma is *Avirati*, or attachment to the things of this life such as food, raiment, lodging, women, or jewels. The unlimited use and enjoyment of any of these gives rise to karma, and the more one limits one's indulgence in them, the less karma one acquires. Karma is also engendered by giving the rein to anger, pride, deceit, or greed (*Kaṣāya*), or any of their sixteen divisions, or the nine Nokaṣāya. Karma is again produced by uniting one's body, mind and speech to worldly things (*Yoga*); and lastly, *Mithyātva*, or false belief, is a fruitful source of karma.

The nine ways of arresting karma.

Karma can be arrested by not using one's own mind, body, or speech; by being careful not to cause any one else to use their mind, body, or speech; and by never approving, or in any other way associating oneself with what another does by mind, body, or speech. That is to say, by never oneself doing any work, however useful or noble; never influencing any one else to do any such work; and never praising any work when done. 'As heat can unite with iron', say the Jaina, 'and water with milk, so karma unites with the soul, and the soul so united with karma is called a soul in bondage.'

Differing views of karma.

We have already seen that it is the inequalities of life and the desire to account for them that have given the Jaina so firm a faith in karma; to prove that the same belief is shared by others they quote a Buddhist śloka, in which a beggar says:

> 'In the prime of life I am deprived of all virility, my leg is injured, and I am a beggar. All this is the result of my karma.'

The Jaina, however, say that they differ from the Hindus in two main points. The Hindus, according to them, believe,[1] that God (*Parameśvara*) inflicts punishment for evil karma just as a judge inflicts the penalties prescribed by the law. On the other hand, the Jaina, who do not believe in a Supreme God who takes any active part in the world's governance, declare that karma accumulates energy and automatically works it off, without any outside intervention.

[1] This, however, would certainly not be true of all Hindus.

The other point of difference they lay stress on is that while Hindus think of karma as formless (*amūrta*), Jaina believe karma to have shape, and to prove this they argue that karma cannot be formless, because formless things can do us neither good nor harm. The sky, they say, like space, is shapeless, and that does us neither evil nor good; but as karma, according to its origin, does inflict hurt or benefit, it must have a form!

To further understand karma we may look at it as easy or difficult to expiate. A scarf may accumulate dust that can be easily shaken off, but if it should get stained with oil it will need much washing; so, according to its nature, some karma is got rid of easily, but some only with great difficulty. As heat is latent in wood, oil in sesame seeds, and ghī in milk, so karma is latent in all actions.[1] Some people ask when karma attaches itself to the soul; this no one knows, but the Jaina say the important thing is not so much to know when the two were united, but how they may be separated; for, just as when gold is found in the earth, the important matter is not to inquire how it became impure, but to free it by heat (representing austerities) from the clay and impurities which cling to it, so in the spiritual sphere, when the presence of karma is detected, the great thing is to free the soul from it.

There is also a difference between Hindus and Jaina with regard to the remembrance of karma. Some Hindus believe that it is owing to Māyā (illusion) that all remembrance of the deeds done in previous births, which led to the accumulation of karma, is forgotten; but Jaina hold that it is owing to Ajñāna (ignorance), and when the soul by means of austerities and good actions has got rid of Ajñāna, it attains omniscience and remembers all the births it has undergone and all that happened in them.

[1] Compare the Hindu saying: 'As fragrance is inherent in flowers, oil in sesame seed, fire in wood, ghī in milk, sweetness in sugar-cane, so wise men should recognize the soul in a body.'

The Jaina divide karma according to its nature, duration, essence and content, quoting the following śloka :

'These are the four parts of karma: its nature, that is, its character; its condition, that is, the time it will last; its constitution, that is called its essence; its scope, or the whole of its content.'

As long as the jīva or ātmā is fettered by karma, so long must it undergo rebirth, and it must be remembered that karma is acquired through good as well as through evil actions. If the karma accumulated in the past life was evil, the soul is bound to the cycle of rebirth by iron fetters, if good, by golden chains, but in either case it is bound, and until the karma is worked out, it must be reborn again and again.

Karma is intimately bound up with the soul; accordingly, when the jīva leaves one body, the weight of its karma draws it irresistibly to another *gati* (state), and there it forms round itself another body. Only when the soul is freed from good and bad karma alike can it attain the highest state and become a Siddha.

Here we notice another point of difference from common Hindu thought: the Jaina believe that once an ātmā has attained the highest state, it is absolutely indifferent to what is taking place on earth, and will never again undergo rebirth; so that the Hindu idea of incarnation in order to help mankind is quite foreign to the Jaina, and they could never use the famous śloka :

'O Bhārata (Arjuna), whenever there comes a decline of faith and irreligion uprises, then I will take birth. In every age for the protection of the good, the destruction of the wicked, and the establishment of faith I become incarnate.' *Bhagavadgītā*, iv. 7, 8.

The Eight Kinds of Karma.

We have discussed various kinds of karma as we have worked laboriously through the long lists of divisions and subdivisions under which the Jaina classify the tenets of their faith; but it will probably make for clearness if, in studying the most popular way of classifying this important doctrine of karma, we begin as it were *de novo* and divide the subject afresh under the eight headings which the Jaina themselves most frequently quote.[1]

i. Jñānā-varaṇīya karma.

The first kind of karma is that which hides knowledge from us. As a bandage bound across our eyes prevents us from seeing, so does *Jñānāvaraṇīya karma* prevent our receiving mental illumination for innumerable oceans of time. It is divided into eight classes: first *Matijñānāvaraṇīya,* which prevents our making a right use of our conscience and intellect; this again is subdivided into *Utpātikī*, which hinders the power of spontaneous thought; *Vainayikī*, the karma which prevents our getting those powers which are obtained by showing deference to our elders; *Pāriṇāmikī*, by which we are hindered from gaining any benefit or knowledge from experience; and lastly *Kāmikī*,[2] a karma which impedes our obtaining any intellectual stimulus from memories of the past or from hope for the future. Perhaps these are nearly sufficient for our purpose, as showing how completely karma can prevent our gaining knowledge; but the Nandī Sūtra goes into the subject at great length, and discusses twenty-eight other minor ways in which Matijñānāvaraṇīya karma may impede learning. It is important also to note the other kinds of Jñānāvaraṇīya karma, which prevent our getting any knowledge from reading the sacred books (*Śrutajñānāvaraṇīya*); or never allow us to know what is passing in the minds of others (*Manaḥparyāyajñānāvaraṇīya*); or what is happening at a distance (*Avadhijñānāvaraṇīya*); and lastly prevent our

[1] For a full analysis of this somewhat confusing subject, see Appendix, p. 309.

[2] Or *Karmajā*.

ever attaining omniscience (*Kevalajñānāvaraṇīya*). But Jñānāvaraṇīya karma not only impedes us in gaining true knowledge and sound learning, but actually gives rise to false and hurtful knowledge and misuse of the intellectual powers. For instance, weapons are invented which eventually kill people owing to *Mati ajñāna*, or the misuse of the intelligence; again the knowledge gained through reading the scriptures may be misunderstood or misapplied (*Śruta ajñāna*), and this might lead to the practice of bhakti (devotion to a personal god) or to obscenity; or karma may hinder and falsify all spiritual insight (*Vibhaṅga jñāna*) as well as physical sight. All this obstruction to knowledge and gaining of false knowledge can be traced back to a former life in which the jīva has been jealous of another's knowledge, or has failed to help another to gain knowledge, or has actually tried to prevent any one from gaining knowledge by employing them in ways which left no time for study, thus acquiring this evil karma.

ii. Darśanāvaraṇīya karma.

The second of the eight great divisions of karma is *Darśanāvaraṇīya*, the karma which prevents our beholding the true faith. As a door-keeper may prevent our getting into the presence of a chief, or a peon hinder our gaining access to an English official,[1] so Darśanāvaraṇīya karma may prevent our ever seeing the true faith, however much we may long to follow it. There are nine divisions of Darśanāvaraṇīya karma which we have already studied. It affects those jīva which in a previous birth have acquired evil karma by showing want of reverence to sacred books or to saints, or by hindering those who would like to believe in Jainism, or by imputing faults to Tīrthaṅkara, or by manifesting ill feeling to other religions.

iii. Vedanīya karma.

Vedanīya karma, the third of the great divisions, causes us to experience either the sweetness of happiness or the

[1] A frequent cause of misunderstanding in India is the way in which a peon often manages to prevent Indians from approaching British officials, until he receives a sufficient *douceur*.

bitterness of misery.[1] The Jaina think of this life as resembling two sides of a sword, the one smeared with honey and the other with opium, and it is Vedanīya karma which determines which side we taste. *Śātavedanīya* is the karma that leads to happiness, and *Aśātavedanīya* that which produces the reverse. One ensures happiness, or Śātavedanīya karma, by showing reverence to our superiors and serving them, by extending forgiveness and mercy to any who have injured us, and by straightforward dealings with all mankind. But one must remember that good no less than evil karma has to be 'worked off' before one can go to mokṣa, and that though it is well to do good, it is better to do nothing at all after one has reached a certain stage in development, for karma lurks in all action. It may perhaps be owing to the influence of this belief, so inimical to anything like public spirit, that the Jaina have shown such apathy during the famines that from time to time have devastated India. They have a saying that one needs the ship of good deeds or puṇya to go from one harbour to another, but after reaching the harbour the ship is no longer needed; meditation alone will transport us to our native village or mokṣa.

iv. Mohanīya karma.

Just as wine, say the Jaina, prevents a man speaking or thinking clearly, so does Mohanīya, the fourth and most dreaded karma, bemuse all the faculties. It results, generally speaking, from worldly attachments and indulgence of the passions, but each of the twenty-eight divisions of *Mohanīya karma* springs from some special cause. We have already (fortunately for the reader!) discussed most of these divisions, and only a few remain. The first of these, *Mithyātvamohanīya karma*, induces a man to believe good things to be unwholesome, or falsehoods to be true, just as a patient who is delirious often longs for

[1] Dr. Bhandarkar follows Govindānanda in believing Vedanīya karma to mean, 'the belief that there is something which one has to know'. Jaina, however, seem to give it in this connexion the meaning rather of experience. *Search for Sanskrit Manuscripts*, p. 97.

harmful things and declines health-giving food; another type of this karma, *Miśramohanīya karma*, forces us to vacillate, resting our faith sometimes on what is true and sometimes on what is false; while, owing to *Samyaktvamohanīya karma*, though we know which faith is true, we cannot attain to full devotion and consecration to it. The Jaina liken the influence of these three classes of Mohanīya karma to the results arising from taking the grain Kodaro. If this grain be eaten without any preparation, it causes the most intense giddiness such as quite to bewilder the eater. Such is the effect of Mithyātva; if the husk of the grain be removed, the result is less stupefying and resembles that of Miśra; whereas, if the grain be thoroughly cleansed, the occasional slight uneasiness it may cause is comparable to Samyaktva. Another karma, *Darśanamohanīya karma*, arises from taking life in the name of religion (as Hindus and Mohammedans do when they slay goats at their religious festivals), or from misappropriating funds or falsifying true religion. Again, taking part in state intrigues, acting immorally, administering evil medicines, spreading false superstitions and giving full play to all the passions give rise to *Čāritramohanīya karma*. Only when Mohanīya karma, the greatest of them all, is extinguished, can the soul reach mokṣa.

v. Āyu karma.

The fifth great division, *Āyu karma*, determines the length of time which a jīva must spend in the form with which his karma has endowed him, for not only the prison but also the term of imprisonment varies according to the weight of karma acquired. There are four divisions of this karma, one of which (*Deva āyu karma*[1]) decides how long a jīva who has become a god[2] shall remain one. The Jaina believe in four classes of gods: those who inhabit the

[1] Or *Devāyuḥkarma*.

[2] It should be noticed that though the Jaina use the same names for the gods as the Hindus employ, the words have often a different connotation; e.g. whereas the Hindus use the word Indra to denote the rain-god, the Jaina believe in not one but sixty-four Indras, who have nothing to do with rain, but who are the rulers of sixty-four different kingdoms.

planets (*Jyotiṣī*), evil ghost-gods (*Vyantara*), gods who travel in the celestial car (*Vaimānika*), and lastly *Bhavanapati*, the lords of the lower regions, who inhabit the space above hell. Each of these gods has a different āyu or term to serve.

Another branch of Āyu karma determines how long a jīva can wear a human form (*Manuṣya āyu karma*[1]). There are two classes of human beings on this earth, those who live in the land where work is done (*Karmabhūmi*[2]) and who exercise themselves in warfare (*asi*), in commerce, religion, or writing (*masi*), or in agriculture (*kasi*); and those who live in the land where no such work is done (*Akarmabhūmi*), but where all needs are supplied by the ten kinds of desire-fulfilling trees; both classes of men only hold their position for the length of time their Manuṣya āyu karma determines. Again Āyu karma decides how long a jīva can be forced to inhabit the form of an insect, a bird, or a lower animal (*Tiryañć āyu karma*[3]).

The fourth division of Āyu karma determines the period for which a jīva must dwell in one of the seven hells (*Naraka āyu karma*[4]).

The comforting thing about all four divisions of Āyu karma is that it can never be accumulated to last beyond one re-incarnation, and that it can be acquired only once in one's life, generally at the period when about a third of life remains. It is accumulated in the following ways: a man wins Deva āyu karma, which will keep him in the position of a god for a certain time, by straightforward dealing, by avoiding anger, pride and greed, and by practising celibacy. In the same way, by being always gentle and honourable and checking all tendency to anger, pride and greed, a jīva gains the privilege of being a man for a period that varies according to his past virtue

[1] Or *Manuṣyāyuḥkarma*.

[2] Dr. Jacobi practically limits the activities of Karmabhūmi to practising religious duties. This would ignore asi and kasi entirely. *Āćārāṅga Sūtra*, *S. B. E.*, xxii, p. 195.

[3] Or *Tiryagāyuḥkarma*.

[4] Or *Narakāyuḥkarma*.

(Manuṣya āyu karma), and also enters a state in which he understands which gurus and gods are true and which books reliable, and in obedience to them he protects all life and follows the dictates of the Jaina religion. But a man who gives way to craftiness and intrigue will be sentenced to pass some of his next life as a bird or beast (Tiryañc āyu karma); another by indulging in any of the following sins: gambling, drinking intoxicants, eating flesh, unchastity, thieving, or hunting, is determining the time he will pass in hell (Naraka āyu karma).

vi. Nāma karma. In studying Āyu karma we have seen that a jīva may be sentenced to spend a certain time as a man, a god, an insect, or a hell-being. Each of these four states or conditions is called *gati*, and it is according to our past deeds that we are born in the Manuṣya gati, Deva gati, Tiryañċ gati, or Naraka gati, the karma that decides which of these four shall be our particular gati, i.e. in which prison we shall dwell, being called *Nāma karma.*[1] There are one hundred and three divisions of Nāma karma, many of which we have already discussed when we were studying the categories of Pāpa and Puṇya.

vii. Gotra karma. An Indian's whole life, his occupation, the locality in which he may live, his marriage, his religious observances and even his food and fellow diners are determined by the caste into which he is born; so that it is small wonder if a Jaina attach the greatest importance to the accumulation of *Gotra karma*, which, as he believes, determines his caste in his next and subsequent lives. There are two main divisions of this karma: it decides whether the jīva shall be born in a high- or in a low-caste family. Pride is one of the chief factors in determining a man's future caste: if he indulge in pride about his high caste, his

[1] Dr. Bhandarkar quotes Govindānanda's saying: 'Nāmika, i.e. the belief that I am a person bearing such and such a name; Gotrika, i.e. the knowledge that I now belong to the family of the pupils of the worshipful Arhat.' Loc. cit., p. 97. None of the Jaina that the writer has consulted accept these translations as correct.

form, his learning, his family, his fame, his strength, his success in commerce, or his austerities, he is laying up the inauspicious Gotra karma which will surely cause him to be born in a low-caste and despised family in the next life; if on the other hand he sternly curbs his conceit and that constant criticizing and censuring of others which is the surest proof of pride, and also in every possible way takes care of animals, then birth into a high caste will be his reward.

viii. Antarāya karma.

All of us have been bewildered by the ineffectiveness of some people; they seem to have everything in their favour and yet they muddle away every opportunity that life offers them. The Jaina find the answer to this puzzle in their belief in *Antarāya karma*, the karma that always hinders. If we are wealthy and so generous that we long to revel in the keen joy of giving, and yet never do give, we know that in a past life we accumulated the karma that prevents giving (*Dānāntarāya karma*). If we realize the profit that is sure to follow a certain course of action, and yet we never act on this realization, we must have accumulated *Lābhāntarāya karma*. If in spite of our wealth we never really enjoy our possessions or our luxuries, either continuously or even for an instant, the cause is either *Bhogāntarāya* or *Upabhogāntarāya karma*. The last hindering karma (*Vīryāntarāya karma*) prevents our using our will or our bodily strength as we should like to do. The convenience of this belief is obvious. Life in India is for Indians, as it is for Europeans, a constant and unending fight against slackness, in which Europeans have the advantage of periodic visits to a cool climate to brace their moral as well as their physical fibre, and have also a tonic belief in the dignity of work and the gospel of exercise. Jaina have none of these advantages, but recline on the enervating doctrine of Antarāya karma, which provides those of them who are lazy with an excuse for every sort of inertia.

The Arrangement of the Eight Karma.

The Jaina have a special reason for the way they arrange the eight karma: they say that the first thing necessary is knowledge (*jñāna*); without this we cannot behold the true faith (*darśana*); if we possess both knowledge and faith, we are indifferent to pain or pleasure (*vedanīya*); *mohanīya* follows, because through pleasure or fear of pain we may become entangled in worldly attachments; that is the chief cause which determines the length of each imprisonment (*āyu*); when this has been determined, there still remains to be decided the state in which we shall be imprisoned (*nāma*); on that again depends the caste and family (*gotra*); and a man's caste and family are after all either his greatest help or his greatest hindrance (*antarāya*).

Ghātin and Aghātin Karma.

The eight karma are also classified into the *Ghātin karma*, which can only be destroyed with great labour, and which include Jñānāvaraṇīya, Darśanāvaraṇīya, Mohanīya and Antarāya karma: and the *Aghātin karma*, namely Vedanīya, Āyu, Nāma and Gotra karma, which, important as their results are, can yet be more easily destroyed. The Jaina say that if the Ghātin are once burnt up in the burning glow of austerities (tapa), the Aghātin can be snapped as easily as a piece of burnt string.[1]

Three Tenses of Karma.

The Jaina also divide karma according to the period when it was acquired, is being experienced, or will be experienced. The karma which we accumulated in past lives they call *Sattā*; that which we are even now in this present life sowing, and of which we shall reap the harvest in a future

[1] Here again will be noticed a difference from the interpretation of Govindānanda (who thinks four karma 'are of use to enable one to know the truth; therefore they are Aghātins, i.e. not injurious, favourable'); and from Dr. Bhandarkar, who considers the Ghātin Karman to mean 'the disabling Karmans'. Loc. cit., pp. 97 n. and 93.

life, is named *Bandha*; and the karma whose fruits, good or evil, are now ripening and being experienced is *Udaya.*[1] The Jaina illustrate these three divisions of karma by the three stages the water in a well passes through. When the water is in the well, they liken it to Sattā karma; when it is in the leathern bucket that draws it up from the depths of the well, to Bandha karma, and as it flows along to the plants, to Udaya karma.

Nikāčita and Śithila karma.

The whole teaching of Jainism on karma would lead to fatalism of the most mischievous kind, were it not for the belief that there are two great types of karma. One type, *Nikāčita karma*, we have stored up for ourselves and we are bound to experience; but a ray of hope comes through the existence of *Śithila karma*, or that destiny which we may by extraordinary exertions evade. Only the Kevalī know to which class a mortal's karma has been assigned, so that every man is left free to hope that he may by present exertion escape some of the suffering he has earned in his past history. It was probably seeing the tragic effect of absolute fatalism on Gośāla which led Mahāvīra to incorporate this tenet into the body of his doctrine.

The Fourteen Steps to Liberation from Karma.

So long as the soul is bound by karma, it can never attain deliverance, but the Jaina believe that there is a ladder of fourteen steps (*Čauda Guṇasthānaka*[2]) by which a jīva may mount to mokṣa.

i. Mithyātva guṇasthānaka.

The Jaina believe that the soul while on the first step (*Mithyātva guṇasthānaka*) is completely under the influence of karma, and knows nothing of the truth. There are two divisions of this step: when a soul is on the lower (*Vyaktamithyātva guṇasthānaka*), other people can see that it is mistaking false religion for the true faith; when one has advanced to the slightly higher step (*Avyaktamithyātva*

[1] It is interesting to compare these three divisions with the Vedānta *Sañčita*, *Kriyamāṇa* and *Prārabdha karma*.

[2] Or *Guṇasthāna*.

guṇasthānaka), though one may continue in this mistake, one is not doing it so unhesitatingly as to be obvious to others. Just as taking an intoxicating drug prevents one's distinguishing white from yellow, so a soul on this step makes mistakes. A Jaina śloka says:

> 'As a man blind from birth is not able to say what is ugly and what is beautiful, a man on the Mithyātva guṇasthānaka cannot determine what is real and what is false.'

ii. Sāśvāsadana guṇasthānaka. The soul, whirled round and round in the cycle of rebirth, loses some of its crudeness and ignorance, and attains to the state (called *Granthibheda*) when it begins to distinguish a little between what is false and what is true; unfortunately, it next moves into the state (named *Upaśama saṅkita*) when, though it knows there is a distinction, it forgets it, and so is not able to put it into practice; but when some faint remembrance comes back, it has arrived at the second step (*Sāśvāsadana*[1] *guṇasthānaka*) of the stairs to mokṣa. The Jaina say that Upaśama saṅkita resembles fire hidden under ashes, for though a man's bad qualities may be hidden and under control for a long time, they are bound to blaze out at last.

iii. Miśra guṇasthānaka. A soul that mounts to the third step (*Miśra guṇasthānaka*) is in an uncertain condition, one moment knowing the truth and the next doubting it. It is like the mixture formed by stirring together curds and sugar to make the sweetmeat called śrīkhaṇḍa, which is half sour and half sweet. No one will die in this mixed condition, but will either slip back to the second step or proceed onward to the fourth.

iv. Aviratisamyagdṛiṣṭi guṇasthānaka. The man at the fourth stage, *Aviratisamyagdṛiṣṭi guṇasthānaka*, has either through the influence of his past good karma, or by the teaching of his guru, obtained true faith. A famous śloka runs:

> 'Liking for principles preached by Jina is called true faith, it is derived either from nature or from knowledge given by the guru.'

[1] Or *Sāsvādana*.

The soul is still unable to take those vows which help in the fight against karma (which we shall discuss in the next chapter) and so the step is called Avirati. He can now, if he likes, control anger, pride and greed and three branches of Mohanīya karma (Mithyātva, Miśra, and Samyaktva), and it is a very dangerous thing not to destroy all of them, for they may lead to a man's falling back to the second step. Whilst on this fourth step, the jīva gains five good things: the power of curbing anger (*Śama*); the realization that the world is evil, and that since it is a place in which one has to reap the fruits of one's own karma, one need have little affection for it (*Śamavega* [1]); he also realizes that his wife and children do not belong to him (*Nirveda*); and that he must try and relieve any one who is in trouble (*Anukampā*); and lastly he gains complete faith in all the victorious Jina (*Āsthā*). We have seen that the distinguishing mark of this stage is that a man does not yet take the vows; he may wish to do so, but though he has destroyed excessive anger, pride and greed, he has not yet entirely escaped from their influence.

v. Deśavirati, or Saṁyatāsaṁyata guṇasthānaka.

The fifth step, *Deśavirati* [2] *guṇasthānaka*, or the step of merit, as it is often called, is specially interesting, for up till now faith has been the chief point that has exercised the thoughts of the climber, but now he realizes the great importance of conduct, and so can take the twelve vows which, as we shall see, deal largely with questions of behaviour. The step has three parts. First (*Jaghanya deśavirati*), a man promises not to drink intoxicants or to eat flesh, and he constantly repeats the Māgadhī salutation to the Five Great Ones (Pañĉa Parameśvara): 'A bow to Arihanta, a bow to Siddha, a bow to Āĉārya, a bow to Upādhyāya, a bow to all the Sādhus of this world.' Then, though still on the fifth step, he may advance a little higher on it (*Madhyama deśavirati*) and, keeping all the twelve vows, take special care only to make money in righteous ways.

[1] Or *Saṁvega*. [2] Otherwise *Saṁyatāsaṁyata*.

Every day he should be very careful to keep the six rules for daily life, which are describcd in a well-known śloka:

'One must worship God, serve the guru, study the scriptures, control the senses, perform austerities and give alms.'

Thirdly, while still on this step, he may advance to *Utkṛiṣṭa deśavirati*, eating only once a day, maintaining absolute chastity, resigning the society cvcn of his own wife, eating nothing that possesses even one life, and finally forming the determination to become a sādhu. This is thc highest stcp that a layman can reach as such, for if it be successfully surmounted, hc will becomc a sādhu.

At this stage, too, *moderate* anger, deceit, pride and greed are controllcd and sometimes destroyed.

vi. Pramatta guṇasthānaka.

We now come to the sixth step on the ladder, *Pramatta guṇasthānaka*, which can only be ascended by the professed ascetic. Even slight passions are now controlled or destroyed, and only certain negligences (*Pramāda*) remain.

'These five Pramāda: Pride, Enjoyment of the senses, Kaṣāya, Sleep and Gossip, torment the soul in this world'

runs a Māgadhī śloka, and the Jaina believe that if a soul is to mount the next step, he must never indulge any of these for more than forty-eight minutes at a time; if he does, he will not mount, but on the contrary will deścend to the lowest step of all.

vii. Apramatta guṇasthānaka.

At the seventh step, *Apramatta guṇasthānaka*, anger is either absolutely quiescent or actually destroyed, and only in a slight degree do pride, deceit and greed remain. The soul's power of meditation incrcases, for the bad qualities which lead to sleep are absent, and lastly one is freed from all negligence.

viii. Niyatibādara (or Apūrvakaraṇa) guṇasthānaka.

Among the Digambara some say that women can only mount as high as the fifth stage; others believe they can reach the eighth step, which is called *Niyatibādara guṇasthānaka*. It is also called the *Apūrvakaraṇa*, because the man who has his foot on this stair experiences such joy as he has never known before in all his life. As anger disappeared on the seventh step, so does pride now, either temporarily or for ever. A man at this stage increases his powers of meditation by Yoga, and the fetters of karma arc fast becoming unloosed; in fact so elevated is this step, and so few attain to it, that it is also called 'the Unique'.

ix. Aniyatibādara guṇasthānaka.

It is interesting to notice that the Jaina think it easier to get rid of anger than of pride, and that deceit does not disappear till the man has reached the ninth step (*Aniyatibādara guṇasthānaka*), whilst greed persists longer than any of the other Kaṣāya; any one who has watched the charactcrs of Indians develop and improve would acknowledge how extraordinarily true this psychological succession is. Not only does the man attain freedom from deceit at this stage, but he becomes practically sexless. One great difficulty still persists, for he is haunted by the memories of what he did and saw before he became an ascetic.

x. Sūkṣmasamparāya guṇasthānaka.

The description of the tenth step, *Sūkṣmasamparāya guṇasthānaka*, emphasizes the enormous difference between the Jaina and the Christian notions of asceticism, for this stage is only reached by the advanced ascetic, who thereupon loses all sense of humour, all pleasure in beauty of sound or form, and all perception of pain, fear, grief, disgust and smells. One contrasts with this a certain Cowley father's saying about 'the sheer fun it was to be a Christian'; and many devout Christians tell us that, having made the great renunciation, they have found almost unexpectedly that the surrender of worldly ambition and the wire-pulling it entails has endowed them with an entirely new appreciation of the beauty of nature, the treasures of art and the joy of living, besides giving them a deeper power of suffering with others. In short, Christian asceticism is a development of personality, whilst Jaina asceticism amounts to self-stultification.

Some slight degree of greed still remains to the Jaina ascetic who has reached this stage. It must be remembered that the Jaina sādhu generally comes from the commercial class, and often from a money-lender's family. This helps us to understand how difficult some ascetics find it to get rid of greed, and, whilst professing to give up everything, contrive by hook or crook to retain their fortune, sometimes, as we have noted, even keeping it in paper money hidden on their persons, to the great disgust of their fellow Jaina. Those who manage absolutely to destroy every trace of greed will pass straight to the twelfth stage, whilst others have to pause at the eleventh.

xi. Upaśāntamoha guṇasthānaka.

When a man has attained to the eleventh stage, *Upaśāntamoha guṇasthānaka*, he has reached a really critical point, where everything depends on how he deals with the sin of greed. If he destroys it, and it becomes quite extinct, he is safe; but if it only remains quiescent, he is in a perilous state, for, like a flood, it may at any moment burst its dam, and the force of its current may carry the soul far down the slope he has been climbing, depositing him on either the sixth or seventh step, or even on the lowest. On the other hand, if he deal successfully with greed, he becomes an Anuttaravāsī Deva and knows that he will become a Siddha after he has undergone one more rebirth as a man.

xii. Kṣīṇamoha guṇasthānaka.

If a man be on the twelfth step, *Kṣīṇamoha guṇasthānaka*, he has won freedom for ever not only from greed but from all the ghātin karma,[1] and though the aghātin karma[2] still persist, they have little power to bind the soul: in fact, so limited is their power, that at death a soul passes at once through the two remaining stages and enters mokṣa without delay. The Digambara believe that at this stage the first two parts of pure contemplation (Śukladhyāna) are developed.

xiii. Sayogikevalī guṇasthānaka.

If a man who reaches the stage of *Sayogikevalī guṇasthānaka* preaches, and forms a community or tīrtha, he becomes a Tīrthaṅkara. He first (according to the Digam-

[1] i.e. those difficult to destroy, or according to another interpretation those which destroy omniscience: Jñānāvaraṇīya, Darśanāvaraṇīya, Mohanīya and Antarāya. Cp. p. 184.

[2] i.e. those easy to destroy, or those which do not destroy omniscience: Vedanīya, Āyu, Nāma and Gotra.

bara) obtains 'eternal wisdom, illimitable insight, everlasting happiness and unbounded prowess'. When this absolute knowledge is acquired, Indra, Kubera [1] and other heavenly beings, including the celestial engineer, Vaiśramaṇa, raise the Samavasaraṇa (or heavenly pavilion) where the twelve conferences meet to hear eternal wisdom from the Kevalī. After prayers have been offered, the Kevalī goes about preaching truth, until, when the day of deliverance approaches, he takes to the third part of pure contemplation (Śukladhyāna). Here the soul reaches every part of the universe and is yet contained within the body, though its only connexion with it now is residence. The last part of contemplation follows when the fourteenth step is ascended, and the body disappears like burnt camphor. This is Nirvāṇa.[2]

Before proceeding, however, to discuss the fourteenth step, we may quote the famous śloka that describes the pomp of a Tīrthaṅkara:

'The tree of Aśoka, the shower of celestial flowers, the singing of heavenly songs, the waving of fly whisks, the lion-shaped throne, the shining of the halo, the beating of celestial kettle-drums, the umbrella, all these eight things attend the Tīrthaṅkara.'

As we have seen, it is the Tīrthaṅkara, the man at this thirteenth stage, that the people worship; for once he passes to the next step, he loses all interest in people, besides parting with his own body. The Siddha alone know exactly where every one is on the heavenward road, but they have lost all interest in the question.

xiv. Ayogikevalī guṇasthānaka.

The moment a man reaches the fourteenth stage, *Ayogikevalī guṇasthānaka*, all his karma is purged away, and he proceeds at once to mokṣa as a Siddha (for no one can remain alive on this step). In mokṣa there is of course no absorption into the infinite, but the freed soul dwells for ever above the land called Siddhaśīlā, from whence it returns no more, and this is mokṣa.

[1] *Or* Kuvera.

[2] A. B. Latthe, M.A., *An Introduction to Jainism*, p. 42.

There 'innumerable delivered souls exist and are to be there for ages that never were begun and which never close'. A śloka describes the qualities of the Siddha thus:

'Omniscience, boundless vision, illimitable righteousness, infinite strength, perfect bliss, indestructibility, existence without form, a body that is neither light nor heavy, such are the characteristics of the Siddha.'

As a soul passes from stage to stage, it gains the three jewels,[1] and the possession of these ensures the attainment of mokṣa.

The writer was recently discussing these fourteen steps with some Jaina friends, and it was most interesting to notice the way they realized that Christians not only believed in an upward, heavenly path, but also in the constant companionship of a Guide who held their hands and steadied their feet over the difficult places. The Jaina of course, denying as they do a Creator, are deprived of the belief in a heavenly Father, who watching over us 'neither slumbers nor sleeps'. The vital difference on this point of the two faiths is well illustrated by the contrast between Christian evening hymns such as:

'Abide with me: fast falls the eventide;
The darkness deepens; Lord, with me abide:
When other helpers fail, and comforts flee,
Help of the helpless, O abide with me.'

—and the following Māgadhī śloka which many devout Jaina repeat after their evening reading from the sacred books:

'The soul is the maker and the non-maker, and itself makes happiness and misery, is its own friend and its own foe, decides its own condition good or evil, is its own river Veyaraṇī.[2] My soul is my Kuḍasāmalī.[3] The soul is the cow from which all desires can be milked, the soul is my heavenly garden.'

[1] Right knowledge, right faith and right conduct. See p. 245.
[2] Or Vaitaraṇī: the river in which hell-beings are tormented and drowned by Paramādhāmī.
[3] A tree under which souls are tormented by Paramādhāmī.

CHAPTER IX

THE LIFE STORY OF A JAINA

Baby-hood.

THE importance of being born a man is early emphasized in Jainism; for the moment a child is born, if it be a boy, a brass tray is beaten by the proud father or other relatives in order to announce the happy event, and also, they say, to get the child used to noise from the first and to ensure that it shall never be frightened.

Whether the child be a girl or a boy, the exact moment of its birth is noted, that the astrologer may later on be able to draw its horoscope, on which its future marriage will depend.

The baby is then bathed in water and its little mouth is washed with wool dipped in a mixture of sugar-cane water and melted butter.

If the child be the first-born son of the household, the parents send presents of such things as sugar, sweets and fruits to their friends, but of course no such extravagance is indulged in if it be a girl.

Fifth day.

When the little mite is five days old, its friends bind white threads round its neck, its hands and its feet for luck, and send presents of cooked sweetmeats to their friends.

Sixth day.

The Jaina believe that a boy's whole future is decided the night that he is six days old, and on that night Mother Chaṭṭhī is worshipped. A little stool in the sleeping-room is covered with a piece of white cloth, and on it are placed a white sheet of paper and a white pen, a lamp of melted butter is lighted, and then some relative takes the baby on her lap, covers its head, and worships both the stool and its contents before the family retire to rest. When all is quiet they believe that Chaṭṭhī or Vidartha will come and write secretly on the paper a description of the sort of fortune that will meet the child during life, and the length of time it will live, but no one is ever able to see, much less decipher, the mystic writing.

Ninth day.

On the ninth (or with some sects the eleventh) day after the child's birth the mother is bathed. After the bathing she stands so as to face the sun and shakes from her finger a drop of kaṅku (turmeric).

Naming ceremony.

When the baby is twelve days old, it is named with much ceremony. In a silk sārī (the shawl-like overdress of Indian women) are placed some grain, the leaf of a pipaḷa tree, a copper coin and a sopārī nut, and then four boys (or, if the child be a girl, four girls) are called, and each seizes a corner of the sārī and begins to rock it. The baby meanwhile is lying in the arms of the father's sister, and as the children rock the sārī and sing

'Oḷi jhoḷi pīpaḷa pāna
Phaie pāḍyuṁ [*Rāmjī*] nāma,'

the aunt at the right moment declares the child's name, and of course also gives it a present; for while all the world over the profession of aunt is an expensive one, it is nowhere more so than in India.

Fifteenth day.

Fifteen days after the child's birth, the mother goes to the river to fill the water-pots for the house. She takes with her seven different kinds of grain and a cocoa-nut. Arrived at the river, she lights a tiny earthenware saucer containing ghī, splits open the cocoa-nut, and, after arranging the grain in seven rows, she fills a water-pot from the river, and then, picking up one of the seven rows of grain, she puts it in her lap, and as she walks home carrying the filled water-vessel, she scatters the grain.

Hair-cutting.

The next thing of great importance is the cutting of the child's hair. This is done when he or she has attained either the third, fifth, seventh, or ninth month of its first year. (The particular month is not of great importance, provided it be an uneven number.) The barber is called, and after the operation is over, he is given a special present, and a lucky mark is made on the child's forehead.

On some auspicious day during the early months the feeding ceremony (*Abotaṇa*) takes place, at which the father's sister again presides, but this time she gains, instead of giving, a present. The aunt takes the baby on her lap and places some dudhapāka[1] on a rupee, and seven times over takes some of this and places it in the child's mouth, whereupon the father makes her a present. Feeding ceremony.

In another ceremony, *Gotrījhāraṇāṁ*, which takes place when the child is three (or sometimes five) months old, the aunt is once more the gainer. This time all the women of the household join in preparing specially dainty food in readiness for a feast, and then place on a stool some grain, some sopārī nut, some small copper coins and a silver coin; the baby is made to bow to this collection, and then the father presents the piece of silver to his sister and feasts all his friends. Very much the same ceremony is repeated when the child goes to school in either his fifth or seventh year. Gotrījhāraṇāṁ.

The whole thought of a household in India seems to an outsider to centre round marriage and motherhood, and all the steps that lead up to them are marked with ceremonials. The age of betrothal (*Sagāi*) is steadily rising, and though it varies in different localities, a boy among the Jaina is usually betrothed about fifteen or twenty and a girl somewhat earlier. The parents on both sides look out for a suitable match, and when one has been discovered, the girl's father sends to the boy's father as a token of his intentions a cocoa-nut and a rupee, and a priest is called in to mark the forehead of the boy and his relatives with a ċāndalo or auspicious mark. A lucky woman (i.e. one whose husband is living and who has never lost a child) or a virgin then takes the cocoa-nut and marks a ċāndalo on it and on the rupee, and the boy's father summons all his friends to a feast, to which each of the guests brings a cocoa-nut. After two or three days a present, Betrothal.

[1] A favourite Indian dainty resembling milk pudding.

consisting of a cocoa-nut and ten rupees, is sent back to the girl's house as a sign that all goes well.

This, however, is only the beginning of the presentations, and in a few days another gift from the boy's house follows, consisting of a complete costume in silk (sārī, skirt and bodice), five rupees in money, half a maund of crude and half a maund of refined sugar; hidden in the refined sugar are two rupees. Not to be outdone, the father of the girl sends something, though of less value: his gift consists of half a seer of crude and half a seer of refined sugar and the two rupees returned.

Jamaṇa. Then follow two children's parties (*Jamaṇa*). First the boy's father invites the little fiancée and some other children to a feast and gives her three silken garments, and afterwards the girl's father invites the boy and some children to a feast in his house and makes him a present.

Samurata. After a short interval the boy's father sends two more sets of silk clothes and some ornament worth perhaps Rs. 300, and the girl's father replies with a substantial tip to the lucky servant who has brought the gift.

Laganapatra. By this time the parties are beginning to think of the actual wedding. An astrologer is called in who decides when everything will be auspicious and fixes the day, and this date is written in old ink and carried by some children from the bride's house to that of the boy's parents. When the bridegroom's dwelling is reached, the child who bears the paper is placed on a stool, and one of the ladies of the house comes and takes the paper from him and gives him sugar in return. All the children are feasted, and that night auspicious songs are sung in both houses.

On either the fifth or the seventh day after this five 'lucky' women wreathe the future bride and bridegroom with flowers and rub them with powder.

Maṇḍapakriyā. About three days before the actual wedding ceremony a booth or maṇḍapa is erected, when appropriate songs are sung, and dates and sugar are divided amongst those who are present. The carpenter who is to erect the booth brings with him a special piece of wood, and on it is placed a green stick and some fruit, all of which are carefully placed in the hole dug for one of the poles that support the booth. A Brāhman next mixes together some curds, milk and sopārī nut, repeating as he does so appropriate mantras, and the bridegroom takes this mixture in his right hand and pours it over the pole of the booth. For a week from the date of the erection of the booth all near relatives of the bride and bridegroom are feasted.

Gaṇeśa worship.

One of the most popular of the Hindu gods is Gaṇeśa, the remover of all hindrances, and at wedding times he is worshipped, not only by the idol-worshipping, but even by the non-idolatrous, sects among the Jaina. Accordingly the day after the erection of the booth even Sthānakavāsī Jaina bring an idol of Gaṇeśa to the maṇḍapa. A heap of grains, sopārī, rice and wheat is arranged on a stool covered with a white cloth, and Gaṇeśa is placed on the pile. Then around the stool they place twenty-five lāḍus in heaps of five, and twenty-five dates, and when this is done, two virgins carrying cooked rice in their hands come and worship the idol and mark it with auspicious marks. The relatives have also been summoned to come and worship Gaṇeśa, and they obey, bringing both wheat and rupees with them to offer to the idol. (After the wedding the paternal aunts of both bride and bridegroom will have the right to these rupees.) The bride and bridegroom are seated on stools near the god, and now a 'lucky' woman takes four pieces of wood, dips them in oil, and touches the bride and bridegroom's heads with them. The paternal aunt plays an important rôle in the wedding, as she did in the other ceremonies, and she now comes forward and ties an iron ring on the bridegroom's ċoṭalī[1] and gives him two rupees, and then an uncle of each of the couple lifts them down from

[1] The lock of hair that most Hindus leave uncut.

their stool and gives them a few rupees. Sometimes seven lucky women come to the pair whilst they are still standing on the stool, and seven things are poured into their laps.

Ukaraḍī Notarī. Occasionally on the night after the booth was erected girls go outside the great gate of the house and, after singing auspicious songs, dig a little hole in which they place small copper coins and grains, carefully covering them afterwards with earth, and then re-enter the house singing.

Ċāka. About this time also the girls of the family go to a potter's yard and mark his wheel with red powder and throw rice on it. The potter gives them some pots, which they bring back to the booth and place near the idol of Gaṇeśa.

Wedding day. When the actual wedding day arrives, the family goddess is worshipped, and fourteen girls are fed. The potter is again visited, and in exchange for a present of some three pounds of wheat, some dates and a cocoa-nut he provides four water-pots. Either the bride or the bridegroom is now seated in the booth, and 'lucky' women come and either bathe them or else content themselves with at least bathing a toe. The all-important aunt now comes forward and ties a silver ring where the iron one had been in the boy's hair, and the maternal uncle gives some money to the lad and lifts him down from the stool.

The bridegroom is then dressed in his most magnificent clothes, and, carrying a cocoa-nut in his hand, goes on horseback in procession towards the bride's house, but is met half-way by a procession from thence.

The actual marriage ceremony takes place after sunset, and is the occasion for some mild horse-play. The bride's sister, for instance, goes out to meet the bridegroom's procession, bearing a water-pot and a cocoa-nut. She makes the auspicious mark on the forehead of the bridegroom and then pinches his nose, and the groom's party put some rupees in the water-pot. Some one then lifts the bridegroom down from his horse, and the lad raises the garlands from the doorway and passes in.

The bridegroom and his friends feast at some house quite close to the bride's house, ladies present him with four lāḍus, and the barber powders his toe and then washes it. Sometimes the bride also goes and receives a sārī and some rupees whilst the bridegroom is feasting. When the dinner is over, the groom mounts his horse and goes to a temple to worship, and then returns to the bride's house.

Tamboḷa ċhāṇṭa-ṇāṁ.

The bride, who is now sitting behind a curtain, spits betel-nut juice at the bridegroom, whilst his mother-in-law marks him with the auspicious ċāndalo, and then throws balls made of rice and ashes over him, and also waves water in a vessel round his head.

The bridegroom next takes his seat in the booth, and his friends bring his gift of clothing and ornaments, and after showing them to the committee of leading Jaina in the town (Mahājana), give them to the bride's friends. The bride and bridegroom are now sitting side by side under the booth, and, after they have shaken hands, her sārī (shawl) is tied to his scarf, and he gives her some rings and other jewellery. The father and mother of the bride then offer some clothing and jewellery, and the father washes the hand of the bridegroom whilst the mother washes the bride's hand, and when this is finished, the mother places the hand of the bride in that of the groom.

Kanyā-dāna.

In the centre of the booth a special fire has been lit, round which the boy and girl walk four times from left to right, the boy offering handfuls of sopārī nut to any lucky women he sees. The Brāhman cooks who are present and the mother-in-law offer sweetmeats to the couple, who, however, must refuse to take them. The young pair next go to the bride's house and worship her gotrīja, and then to the house where the bridegroom had been staying and worship his gotrīja, after which the bride returns to her house laden with lāḍus, dates, rupees, and the kernels of four cocoa-nuts

The feasting is kept up for three or four days, and then the bride's parents summon the Mahājana, and in their presence give a suitable quantity of ornaments and clothing to the bridegroom, who distributes money in charity. After this is done, the bride's parents give her leave to go and live in the bridegroom's house.

As the bride leaves her home, she marks its walls with the imprint of her hands dipped in red powder; and when the couple pass the marriage booth, they stop at the stool and mark one of the groom's party with the auspicious mark, a sārī being presented to the bride. The bride gets into the carriage holding a cocoa-nut, and a cocoa-nut is also placed under the wheel of the carriage in such a way that it shall be crushed and broken when the carriage starts. The moment this happens, the pieces are picked up and offered to the bride with four lāḍus and two brass vessels, and the wedding ceremonies are completed.

The first child.

The whole position of the new daughter-in-law will depend on her bearing children, and the young mother is guarded in many ways from the supposed influence of evil spirits before and after the child's birth.

Rākhaḍī bandhana.

One of these protective ceremonies takes place during the fifth month, when the husband's sister binds a little parcel done up in black silk by a white thread to the wrist of the expectant mother. In the parcel are a cowrie shell, a ring of iron, a piece of black silk, some earth from the junction of three roads, some dust from Hanumān's image and seven pulse seeds. (Some Jaina prefer the parcel to be done up in green or red or yellow silk rather than black, which they regard as unlucky.) If the husband had no sister living, a priest would be called in to tie on the parcel, and in return would expect enough food to last him for a day. Whilst tying on the parcel, he would probably bless the woman in words that might be translated: 'Auspicious time, auspicious junction of the planets, happiness, welfare, freedom from disease, good:

let all these be yours without hindrance.' No man older than the husband is allowed to be present at this ceremony, and it is considered better for the husband not to be in the house at the time of any of these functions. The father and mother of the girl feast all their relatives at this time; and from now on the expectant mother is not allowed to do any drudgery or hard work about the house.

Sīmanta or Kholo bharavo.

A very important ceremony takes place on some auspicious day in the seventh month. The bride's mother sends special clothes for the occasion, and the bridegroom's relatives also give presents, including three pounds of rice. The expectant mother fetches seven water-pots, and then goes and worships the gotrīja. Then the auspicious direction for that particular day being settled, she is taken to a room facing that quarter and there bathed, whilst she sings and is fed on sweetmeats. A little boy is also brought into the room and seated beside her whilst she bathes, and is afterwards presented with a rupee by the bride's parents. The girl's own mother, or her representative, comes into the room whilst she bathes, and parts the young wife's hair; she is then dressed in the special clothes sent by her parents, her hands and feet being coloured red. A rich piece of cloth is spread outside the bathing-room, and on this the girl steps very slowly and majestically, bearing a cocoa-nut in her hands. For every step her father will have to give a present to the ubiquitous husband's sister, but the gifts progressively decrease in value, for whereas the first step will cost her father a rupee, the next will be valued at only eight annas, the third at four, and so on. When the edge of the carpet is reached, the husband's relatives offer the wife one rupee and throw over her balls of ashes and rice.

She then sits on a stool near the family goddess, and some milk is poured out on to a plate, which she drinks; the two fathers give her two rupees, and she also asks her mother-in-law for some money. Her husband's youngest brother then makes the auspicious red mark on her forehead and slaps her seven times on her right cheek, for which kind office the girl's parents pay him handsomely in rupees! The husband's sister plays yet another part, for she now ties a silver and gold thread on the young wife's right hand (which she will take off, however, the next day). A lucky woman then presents rice, lotus seed and a pomegranate to the girl, who gets up and bows to her mother-in-law and other elders as a sign that the ceremony is complete.

The next day the young wife receives sweetmeats from her father's house and distributes them amongst her husband's relatives, and on the third day she goes to her own old home and stays there till the child is born. She does not usually return to her husband's house till the child is three months old, and then the maternal grandfather makes a handsome present of jewellery.

Death ceremonies.

When a Jaina seems to be dying, his relatives summon a monk or nun to preach to the patient. As the ascetic is not allowed to sit, he cannot preach for very long at a time, so a devout layman or laywoman may be called in to supplement his work. In a case the writer knew, where a Jaina lady was dying of consumption, this religious instruction was given for three hours a day for twenty-two days.

As death approaches, the patient is urged to take the vow[1] of giving up all attachment to worldly things and of abstaining from all food. Enormous sums are given in charity by the dying man or his relatives to ensure his happiness in the next world. (Recently in the writer's town, for instance, one gentleman gave Rs. 70,000 on his death-bed, and the sons of another, who was killed in a railway accident, immediately gave Rs. 15,000 in their father's name.) Then the name of Mahāvīra is repeatedly whispered in the dying man's ear, till all is over.

[1] See Santhāro, p. 163.

As soon as death has taken place, the body is moved from the bed and placed on the floor, which has been previously covered with a preparation of cow-dung to make it hallowed ground. The corpse is so arranged that the face of the dead is turned towards the north, and a lamp filled with ghī is lighted beside him. In memory of the deceased even animals are made happy, for sweets are given to the pariah dogs of the village and grass to the cows; nor are the poor forgotten, for grain is distributed amongst them.

Funeral ceremonies.

Directly a Jaina dies, all his relatives weep as loudly as possible, and so advertise the fact that death has taken place. If it be a woman who has died, she is dressed in her best, probably in a sārī with a gold border, a silk bodice, and a petticoat of silk. Formerly these things used to be burnt with her, but nowadays they are removed before the actual burning takes place, so the corpse is swathed with green cloth from knees to waist underneath the silken garments. If the corpse be that of an ordinary widow, she is dressed not in silk but in black, but if the woman had been what is known as a *veśa* widow (i.e. one under thirty whose husband had died whilst she was still a little child), her corpse is not dressed in black.

When a man dies and leaves a widow, her ivory bangles are broken, one of them being tied to the bier and the other taken to the river by some women. Even if the wife he leaves behind be a virgin, she must take off her jewels and wash off the red auspicious mark from her forehead, and never use either again. She is not, however, always compelled to wear black garments, abstain from sweetmeats, or sleep on the floor, until she attains womanhood.

The corpse in the case of a man is dressed only in a loin-cloth, a costly cloth being wrapped over all. Four cocoanuts, a ball of flour and four small flags are placed on the bier, and two annas are put in the dead man's mouth, which will later on be given to the sweepers as rent for the ground on which the corpse is burnt.

The dead body is now lifted on to the bier and carried by near relatives to the burning-ground, where a pyre has been arranged, which is lit by the son of the dead man. Women can follow the bier no further than the threshold of their house.

The fire to light the funeral pyre is taken from the house, and special attention is paid by the relatives and friends to the manner in which the fire is carried from the dead man's home to the burning-ground. If it is carried in a cup, it is an intimation that the feasting and funeral expenses generally will be moderate, but if the fire is carried on a plate, it is a sign that a great feast will be given.

Curiously enough, as the Jaina carry the corpse to the burning-ground, they call aloud 'Rāma Rāma',[1] just like ordinary Hindus, but the writer has been assured that they are not then thinking of the god Rāma of the Rāmāyaṇa, but simply use the word as synonymous for Prabhu or Lord, and in their own minds are thinking each of his own particular god.

When the body is burnt to ashes, most of the relatives return, but one of the party goes to a potter and gets a water-pot, and the next-of-kin fills it four times at the river and pours it over the ashes four times, and after the fourth time he leaves the pot lying there.

On the second day after the death the near relatives all go to the Apāsaro and listen to sermons.

[1] They do not, however, use these words as an ordinary salutation. Jaina, when they meet, greet each other with the words *Juhāra* or *Jayajinendra*; Brāhmans usually say *Jayajaya*; other Hindus *Rāma Rāma*; Mohammedans *Salām*; while, in Gujarāt at least, the Christian greeting is *Kuśaḷatā*.

CHAPTER X

THE JAINA LAYMAN AND HIS RELIGIOUS LIFE

The Twelve Lay Vows.

THE Jaina, though they do not know of any dynamic power such as would give a man strength to keep his promises, nevertheless firmly believe in the helpfulness of taking vows.[1] Through these, they say, a man is aided towards keeping the third jewel, that of Right Conduct, and by failing to take them he acquires karma from which they might have saved him.

We have seen that it is only after he has made some progress in the upward path that a man wishes to take these vows,[2] though after a certain time he is able to keep the spirit of the vows without needing to renew the vows themselves. Not only must the candidate have reached the fifth step, but he must also have attained to firm faith in a true Tīrthaṅkara, true guru, and true religion.

Pañča Atičāra.

Further, he cannot take any vow unless he has first renounced five faults (*Pañča Atičāra*) and so has no doubts (*Śaṅkā*); no desire to belong to another faith (*Kāṅkhā*); no questioning about the reality of the fruits of karma (*Vitigiččhā*); undertakes not to praise hypocrites (*Parapākhaṇḍa paraśaṁsā*); and not to associate with them (*Parapākhaṇḍa santhana*).

The five Anuvrata.

i. Prāṇātipāta viramaṇa vrata.

If all these conditions be fulfilled, the man may take the first vow (*Prāṇātipāta viramaṇa vrata*), promising never intentionally to destroy a jīva that has more than one sense. This vow would not prevent a king leading an army

[1] Other Indians also believe strongly in the virtue of the Jaina vows. It is said, for instance, that the mother of Mr. Gāndhī, the South African leader, though herself a Vaiṣṇava, persuaded her son before he left Rājkot for England to vow in front of Pūjya Bečarajī, a famous Jaina sādhu, that he would abstain from wine, flesh and women.

[2] See p. 187.

in defence of his kingdom, but would prevent one's fighting with a lunatic, or a blind man who had hurt one unintentionally. The vow also forbids the killing of weak creatures like mosquitoes and any other troublesome insects, and prohibits acting as 'agent provocateur'.

The man who takes this vow must avoid five faults in the treatment of animals: he must never tie an animal up too tightly; beat it unmercifully; cut its limbs; overload or overwork it; or neglect to feed it properly.[1]

The vow is infringed by planning to kill any one, even if the evil purpose be never carried out. It also forbids animal sacrifice, the Jaina arguing that, if mokṣa be attained by sacrifice, we had better sacrifice our fathers and mothers! If an animal is in pain, it is not permissible to kill it in order to end its sufferings, for who knows that it will not suffer worse things in the next life?

The reason the Jaina give for their horror of killing (hiṁsā) is not, as some say, the fear of being haunted by the dead animal's ghost, but the realization that every jīva has two bodies, Kārmaṇa and Taijasa, and also a third which may be Audārika (i.e. human or animal) or Vaikreya (i.e. a demi-god or a hell-being). Every jīva (save a Siddha) forms round it through its karma a body, which is called its kārmaṇa body, and also another invisible body, taijasa, which at its death will enable it to assume a new form; these two unseen bodies are indestructible and loathe being separated from the third body, which is destructible, be it audārika or vaikreya. If, therefore, we destroy a living body, it is like destroying the beloved home of the taijasa and kārmaṇa bodies.

The actual words used in taking this first vow are, in the case of Sthānakavāsī Jaina, mixed Gujarātī and Māgadhī, and might be translated:

'I will desist from destroying all great lives such as Trasa jīva (i.e.

[1] It would surely seem advisable to quote these five faults in the publications of the Indian Society for the Prevention of Cruelty to Animals.

lives of two, three, four and five senses), either knowingly or intentionally, excepting offending lives living in my body which give pain; but I will not with evil intent destroy vermin or lunatics, and I also vow not to destroy minute one-sensed lives. As long as I live I will not myself kill; nor cause others to kill; nor will I kill by mind, speech, or body.

Thus have I taken the first vow, so I must know the five Atičāra concerning it, but I must not commit them. I repeat them in their usual order: binding, killing, mutilating, overloading, wrong feeding.'

Another thing forbidden by this vow is the burying of people in a trance; for, as the Jaina sagely remark, it is very likely to kill them!

The Jaina prophesy that certain penalties will be accumulated by acting contrary to this vow. For instance, if a man commit murder, he may die even in this life in an untimely fashion. (The British Government has a knack of seeing that this prophecy is fulfilled!) He may also be drowned, or become a leper, or lose his hands and his feet, if not in this birth, at least in the next.

ii. Mṛiṣāvāda viramaṇa vrata.

The second vow (*Mṛiṣāvāda viramaṇa vrata*) of the Jaina layman is directed against falsehood or exaggeration. In a country where the women live in purdah, one can see how easy a thing it would be to spread untrue or exaggerated reports about them; and so a man who has taken this vow must never tell lies about any girl, including his own daughter, never for example, in order to marry her well, saying that she is younger or prettier than she is, or denying her bodily defects; he must likewise be careful never to speak against a prospective bridegroom. The vow is also concerned with commercial honesty, and forbids a man, for instance, when selling cows or buffaloes to say that they give more milk than they actually do, or when selling land and houses to describe the boundaries or the number of trees on the estate falsely. If the man taking the vows is a banker, he must keep any deposit honestly and give it back when demanded, even if no receipt be producible. If he have to take part in the courts or in the *Pañča*,[1] he must never give false evidence.

[1] Village Council.

Now this vow is notoriously difficult to keep, and so Jaina laymen are advised always to guard against five things: rash speech; revealing secrets; running down one's wife; giving false advice; and cooking accounts. (In this list the Digambara substitute forgery for false advice.)

When one meets a dumb man, or a man with a bad stutter, one knows that he has broken this vow of truthfulness in a previous life.

The actual words of the vow might be rendered:

'I take a vow not to utter great falsehoods, such as lies concerning brides, cattle, estates, deposits, and [not to bear] false witness. I will abstain from all such lies. As long as I live . . . [and then it goes on as in the first vow down to] the five Aticāra, which are rash speech, revealing secrets, speaking ill of one's spouse, giving bad advice, falsifying accounts or forging documents.'

iii. Adattādāna viramaṇa vrata.

Stealing or taking what is not given is renounced in the third vow (*Adattādāna viramaṇa vrata*), which includes stealing from a house, taking from bundles, highway robbery, opening any one's lock with one's own key, or appropriating lost property. In especial, a man is warned never to buy stolen property, never to encourage another in thieving, never to act seditiously, to smuggle or to work in any way against the Government, not to use false weights or measures, to adulterate goods or to sell them false to sample. The penalty for breach of this vow is either to be born in a condition of poverty or (if the offence was very rank) in a state of actual servitude.

A free translation of the actual words used in taking the third vow might run:

'I take a vow not to thieve in any of the following ways: not to steal from a house, not to steal from a bundle, not to steal on the highway, not to open another's lock, not to appropriate lost property. I will abstain from such forms of thieving. I take a vow not to steal, except in things relating to trade and things belonging to my relatives which will not give rise to suspicion. As long as I live [and then as in the other vow to] the five Aticāra, which are buying stolen property, encouraging others to thieve, committing offences against Government, using false weights and measures, adulterating or selling goods false to sample.'

The vow of chastity (*Maithuna viramaṇa vrata*) follows, by which a man promises to be absolutely faithful to his own wife at all times and never to allow any evil thoughts in his own mind about goddesses. The vow may be broken in five ways: consummating marriage with a young child, or forming a temporary connexion with a widow or other woman whom it is impossible truly to marry; unfaithfulness before marriage; match-making and marriage brokerage; excessive sexual indulgence; and lastly, evil talk. The breaking of this vow carries with it penalties too horrible to put on paper. Many of the enlightened Jaina are beginning to feel very strongly the evils of early marriage; and here again one would venture to suggest to them that their protest cannot be fairly termed an innovation when the abuse of early marriage is expressly forbidden in this vow. iv. Maithuna viramaṇa vrata.

The Jaina have shrewdly realized that the true way of increasing our wealth is by curbing our desires. The fewer things we allow ourselves to use, the fewer our desires become, and, safe within the circumscribing walls we ourselves have built round our potential possessions, we find not only peace of mind but also safety from many temptations. Why should we steal when we already have all we desire, or why cheat and defraud in the race for wealth, if we already are as wealthy as we will ever allow ourselves to become? After all, few people forge or gamble to gain money to give in alms. When we remember that the Jaina creed has forced its holders to become a commercial people, we see the special value this vow of limitation, *Parigraha viramaṇa vrata*, might have, if it were really lived up to. Unfortunately it has not been kept sufficiently to prevent the name of Baniyâ being considered a synonym for a money-grubber. v. Parigraha viramaṇa vrata.

The vow may be translated:

'I take a vow not to possess more of the following things than I have allowed myself; a certain fixed quantity of houses and fields, of silver and gold, of coins and grain, of two-footed or four-footed creatures, furniture and plenishing. Beyond this limit I will regard nothing as my own possession. As long as I live I will not myself regard in body, mind, or speech things beyond these as my own. . . . [The five Aticāra are] transgressing the limit fixed in houses and fields, silver and gold, coins and grain, two-footed or four-footed creatures, furniture and plenishing.'

The man who takes this vow promises that he will never allow himself to retain more than a certain fixed quantity of houses and fields, gold and silver, cash and corn, servants and cattle, furniture and plenishing. The vow is broken by passing beyond the self-prescribed limits by means of such devices as banking the superfluous money in a daughter's name, or substituting four big houses for the four small houses originally agreed on. As a proof of how this vow is observed the Jaina are fond of quoting the recent case of a Mr. Popata Amaraćanda of Cambay, who when quite a poor man had promised that he would never possess more than 95,000 rupees. He became a very successful man of business, but as soon as he had made the prescribed number of rupees, he gave to the building of temples or the founding of animal hospitals all the extra money he made.

These five vows are called the five Anuvrata, and they resemble in their content, as we shall see, the five great vows a monk takes. If a layman keeps all five Anuvrata and has also abandoned the use of intoxicants, animal food, and honey,[1] he possesses the eight primary qualities of a layman and is rightly called a Śrāvaka.

The three Guṇavrata.

The first five vows are followed by three *Guṇavrata*, which 'help' the keeping of the first five vows.

[1] Honey seems to the Jaina to resemble hiṁsā, the depriving a jīva of his house, and, moreover, by the brutal way in which honey is gathered in India by burning a torch under the comb, the bees and their eggs are destroyed. Jaina are therefore most interested to learn that Europeans actually build houses for bees in which the arrangements are so efficient that the eggs and bees are not injured when the honey is removed, and also that sufficient food is left to the bees. So strongly do the Indian villagers feel about their own destructive way of taking honey, that they have a proverb: 'The sin incurred in destroying one honey-comb is as great as that accumulated by destroying twelve villages.'

We saw how the Jaina believe that the limitation of desire curtails sin by limiting the motives for sinning; they also believe that setting bounds to one's travels (*Diśi-vrata parimāṇa*) curtails sin by restricting the area in which one can sin. vi. Diśivrata parimāṇa.

The vow taken runs:

'I fix a limit of height and depth and circumference. If I have to pass this limit, willing and in my body, I vow not to indulge any of the five āśrava. . . . [The five Atiċāra are] transgression of the limit above, below or around, altering the position of the bounds fixed by increasing one and decreasing the other, and proceeding further when a doubt arises as to the limits.'

It is only laymen who take this vow. A sādhu does not vow that he will limit the possible places to which he may wander, for the farther he wanders the fewer intimate friends he can make; and friendship is forbidden to a sādhu, lest it lead to love. But he does promise never to make his wanderings an excuse for luxury by sitting in a boat, a carriage, a cart, or a train, or riding on a horse.[1] Breaking this vow leads to excommunication.[2] A sādhu of the Tapagaċċha sect travelled constantly by train and was therefore excommunicated. He still continues to go by rail wearing sādhu dress; but seeing him in a train

[1] The writer had an opportunity not long ago of seeing how strictly the ascetics keep this vow. An aged nun was very ill, and the community was most anxious that she should go and see an English lady doctor. She refused to be conveyed to the hospital by carriage or in a litter, and at length in despair her friends asked the writer to request the doctor to go and see her at the Apāsaro.

[2] Excommunication of sādhus is still fairly common; for instance, a Sthānakavāsī sādhu in Rājkot bit his guru and was excommunicated in consequence. The Sthānakavāsī laymen ordered a coat and trousers to be made for him and forced him to abandon his sādhu dress and don these. They then gave him a railway ticket to Thān (a station about forty-four miles distant) and sent him away. They told the writer that they could do this because this cannibal *bonne bouche* had been enjoyed in a native state; they would have been afraid to act so sternly in British territory. This sādhu repented most deeply and implored forgiveness in Rājkot, but the laymen refused it. In other towns he was, however, acknowledged as a sādhu, and he died wearing sādhu dress.

P 2

no Jaina layman of any sect will acknowledge him as a religious person or salute him.

The layman vows not to go beyond set limits, such as Ceylon in the south, the Himalayas in the north, England in the west, and China in the east. The vow can be broken in five ways: by climbing too high; descending too low; going obliquely; increasing the limits fixed; and forgetting these limits.

vii. Upabhoga paribhoga parimāṇa.

The second of the assistant vows, *Upabhoga paribhoga parimāṇa*, is intended to help people to keep their vows against lying, covetousness and stealing, for it limits the number of things a man may use.

This vow is taken in words somewhat as follows:

'I take a vow of indulging only to a certain fixed extent in things to be enjoyed once and in things to be enjoyed from time to time, such as towels, things for cleaning teeth, the anointing of oneself with oil or such like, washing oneself with soap, bathing, clothing, besmearing oneself with saffron, sandalwood, &c.; decorating, incense-burning, drink, eating of sweetmeats, of rice, pulse, nutritious things (milk, butter, ghī and the like), vegetables, indulging in sweet drinks (such as grape-juice, sugar-cane juice), ordinary meals, drinking-water, sleeping on beds, [eating] raw things containing lives, and other miscellaneous things. I have fixed certain limits in respect of the above twenty-six things. In transgression of these limits I will never indulge in things to be enjoyed once or from time to time with a view to seeking pleasure therefrom. I will observe this vow as long as I live; and I will not go beyond the limit for personal enjoyment, in mind, speech or body.

As a layman, I must have knowledge of the five following Atiċāra, and avoid acting according to them, and I repeat them in their usual order: Eating things containing life; eating things partially animate and partially inanimate; eating things having some remnants of life in them (such as partially ripe fruit, the unripe part having life but not the ripe part); eating highly spiced things; eating things in which the greater part has to be wasted (such as sugar-cane).

I, a layman, must have knowledge of the fifteen Atiċāra concerning means of livelihood, and must avoid putting them in practice. I repeat these in their usual order: Burning a kiln; cutting jungles or getting them cut; making carts and selling them; receiving rent of houses; digging the earth; trading in ivory; in hair (such as fly-whisks); in liquid things; selling poison; dealing in sealing-wax; owning a mill or working with a machine; mutilating or cutting the limbs of animals;

burning jungles; wasting the water of a pond, spring or lake; taming (dogs, cats, and such) obnoxious animals and selling them.'

In practice a man frequently agrees only to use twenty-six things, viz.: a towel; tooth-brush; fruit; soap; water for washing; wearing apparel; tilaka (mark on forehead); flowers; ornaments; incense; drinking-vessels (nowadays these include tea-things); sweetmeats; wheat and grain; peas; ghī; oil and milk; vegetables; dried fruit; dinner; drinking-water; pāna, sopārī, &c.; conveyances, railway trains, and horses; boots; beds, tables, chairs, &c.; anything unmentioned that turns out to be really necessary; anything that has no life. The grouping of this list is very curious, and under the last two items considerable latitude is allowed to creep in; it is only through these, for instance, that any books are permitted.

In trying to keep this vow one must be on one's guard about both food and commerce: for with regard to food, one might sin through eating unripe vegetables, or eating ripe and unripe together, or partaking of food that needs a lot of fire to cook it, or food like sugar-cane of which only a small portion is eaten and the greater part has to be thrown away; of course onions, potatoes, and all roots, being inhabited by more than one jīva, must never be eaten. In the same way one vows to be very careful, in choosing a profession, to avoid any business which involves the taking of any life, however low in the scale. One should therefore never be a blacksmith, a limeburner, or a potter, or follow any other trade in which a furnace is used, for in a fire many insect lives are destroyed; wood-cutting also often involves the accidental death of many minute lives, so a Jaina should never cut down a forest; in the same way he must never make a railway carriage, or even an ordinary cart, for railway trains sometimes run over people[1] and often run over animals and insects.

[1] Especially in India where railway employees *will* go to sleep with their heads on the rails!

One must never sell artificial manure (as it is sometimes made of the bones of dead animals), or take any contracts for building houses or sinking wells that involve much digging (for one might dig an insect in two). One has to be very much on one's guard if one thinks of selling anything: one must never sell ivory (for that might be made of elephants' tusks), or butter or honey (the latter involving the destruction of bee life), or fur or hair (lest any jīva should have been pained), or sealing-wax (for insects might be killed by it). A Jaina may not sell opium or any poison (lest the buyer should use it to take life), neither may he sell mills (for machinery causes many insect deaths). He is very hampered with regard to agriculture: he may not dig, burn weeds in a field, drain water from land, wells, or tanks (lest fish should die), or even rent land that has been drained by some one else. All of these restrictions on trade and agriculture have had the very doubtful benefit of forcing Jaina more and more into the profession of money-lenders; but the last clause of the vow has certainly proved beneficial, for it forbids slave-owning and the keeping of any animal or woman for any cruel purpose, and is considered so important that it is rehearsed every day.

viii. Anartha daṇḍa vrata.

The eighth vow, the *Anartha daṇḍa*, is designed to guard against unnecessary evils. It runs:

'I take the vow called Anartha Daṇḍa Viramaṇa, which has four divisions: not to do the two evil meditations, not to be careless about keeping or using weapons, not to persuade people to do evil.'

The vow contains four divisions: first, one promises (*Apadhyāna*) never to hope that evil may befall some one else, or to think evil of any one; next (*Pramāda ċaryā*), to be as careful as possible not to take life through carelessness, but to cover all oil, milk, or water in which a fly might be drowned; again, remembering the injuries that are often accidentally inflicted through weapons, one promises (*Hiṁsādāna*) not only to keep as few actual weapons as possible but also as few knives or other things that could be used as weapons; finally one promises (*Pāpopadeśa*) never to use one's influence for evil or to persuade any one else to do so. In keeping this vow five special faults must be guarded against, the vow being broken if one writes an immoral book, sells evil medicines, or indulges in evil conversation; if one takes part in buffoonery; indulges in vile abuse; leaves one's guns lying about when loaded or in any way is careless about them; or lastly, if one thinks too much about things to eat or drink.

The four Śikṣāvrata.

The remaining four of the layman's twelve vows are called *Śikṣāvrata*, and they are all intended to encourage the laity in the performance of their religious duties.

ix. Sāmāyika.

The ninth vow is taken in the following words:

> 'I take the ninth, Sāmāyika, Vow which teaches me to avoid all evil actions. I will sit in meditation for forty-eight [minutes], ninety-six, or whatever period I may have previously fixed upon. Whilst I am sitting in meditation I will not commit, or cause any one to commit, any sin in the space of the whole world by mind, speech, or body.'

A man hereby promises to perform Sāmāyika, i.e. to spend at least forty-eight minutes every day in meditation, thinking no evil of any one, but being at peace with all the world, to meditate on what heights one's soul may reach. One may observe as many periods of forty-eight minutes as possible (e.g. ninety-six minutes or one hundred and forty-four), but forty-eight minutes is the least unbroken period one may spend. A Jaina should engage in Sāmāyika every morning, afternoon and evening, but of these the morning Sāmāyika is considered the most important. Whilst doing it, one must neither sin oneself, nor cause any one else to sin, but, sitting with one's legs crossed, one should fix one's gaze on the tip of one's own nose. (Nowadays, however, Jaina quite often just sit or stand comfortably whilst they are doing it.) The usual place for Sāmāyika is the temple or the Apāsaro (there used to be an Apāsaro in every man's house). If an idol be there, they kneel in front of it, and if a guru be present, kneel before him and ask his permission. Three times they kneel (*pañcāṅga*) in front of idol or guru, and three times also they perform *āvartana*, i. e. make a circle before their faces from the right ear round to the left ear, holding a mouth-cloth or other piece of material in front of their mouths, and repeat the *Tikkhutto*, which may be translated:

'Making āvartana from the right ear to the left three times, I salute and bow, and I worship and adore you; you are a guru [or a god], you are auspicious, you do good, you are full of knowledge, so I serve you.'

If no image and no guru be there, the Jaina kneel towards the north-east (in which direction they believe the country of Mahāvideha, where certain Tīrthaṅkara live, to be situated) and then ask permission of the first of these, the Sīmandhara,[1] before repeating the Tikkhutto. During the forty-eight minutes they not only meditate but also read the scriptures, and at the end of the forty-eight minutes they repeat the particular pāṭha for closing Sāmāyika which refers to five special faults which may be committed during meditation, namely; failing to control thoughts; mind; actions; failing to observe the fixed time; and not repeating the pāṭha correctly.

x. Deśāvakāśika vrata.

The tenth vow, *Deśāvakāśika vrata*, which resembles two that we have already discussed, is taken in the following words:

'I take the tenth vow called Deśāvakāśika. I will not go beyond the limit fixed by me in any of the four directions in mind or body, and will not open any of the five āśrava [channels] for sin. In the limit that I have fixed I will not enjoy any of the things which I have vowed not to enjoy. I will not transgress nor cause others to transgress it by mind, speech, or body; and I will not enjoy such things in mind, speech, or body for one day and night.'

In taking this vow a man promises for one particular day to still further contract the limits he has undertaken not to transgress, and he may bind himself during that day

[1] Sīmandhara was the earliest Tīrthaṅkara from the land of Mahāvideha, just as Ṛiṣabhadeva was the first in Bhārata (India).

never to go outside the Apāsaro or the village, and only to have one meal, or to drink nothing but water. At the same time he promises that he will spend longer in meditation. He must guard against infringing the vow by extending the number of things used; borrowing some one else's things; sending a servant to fetch things or asking some one he meets in the road to do so; or by making signs and so asking even without words; or by throwing stones to attract people's attention and then getting them to fetch it.

xi. Poṣadha vrata.

We have seen how Mahāvīra realized the importance of connecting the laity closely with the ascetics, and how this close connexion saved Jainism when Buddhism was swept out of India. The eleventh vow, *Poṣadha vrata*, is one of the links that bind the two sections of the Jaina community together, for the taking of it compels a layman to spend some of his time as a monk. He promises that for twenty-four hours he will touch neither food, water, fruit, betel-nut, ornaments, scents, nor any sort of weapon, and will commit no sort of sin, but observe celibacy. He further promises that by day he will only wear three cloths (a cloth over his legs, one over his body, and a mouth-cloth), and that at night he will use two cloths only (one spread above him and one below him).

Devout laymen usually perform Poṣadha four times a month, but those who hope eventually to become sādhus observe it six times a month at least.

The Digambara keep this vow more strictly than any other Jaina, for they begin to observe it the night before the twenty-four hours fixed (i. e. they keep it for two nights and the intervening day), and during all that time they never even touch water. Neither do they go to an Apāsaro, but choosing some lonely place they read the scriptures and meditate there.

The other Jaina go to their Apāsaro, read the scriptures, sing the praises of the Tīrthaṅkara, and ask questions of their sādhus—in fact, as a Jaina friend said to the writer, 'We use the time to cram the points of our religion'.

In keeping this vow there are five faults which must be avoided: neglecting to search the clothes for vermin; failing to remove it carefully out of harm's way when found; any other carelessness which may result in injuring insect life; not fasting as one has vowed; and allowing oneself to sleep in the day instead of meditating. The keeping of this Poṣadha vow is considered one of the highest of religious duties, and at the solemn yearly fast of Pajjusaṇa even careless people keep it most strictly. As a rule it is more scrupulously observed by women than by men.

The following is a literal translation of the actual words used when this vow is taken:

> 'I take the eleventh vow called Poṣadha, in which I promise to abstain for twenty-four hours from food, drink, fruits, sopārī, sex enjoyment, from wearing ornaments (gold, silver, or diamond), from wearing a garland or anointing my body. I will not use weapons, or a heavy club, or any destructive missile. This I will observe for twenty-four hours and will not infringe it myself, nor cause others to infringe it, in mind, body, or speech.'

xii. Atithi saṁvibhāga vrata.

The twelfth vow, or *Atithi saṁvibhāga vrata*, which the Digambara call the *Vaiyā vrata*, runs as follows:

> 'I take the twelfth vow, the Atithi saṁvibhāga vrata, by which I promise to give to Śramaṇa or Nirgrantha any of the fourteen things which they can accept without blame, namely: food, drink, fruits, sopārī,[1] clothes, pots, blankets, towels, and things which can be lent and returned, such as seats, benches, beds, quilts, &c., and medicine.'

The purpose of this vow is to encourage the laity to support the ascetic community, on whom they bestow in alms food, water, clothing, pots, blankets, and towels for the feet, and also lend them beds, tables and other furniture. They must never give a sādhu unboiled water, bread hot from the fire, bread on which green vegetables have rested, or anything that has gone bad. Neither must they call

[1] Monks may not take betel-nut whole, but may take it chopped.

a servant and tell him to give the alms to an ascetic, but they must get up and give them themselves, and must give without conceit.

The sādhu on his part must never send notice beforehand of his coming, for a layman must always be prepared to give; neither will most Jaina laymen (except members of the Tapagaććha sect) invite an ascetic to their house, as this is thought by them to be forbidden in their scriptures; but they will invite a layman who has just completed Poṣadha to dine,[1] since feeding such brings puṇya to the host if done with that intention; if, however, he gives the invitation simply thinking it to be his duty to do so, he will obtain nirjarā.

That some benefit is always obtained by giving alms, the following legend shows. Once upon a time in the state of Rājagṛiha there was a poor lad, so poor that he rarely tasted rich food; but once as a great treat his mother prepared a dish magnificently formed of rice and milk and sugar! Just at that moment a sādhu came by, and the model youth passed on the tempting dish to him. As a reward the pleasing lad was born in his next incarnation as the son of a rich merchant, and, determining to become equal to a king, he became a sādhu, and in his next birth will proceed to mokṣa.

How a layman takes the twelve vows.

When a Jaina, proceeding on the upward path, has reached the fifth step[2] in the Ċauda Guṇasthānaka, he necessarily desires to take the twelve vows, and accordingly goes to the Apāsaro and tells a guru of his wish. The guru reads out the vows and gives him an instruction on each one and its infringement similar to the foregoing notes on the vows. The layman assents to the instruction and fixes the limits of the distance he will travel, the amount of money he will

[1] A friend of the writer's recently invited a Khojā who had become a Jaina to dine with him, after he had performed his Poṣadha vow. She was told that such a convert could be invited to dine with the *saṅgha* but not with the *nāta*, i. e. he was asked to their religious feasts (though even there he had to sit separately) but not to their caste dinners.

[2] See p. 187.

allow himself to use, &c. These limits he writes down in his note-book, and at the great yearly confession, Saṁvatsarī, he goes to any guru who happens to be present, confesses any infraction of the vows and accepts the penance given. Besides this, every day of the year when he performs Paḍikamaṇuṁ he privately confesses his transgressions against the vows. Every day also both morning and evening the layman repeats the vows. The period for which they are taken varies: some Jaina promise to observe them as long as they live, others fix a certain period, consisting very frequently of two years, and at the expiry of that time take them afresh if they feel inclined.

The advantage of the vows. The Jaina believe that great advantages flow from keeping the vows: physically, since the moderation they enjoin keeps the body in training and health; and morally, because they free the soul from love or enmity, and ultimately lead it to mokṣa. A layman who keeps all these twelve vows is called a *Deśavratī*, or one who keeps the vows in part; a sādhu, who as we shall see keeps them in a more stringent form, is called a *Sarvavratī*, one who keeps all the vows.

Santhāro. When a layman realizes that he is growing old and that his body is becoming very frail, he spends more and more time in the Apāsaro and tries to use fewer and fewer things, and daily after Paḍikamaṇuṁ repeats the old-age vow or *Santhāro Pāṭha*, which contains the promise of dying by voluntary starvation. He does not vow not to take food, however, until he feels that death is approaching.

Before repeating the words, he should seat himself cross-legged on a stool of *darbha* grass, with his face turned to the north-east, and folding his hands he should encircle his face with them (*āvartana*) and say as follows: 'I bow to all the adorable Arihanta who have attained to the highest state.' He then repeats all the twelve vows, and determining to keep himself free from all sin, particularly hiṁsā (against which he takes a special vow), he promises never to lie, thieve, &c., as long as he lives.

'I will be from henceforth till death quite indifferent about this my body which once was dear and beautiful to me. It was like a jewel-case which I carefully protected from cold, heat, hunger, thirst, serpent-bite, the attack of thieves, insects, diseases such as cough and high fever.'

Then he should meditate on the five Atiĉāra which would infringe the vow and should strive to avoid them: that is to say, he should not wish to be a king or a rich merchant or a deity in his next life; he should not wish for long life; nor, being weary with the dreadful hardship of Santhāro, must he desire immediate death. He must then quietly wait for death, longing for mokṣa, but not for any amelioration of his present state.

Every Jaina hopes to make a Samādhi death, i. e. to die by self-immolation. It is true that near relatives, standing by the death-bed of a younger man, will often not permit him to give up all hope of life and decline to take food, but if an old man is evidently dying, and if he wishes it, he repeats the Santhāro Pāṭha, and, before promising indifference to his body, he says:

'I take a vow to abstain from food and drink and fruits and sopārī as long as I live.'

The same words are also used when this terrible vow is taken voluntarily in good health by ascetics who wish to reach the highest point of holiness.[1] After his death a man who has done Santhāro is called Samādhistha and held in the highest honour, and while he is suffering the dreadful pangs of thirst before his death, his relatives and friends encourage him to carry out his resolve by every means in their power.

The Eleven Pratimā.[2]

We have already noticed that the Jaina aim seems to be to close as many as possible of the channels which love and

[1] The Jaina consulted by the writer do not agree with those who say that Santhāro is only performed after twelve years of austerities, declaring that there is no time fixed before which Santhāro may not be performed.

[2] Or *Paḍimā.*

affection open, and through which suffering might enter our lives, and to abstain from action, lest karma should be acquired with all its penalties.

The twelve vows were shaped in accordance with the fixed idea of all who hold the doctrine of karma that, though it is well to do good, it is better to do nothing; their aim is also to bridge over the gap between the lay and the ascetic life. The eleven Pratimā bring the approach still closer.

A layman who is desirous of reaching a higher stage in the upward path, or Ċauda Guṇasthānaka, than that attained by keeping the twelve vows will also keep the eleven Pratimā, which lead him gently on towards the point when he will be able to take the five great vows of the ascetic.

i. Darśana pratimā.

By the first, or *Darśana pratimā*, a layman undertakes to worship the true deva (i.e. a Tīrthaṅkara), to reverence a true guru, and to believe in the true dharma (i.e. Jainism). He also promises to avoid the seven bad deeds which are mentioned in a well-known Sanskrit śloka that may be translated thus:

> 'Gambling, eating meat, wine-bibbing, adultery, hunting, thieving, debauchery—these seven things in this world lead to the worst of hells.'

ii. Vrata pratimā.

He next promises to keep each of the twelve vows (*Vrata*); and when death comes, to receive it in absolute peace, and that he will perform Santhāro. (This, the perfect death, is called Samādhi Maraṇa.)

iii. Sāmāyika pratimā.

He goes on to vow that he will engage in *Sāmāyika* at least three times every day.

iv. Poṣadhopavāsa pratimā.

He also vows that he will observe *Poṣadha* at least six times a month (i.e. on the two eighth and the two fourteenth days of the moon, and also on the full-moon night and one dark night).

v. Saċittaparihāra pratimā.

Again, with the object of never even taking vegetable life, the layman promises (*Saċittaparihāra pratimā*) to avoid all uncooked vegetables, or cooked vegetables mixed with uncooked, never to break a mango from a tree, and only to eat it if some one else has taken out the stone.

vi. Niśibhojanatyāga pratimā.

Lest in the darkness he might unwittingly devour some insect he promises (*Niśibhojanatyāga pratimā*) never to eat between sunset and sunrise, or to sip water before daylight. If a guest arrives during the night, the layman may prepare a bed for him, but never offer him food, lest he cause his guest to sin.

vii. Brahmaćarya pratimā.

Getting nearer to the ascetic ideal, the layman next promises (*Brahmaćarya pratimā*) to keep away from the society of his own wife, and never in any way to scent or adorn his body, lest he should cause his wife to love him.

viii. Ārambhatyāga pratimā.

As the layman is now steadily mounting the steps, he must be very careful never to begin anything that might entangle him in such worldly pursuits as involve the destruction of life. So he undertakes (*Ārambhatyāga pratimā*) never even to begin to build a house or take up a trade (like a blacksmith's) which entails the taking of life.

ix. Parigrahatyāga pratimā.

He must also use his remaining days in the world as a sort of novitiate; and first he must be careful not to have any attachment for his worldly possessions (*Parigrahatyāga pratimā*), and to avoid it he should divide his property, for instance money or grain, amongst his children, or give it away in charity. He must also prepare for the hardships he will have to face by never allowing his servants (if he has any) to work for him, but should always wait on himself and only allow the servants to wait on his children. Having made this resolution, he should endeavour in every way to lead a quiet unambitious life.

x. Anumatityāga pratimā.

The next resolution (*Anumatityāga pratimā*[1]) shows a further step taken towards a sādhu's life, for the erstwhile layman promises to keep the sādhu rule of never allowing any special cooking to be done for him, and only to take what is over when others have dined, and, if none remains, just to fast. He also vows that he will never give advice

[1] Or, according to the Digambara Jaina, *Anumodanavrata pratimā*.

in any worldly or household matter, but will keep his mind free from all thoughts about such things.

xi. Uddhiṣṭa pratimā.

When he has taken the last (*Uddhiṣṭa* or *Śramaṇabhūta*) pratimā, he is practically a monk, for he has promised to wear a sādhu's dress, to remain apart in some religious building (when the Digambara call him a Kṣullaka Śrāvaka) or in the jungle (when they name him an Ailaka Śrāvaka), and to act according to the rules laid down in the scriptures for sādhus to follow.

The twenty-one qualities of the ideal gentleman.

As a layman endeavours to attain to this exalted stage, he will strive to develop those twenty-one qualities which distinguish the Jaina gentleman. He will always be serious in demeanour; clean as regards both his clothes and his person; good-tempered; striving after popularity; merciful; afraid of sinning; straightforward; wise; modest; kind; moderate; gentle; careful in speech; sociable; cautious; studious; reverent both to old age and old customs; humble; grateful; benevolent; and, finally, attentive to business.

Only the very best of men ever possess the full complement of the whole twenty-one virtues, but ordinary mortals strive to possess at least ten.

CHAPTER XI

THE JAINA ASCETIC

THE layman has now reached the summit of his ambition, and is prepared to take those five celebrated vows which Mahāvīra himself laid down as the only entrance through which a man can pass to the ascetic state.

As one reads the biographies of the great Jaina saints, or even studies the lengthy route we have just been following, one can see that, though the Jaina did not insist on their candidates taking a long training like that of the Vedic schools, they nevertheless did not intend their monks to be the ignorant, ill-prepared and undisciplined men they often are at present. The Jaina openly wish that they could insist on a thorough preparation for their sādhus such as is customary for the Christian ministry.

The Life Story of an Ascetic.

The life story of an ascetic may be said to begin with his initiation or *Dīkṣā*, and the writer is indebted to a Śvetāmbara monk for the following account of a Jaina call and ordination. Initiation.

The man in question had heard a famous sādhu preach on the transitoriness of life and happiness and the superiority of the religious over the lay life, and had thereupon followed the preacher for a year as his disciple, and at the completion of twelve months received initiation.

A great procession was formed and he was led through the town to a banyan tree (an aśoka tree would also have served). There a pujārī (officiating priest) had arranged a small three-tiered platform with an image of one of the Tīrthaṅkara at the top. A Jaina layman began the proceedings by performing the ordinary daily worship, and then the candidate took off his jewels and his clothes, and giving them away to his relatives, put on a sādhu's dress.

An ascetic can only retain five garments (three upper and two lower ones), the colours of which vary according to his sect, a Śvetāmbara wearing yellow, or white with yellow over it, and a Sthānakavāsī white. A Digambara ascetic, however, may wear no clothing at all, and such are accordingly to be found only in jungles or desert places outside British states. In Bhopāl my informant met a man claiming to be a Digambara sādhu, but because he wore a loin-cloth, the laymen of his community refused to recognize him as such, and drove him away.

The next step in the initiation is the removal of the hair. A peculiarity of the Jaina cult is that they insist on ascetics tearing the hair out by the roots at least once a year; but when at his initiation a man's hair is removed for the first time, the merciful method of shaving is resorted to, and only a few hairs are left to be pulled out; these are plucked off behind a curtain in private. After this a mixture called Vāsakṣepa is applied to the man's head, and this is the crucial point in the initiation, for until this is applied he is not a sādhu. Whilst the mixture is being put on, a sādhu whispers a sacred mantra in his ear. The newly made sādhu then performs the morning worship, and devout laymen feast the ascetics who are present.

If the ascetic were a Digambara, he would take an entirely new name; if a Śvetāmbara, he might either change his name or add a new one to his old one; but a Sthānakavāsī retains his original name intact.

He is now to be a homeless wanderer, possessing nothing and dependent for his very subsistence on the alms of the charitable. He may possess no metal of any sort: even a needle, if borrowed, must be returned at sunset, and his spectacles, if he wear them, should be framed in wood. A man was once pointed out to the writer at Pālitāṇā as a sādhu who, however, was wearing gold-rimmed spectacles; and when she asked for an explanation, the bystanders all turned and jeered at the discomfited ascetic, declaring, much to his chagrin, that since he had infringed this law, he had no claim to be accounted a monk at all. Constant evasions of the rules against non-possession, however, do take place, to the grcat indignation of the laity, some monks, as we have seen, even retaining their property on their persons in the shape of bank-notes, thus keeping the letter and breaking the spirit of the law.

The ascetic may have some pieces of cloth to strain away any insects from the water he will drink, and also some wooden jugs or somc gourds in which to keep his drinking-water, but no brass vessels. All monks also possess a piece of cloth to wear over their mouths, not, as has been usually thought, to prevent them injuring the minute insects in the air, but to guard against hurting the air itself.[1] The less strict Śvetāmbara only keep this mouth-cloth in their hands, but the Sthānakavāsī always wear it night and day; and the writer found that it always pleased ascetics if she covered her lips with a handkcrchief when speaking with them or when in the presence of any of their sacred objects.

Every Śvetāmbara monk also carries with him five shells; these must be spiral and must turn to the right; shells turning to the left are useless. The shells are consecrated at the time of the Divālī festival.

All ascetics have to guard most scrupulously against the taking of any insect life, so all three sects furnish their monks with something with which they may sweep insects from their path. Amongst the Sthānakavāsī, who are the most punctilious of all the Jaina, the monks have a long-handled brush; the Śvetāmbara ascetics use a smaller brush; and the Digambara a peacock's feather.

We shall later study the five great vows that guide an

[1] See p. 100.

ascetic, and we have already learnt something of his philosophy and his belief in austerity, but it may be of interest here to record the actual daily life of a Śvetāmbara ascetic, as one of their number described it to the writer.

Daily duties.

They are supposed to rise about four o'clock, summer and winter, and perform *Rāyasī Paḍīkamaṇuṁ*, in which in a set form of Māgadhī words each monk confesses the sins of the past night, and especially the taking of any life and any injury he may have inflicted on any sacred thing, or any of the earth, water, fire, air, or vegetable bodies. It is at this time that the laity perform their meditation or sāmāyika, but in many of the Śvetāmbara sects a sādhu performs sāmāyika at the time of his initiation and never again.

After paḍīkamaṇuṁ he engages in a search for any insect life that may be sheltering in his clothing. This search, which is called *Palevaṇa*, is carried out as a religious duty, and any insect found is carefully removed to a place of safety.

The sādhu neither bathes nor cleanses his teeth; he does these things before his initiation for the last time in his life, but now, without waiting for either, he leaves the monastery and goes to the temple to perform *Darśana*. Unlike a layman, he dons no special clothes at the temple gates, but worships in his ordinary ones. When he enters the temple, he stands in front of the idol and bows down to it, and then performs a mental exercise known as *Bhāva pūjā*, during which he meditates on the undoing of karma, the qualities of a Tīrthaṅkara, and similar subjects. He now performs *Pradakṣiṇā*, circumambulating the shrine either four or seven times. If he do it four times, he meditates on the four gati, namely, whether he will be born as a god, a man, an animal, or a denizen of hell; if he walks round seven times, he thinks how he can best escape dwelling in any of the seven hells.

An ascetic can neither cleanse the idol (*jaḷa pūjā*), nor

mark it with saffron (*ċandana pūjā*), nor offer flowers (*puṣpa pūjā*), nor wave incense before it (*dhūpa pūjā*), nor wave a lamp (*dīpa pūjā*), nor offer rice (*akṣata pūjā*), nor sweetmeats (*naivedya pūjā*), nor fruit (*phaḷa pūjā*); neither can he mark his own forehead, as a layman would, with a *ċāndalo* (auspicious mark); but his worship seems to be almost entirely mental and 'interior', and sometimes includes acts of worship known as *Khamāsamaṇa*, *Ċaitya-vandana* and *Jāvantiċayāṇaṁ*. He also usually sings some hymn in praise of the qualities of the Arihanta, and then joining his hands repeats a mantra. After meditating in a particular posture (*Kāusagga*), he tells his beads, making salutations to 'the Five' (*Arihanta, Siddha, Āċārya, Upādhyāya* and *Sādhu*), and to Knowledge, Faith, Character and Austerity. When he has done this and said the *Āvasahī*, which allows him to enter his worldly affairs again, he feels that Bhāva pūjā is complete; with its different parts and their variations it generally lasts about an hour.

After completing his Bhāva pūjā the ascetic goes back to the monastery and either preaches or reads one of the scriptures.

Begging. About ten o'clock in the morning one of the monks goes out on a begging round; as a rule one begs for the whole monastery, whilst the other monks study. Curiously enough the English fashion of tea-drinking has spread so much in India that even monks now indulge in an early cup of tea; and the writer's informant told her that he used not to wait till ten o'clock, but about an hour after sunrise he always went on a preliminary round, and, begging tea and milk for his guru and the other monks, took it back to the monastery. According to their scriptures, ascetics are only supposed to beg once a day, but as a matter of fact they often do so three or four times a day. When the monk goes out at ten, he expects to receive gifts of rice and split peas, bread, vegetables, curry, sweets, and dudhapāka (a kind of milk pudding).

There are innumerable rules that should be observed when begging, with regard to which all the seets and sub-sects differ. A yellow-robed Śvetāmbara sādhu will only accept food from Jaina, and would refuse alms from Brāhmans, Kṣatriya, and even from Vaiṣṇava and Mcsarī Baniyā; on the other hand, thc white-clad Śvetāmbara sādhu will take food from Brāhmans and Kṣatriya, and in Mārwār they will even accept it from a Hajāma (barber), with whom a high-caste Hindu will not eat.

My informant told me that he was most careful to go only to houses in which the door was standing open, and that he always repeated the formula: Dharma Lābha. He was not nearly as particular as thc Sthānakavāsī about the boiled water he took: for whereas they would only aeeept water which has beer. boiled not more than four hours previously, lest new life should have been formed in it, this Śvetāmbara sādhu told the writer that he generally begged enough boiled water in the morning to last the whole day, and that it was only in the rainy season he was particular to keep the water for a shorter time. They are very particular, however, not to take vegetable life; and if on the steps of a house they see a green leaf or a vegetable lying they refuse to pass ovcr it, turn aside and go to another house. In the same way, if they see the woman of the house cleaning rice or wheat, they will not take it, but will only accept ricc or grain cleaned before they came on the scene. If a mother is nursing her baby and offers to leave it to go and get food for them, thcy refuse, lest they should be guilty of making the child cry.

All sects agree in only taking what they may reasonably consider to be food left over after the necds of the household have been satisfied; none will take things specially prepared for them. They never sit in a layman's house, but take the gift back to the monastery, and after showing it to the Head, divide it with the other monks. They will not receive food if it is taken specially to the monastery for them; but a Śvetāmbara will accept an invitation to go and fetch food from a layman's house, a thing which a Sthānakavāsī will never do.

With regard to clothes, the rule is the same: the monk may not ask for clothes, may not accept them if taken to the monastery specially for him, and may only receive them if the householder, as he gives them, explains that he has no longer any need of them.

These rules were clearly drawn up to prevent the order becoming too great a tax on the charitable; but, despite all this care, the numberless 'holy men' in India are a most unfair burden on the earnings of the industrious.

Confession. The begging round is finished about eleven, but before breakfasting the ascetic makes auricular confession (*Āloyaṇā*) to his guru and has a penance appointed.

The monks breakfast as near eleven as possible, for they may not warm up the food, and so eat it as quickly as they can.

Kāḷa. From twelve to one they may not study; this hour is called Kāḷa, and to study during it would be a sin.

Study. From one to three they ought to study, and the laity are so anxious that they shall, that devout Jaina often pay a paṇḍit to instruct the monks in Sanskrit or Māgadhī, but they complain most bitterly of the monks' aversion to intellectual labour.

In the early afternoon, from about three to four, they again perform palevaṇa, searching their clothing for insects.

About half-past four they go out to beg, and after coming in, make confession just as they did in the morning. They dine from five to six on their gleanings from the charitable, generally, as at breakfast, on rice and peas, bread, vegetables, curry and sweets; this meal they must finish before sunset, and during the night they may not even drink water.

They may not leave the monastery after dark, but they perform their evening Paḍikamaṇuṁ there for about an hour. As no light can be brought into the monastery, their day closes about nine o'clock, when they perform Santhārā Porasī, spending about an hour asking the protection of Arihanta, Siddha, Kevalī, and Sādhu.

Nuns.

Female ascetics (sādhvī) are held in the greatest reverence by the Jaina, and their lives follow much the same lines as those of the male ascetics. They always wander about in twos or threes and have of course their own Apāsarā. At their initiation their hair is shaved and pulled out just like a monk's, and the mantra is whispered to them by a sādhvī instead of a sādhu.

They choose the head of their Apāsaro generally for learning; if she be strong enough, she wanders homeless just like the other nuns, but if old and feeble, she is allowed to continue to live in the same nunnery without change.

A nun's day much resembles that of a monk. The stricter ones will only beg once, eat once, and sleep for a few hours in the twenty-four; but these more rigid rules are falling into abeyance, and the nuns the writer has met confess that they do not now rise as they should after a few hours sleep to meditate twice in the night.

The funeral of a nun [1] is carried out with the greatest pomp, and during it childless women strive to tear a piece from the dead sādhvī's dress, believing it will ensure their having children, whilst men anxiously endeavour to acquire merit by carrying the palanquin in which the corpse, covered with a rich cloth, is borne, boys from the Jaina school acting as a guard of honour.

In all the neighbouring towns also, directly the telegram announcing the nun's death is received, a crier would be sent out to tell the news and to ask the Jaina to observe *Amāra*, i. e. not to grind or pound grain or do anything

[1] A full description of a nun's funeral is given in the writer's *Notes on Modern Jainism*, Blackwell, 1910, pp. 28 ff.

that might involve the destruction of life. All the Jaina who know the *Logassa*, or praise of the twenty-four Tīrthaṅkara, would repeat it four times, sitting in the Kāusagga position, either in their own houses or in the Apāsarā, and all the Jaina schools would be closed.

A pathetic case recently occurred in Kāṭhiāwāḍ, when a wealthy old Jaina lady and her husband became ascetics. Their initiation was celebrated with great pomp; but of course the lady suffered most severely by being suddenly deprived of all luxury and comfort; and even when she was ill with fever, it was not possible for her husband to see her, as the two might never meet.

Gorajī.

Amongst the sādhus we have not included the Gorajī or Yati, because the orthodox Jaina do not hold them to be sādhus at all. They are considered to be a fallen class of monks, for they take money, go about in palanquins, and keep watchmen and guards. They exact a tax from their followers of five rupees and upwards, which they annually go out to collect, returning again to their own monastery. Their spiritual heads are called Śrīpūjya, and are to be found in Bombay, Baroda, Māndvī, Māngrol, Jaisalmer, and many other towns. The Gorajī, in fact, much resemble the Śaṅkarāċārya or Vaiṣṇava Āċārya; and orthodox Jaina say they prove the wisdom of Mahāvīra's insistence on constant change of abode, for they have not a high reputation for morality, and strict Jaina will not give them any money or go to their Apāsarā, though ignorant Jaina sometimes contribute through fear of their power to harm, since the Gorajī claim to know many mantra.

The Five Great Vows of Ascetics.

We may now examine the famous five vows taken by all ascetics. They resemble the first five of the layman's twelve vows, and this accordance bears witness to the fact that these are the five points in the Jaina religion which are to be regarded as of supreme importance.

i. Ahiṁsā. The first vow the Jaina monk takes is that he will never destroy any living thing. This is also the first vow that both Buddhist and Brāhman monks take, and it was the resemblance between the vows that led people for so long to deny the early origin of Jainism.[1]

The Jaina ascetic takes a vow of Non-killing (*Ahiṁsā*), which is described as follows :

'Not to destroy life, either five-, four-, three-, or two-sensed, or immovable (i.e. one-sensed), even through carelessness, is considered as keeping the vow of non-killing.'[2]

There are five buttressing clauses (*Pañca Bhāvanā*), the remembrance of which assists a sādhu to keep this vow. First (*Īryā samiti* or *samai*), a monk must be careful never to run the risk of breaking the vow in walking: for instance he must walk by trodden paths, in which the presence of any insect could be detected. He must also (*Bhāṣā samiti* or *Vatiṁ parijāṇāi*), be watchful in his speech and always speak in gentle, kindly ways, such as could never give rise to quarrels or murders. If he were not careful as to the alms he received (*Eṣaṇā samiti* or *Āloi pāṇa bhoyaṇa*), he might infringe some of the forty-two rules as to receiving alms, e.g. by accepting food containing living insects. When a monk receives or keeps anything that is necessary for religious duties, he must see (*Ādānanikṣepaṇā samiti*

[1] The whole question has been authoritatively discussed by Dr. Jacobi, *S. B. E.*, xxii, pp. xix ff.

[2] The words resemble those of the layman's vows with the addition of 'Ekendriya'.

or *Āyāṇabhaṇḍa nikhevaṇā*), that it has no insect life on it. And at night, when putting away all that remains over from the food he has begged, he must deposit it and any other refuse so carefully, that no insect life is injured (*Pratisthāpanā samiti* or *Parithāpaṇikā samai*).[1]

The following śloka sums up these five clauses:

'A man should respect the vow of Ahiṁsā by exercising self-control, examining things taken, always maintaining the Five Samiti, and by inspecting things before he eats or drinks, and before he receives them.'

The Jaina monk further takes a vow against untruthfulness (*Asatya tyāga*) which is defined in the following words: ii. Asatya tyāga.

'Undertaking to speak what is pleasant, wholesome and true is called the vow of truthfulness. Truth is untruth if it is not pleasant and wholesome.'

The five bhāvanā, or strengthening clauses, to this vow supply a remarkable psychological analysis of the causes which lead to untruthfulness. The first (*Aṇubīmabhāsī*) condemns speech without deliberation; then, as wrath often leads to falsehood, monks must never speak when angry (*Kohaṁ parijāṇāi*); nor for a similar reason when moved by avarice (*Lohaṁ parijāṇāi*); nor by fear (*Bhayaṁ parijāṇāi*); finally, they promise never to tell a falsehood for fun, or from the desire to return a smart repartee (*Hāsaṁ parijāṇāi*).

A Sanskrit śloka which sums up these clauses may be translated as follows:

'One should respect the vow of truthfulness by always avoiding jesting, greed, cowardice and anger, and by thinking before speaking.'

The third vow, that of non-stealing (*Asteya vrata*), is defined as follows: iii. Asteya vrata.

'The vow of non-stealing consists in not taking what is not given; wealth is the outward life of man, and if that is taken away the man is undone.'

[1] Some Jaina substitute for this the duty of searching mind, thought and intention (*Manaparijāṇāi*).

The five bhāvanā are as follows: First, a monk must ask permission of the owner before he occupy any one's house (*Miugāha jāti*). Then a junior monk must never use any food without showing what he has received in alms to his guru, and receiving his permission to eat it (*Aṇuṇa vihapāṇa bhoyaṇe*). Again, a monk must not be content to ask permission only once from the owner to use a house, but he must frequently ask if he may occupy it, and also ask how much of it he may use, and for how long a time (*Uggahaṁ siuggāhitaṁsī*). He must not use any furniture, such as beds or seats, that may be in the house, without the owner's permission (*Uggahaṁ vauggahiṁsa abhīkhaṇaṁ*). Lastly, if a sādhu arrives after another sādhu has already obtained permission to use the house, the second arrival must ask the first sādhu to go again and get permission for him also; and if the second sādhu arrives ill, the first must willingly give him all the room he needs (*Aṇuvīi mitoggaha jāti*).

The following śloka describes these clauses:

> 'One should ask for a place of residence after reflection, and renew the request every day: "I only need so much of it." Thus speaking, one should renew his petition. With people of one's own rank one should ask in the same way. One should gain permission before eating or drinking. In these ways the vow of non-stealing is respected.'

iv. Brahmaćarya vrata.

The monks, as their fourth promise, take the vow of chastity (*Brahmaćarya*), and the Sthānakavāsī monks in Kaṭhiāwāḍ every night and morning repeat the following words:

> 'The vow of chastity is eighteen-fold. One should have no dealings with gods, human beings or animals of the opposite sex, should not encourage them, or cause others to do so, by speech, thought or deed.'

This vow also has its five strengthening or protective clauses. To prevent any approach to transgressions of the main vow, monks should not talk about a woman (*Abhikhaṇaṁ itthīṇaṁ kahaṁ kaha itame*); or look at the form of a woman (*Maṇoharāi indiyāi āloetae*); or even recall the former amusement and pleasure women afforded them when they lived in the world (*Itthīṇaṁ puvārayāiṁ puvakiliyāi sumaritae*); they must not, for similar reasons, eat or drink[1] to excess, or partake of too highly spiced dishes (*Ṇātimapāṇa bhoyaṇa bhoi*); nor must they live in the same building as a woman, a female animal, or a eunuch (*Itthī pasu paṇḍaga saṁsatāi sayaṇā saṇāiṁ sevitāe*).

All these rules *mutatis mutandis* apply to nuns.

The śloka that sums up the whole vow and its clauses runs thus:

> 'The vow of chastity is maintained by not sitting on seats previously occupied by women, female animals or eunuchs, and by not living in their vicinity, not participating in exciting conversation about women, not remembering former delights, not looking at a woman's form, not decorating one's own person, not eating or drinking to excess, or partaking of too highly seasoned food.'

This Jaina vow seems limited to negative chastity, which shudderingly avoids its fellow creatures, lest they should prove occasions of stumbling, and it appears ignorant of the sunlit purity that so delights in its walk with God on the open road of life, that it cannot be bored with nastiness.

v. Aparigraha vrata.

The last great vow (*Aparigraha vrata*) consists in renouncing all love for anything or any person. The definition of it may be translated as follows:

> 'Having no possessions consists in relinquishing greed for anything; if we think that a particular thing is our own, the mind is agitated by greed.'

In the Jaina scriptures the vow is held to exclude all likes and dislikes in regard to sounds, colours, or smells, as well as people. In short, the way to maintain this vow is to be indifferent to anything our senses can tell us.

This fifth vow of the monk foreshadows what the condition of the Siddha will be, when all his powers are entirely shrivelled up.

[1] It will be remembered that no Jaina, lay or ascetic, may ever drink wine.

The following śloka tells how the vow is kept:

'Renouncing liking for pleasant touch, taste, smell, form,[1] or word,[2] and for all the objects of the five senses, renouncing hatred for unpleasant objects, these are the ways to maintain the vow of Aparigraha.'

Rātribhojana tyāga.

Certain Śvetāmbara add a sixth vow, that of never dining after it is dark (*Rātribhojana tyāga*), lest they should inadvertently take life, but most Jaina consider this included under the other vows that protect insect life.

Twenty-seven Qualities of the Ideal Monk.

We have seen that the Jaina have a conception of the ideal layman; and in the same way they also show us the picture of a perfect monk, summed up in a Māgadhī śloka:

'The true ascetic should possess twenty-seven qualities, for he must keep the five vows, never eat at night, protect all living things,[3] control his five senses, renounce greed, practise forgiveness, possess high ideals, and inspect everything he uses to make sure that no insect life is injured. He must also be self-denying and carefully keep the three gupti, he must endure hardships in the twenty-two ways, and bear suffering till death.'

[1] i.e. beauty.
[2] i.e. literature and oratory.
[3] Of the six classes.

CHAPTER XII

THE END OF THE ROAD

Pañča Parameśvara.

We have traced the journey of a jīva along the upward path that leads through the destruction of karma, by way of the fourteen upward steps and the keeping of the twelve vows and the eleven Pratimā, to monkhood. It only remains to us to note the different ranks a man may hold as an ascetic before he finally attains mokṣa.

Sādhu.

First, he is just an ordinary ascetic or sādhu; if he be a Digambara, he will wear no clothes and live in the forest, lost to the world and immersed in meditation, eating only once a day and tearing out his hair as it grows. Nowadays one hears of only two or three Digambara ascetics. If he be a Śvetāmbara[1] or a Sthānakavāsī,[2] he will move from Apāsaro to Apāsaro clad in white clothes.

Upādhyāya.

The next step to which he can rise is that of Upādhāya or instructor. An exceptionally clever monk may be chosen from amongst the others as teacher, when he is expected to study the scriptures and teach them to his fellow monks. Amongst the Tapagaččha no monk can be chosen as an Upādhyāya till he has been an ascetic for at least a year, but this does not seem to be always the rule with other sects. The scriptures he will most probably teach are the Uttarādhyayana Sūtra, the Upāsaka Daśāṅga Sūtra, and the Bhagavatī Sūtra. The last, the Bhagavatī Sūtra, holds almost the same position amongst many Jaina that Hindus give to the Bhagavadgītā or Christians to the Gospels.

[1] Unless he be a follower of either Ātmārāmajī or Āṇandavijayajī, when he will wear yellow clothes.

[2] The followers of Śrīlālajī, however, who are found mainly in Mālwā, never live in an Apāsaro lest they should be held guilty of the lives destroyed in building it.

These scriptures most Jaina laymen are familiar with, but the instructor should, according to some Jaina, have also studied the scriptures the laymen have not read, namely, the eleven Aṅga and the twelve Upāṅga or the Ċaraṇaśitarī[1] and the Karaṇaśitarī[2], or, according to others, the eleven Aṅga and the fourteen Pūrva. All teaching and studying is a kind of austerity; if a man studies intentionally to gain merit, he will get merit (*puṇya*); if, however, he studies and teaches to gain and impart knowledge with no thought of acquiring merit, he will destroy certain karma (*nirjarā*).

Āċārya. A still higher rank is attained when a monk becomes an Āċārya or Superior. In many sects the Āċārya is chosen simply by seniority (this is nearly always the case in Kāṭhiāwāḍ), but in others the Āċārya is selected for ability, or powers of leadership, as is generally done in Mālwā.

The choosing of a new Superior or Āċārya is made the occasion of great rejoicing. Jaina laymen come to the Apāsaro, take the twelve vows or renew them, and sing songs and make the greatest noise imaginable. In order to permit of animals sharing in their rejoicing, they pay butchers varying sums to cease killing for those days. An Āċārya is a man of very high dignity: he never travels alone, but is always accompanied by at least two sādhus; and as his fame grows, the number of his disciples increases. When the writer, for instance, had the pleasure in Rājkot of meeting Śivalālajī Mahārāja (who is considered the most learned Sthānakavāsī āċārya of the present time), he had travelled thither with twenty-one attendant sādhus.

The power of excommunication for religious offences lies with the Āċārya[3] acting with the Jaina community or saṅgha, and it is to the Āċārya that, whenever possible, the monks of his saṅgha should make confession. As a rule the Āċārya wears the same dress, eats the same food, and

[1] Or *Ċaraṇānuyoga*. [2] Or *Karaṇānuyoga*.

[3] The Āċārya, acting with the community, excommunicates for religious offences; but for offences against society the Mahājana (committee of leading Baniyā) excommunicates.

follows the same rule as his fellow monks; sometimes, however, his little sitting-board is raised slightly higher from the ground than those of the other monks.

It must not be thought that the ordinary sādhu must gain the rank of Instructor and Superior to go to mokṣa, a simple ascetic can do that; but it is generally easier for the higher ranks of ascetics to attain deliverance than for the lower, because their office helps them to develop the necessary qualities. An Āċārya should, of course, observe with special attention all the usual ascetic discipline.

A Māgadhī śloka describes the ideal Āċārya as possessing thirty-six qualities: he controls the five senses; he is chaste in the nine ways; he keeps the three gupti; he is free from the four kaṣāya; he keeps the five great vows; he observes the five rules of conduct; and he maintains the five samiti: such are the thirty-six qualities of an Āċārya.

Tīrthaṅkara or Arihanta.

The goal of every monk is to become at last an Arihanta or Tīrthaṅkara, the Being who has attained perfection of knowledge, perfection of speech, perfection of worship, and absolute security, for no danger or disease can ever come where he is. Having become a Tīrthaṅkara, the jīva is at length freed from the dread that overshadows every Jaina, the fear in this life of suffering or sorrow, which has to be borne with no Friend at hand to strengthen and comfort, and the dreary expectation after death of the endless cycle of rebirth.

A meaning often given to the word Tīrthaṅkara is that of one who finds a ford (*tīrtha*) through this world (*saṁsāra*) to mokṣa, or one who attains a landing on the other side. But many Jaina say it denotes one who forms four communities (*tīrtha*) of monks and nuns and male and female lay-followers. When a new Tīrthaṅkara arises, the followers of the preceding one follow him, as the followers of Pārśvanātha followed Mahāvīra.

We have noticed[1] the eight glories which surround a

[1] p. 191.

Tīrthaṅkara when he preaches; besides these, the Jaina assign to him an enormous list of attributes. A Tīrthaṅkara, for example, is worshipped by the sixty-four Indra, and has thirty-five special qualities of speech, and thirty-four pertaining to his body, which is distinguished by one thousand and eight specified marks. We shall probably, however, gain a better idea of the Jaina's real conception of a Tīrthaṅkara, not by working through this long bare list of qualities, but by studying one of their prayers of adoration —that surest mirror of a man's mental picture of his god. The writer's Sthānakavāsī friends tell her that every morning and evening during Paḍīkamaṇuṁ they worship the Tīrthaṅkara in Gujarātī words which may be rendered as follows:

'You I salute at various times, the Lord Arihanta. What kind of a Lord is He? He knows what is passing in your mind and my mind. He knows what is passing in the mind of every man. He knows what is going on at various times. He sees all the fourteen worlds as though they were in his hands. He is endowed with these six qualities: boundless knowledge, insight, righteousness, austerity, patience, strength. He is endowed with thirty-four kinds of uncommon qualities. He is endowed with speech. He is endowed with thirty-five kinds of truthful speech. He has one thousand and eight auspicious marks. He is free from the eighteen sins and endowed with the twelve good qualities. He has destroyed four of the hardest karma, and the four remaining karma are powerless. He is longing to get mokṣa. He dispels the doubts of souls [1] with yoga. He is endowed with body, with omniscience, with perfect insight, and has the before-mentioned righteousness. He has the highest kind of saṅkita, which is permanent; he has Śuklaleśyā, Śukladhyāna, Śuklayoga; he is worshipped, adored and saluted by the sixty-four Indra. He is the most learned paṇḍit. He is endowed with these and other endless qualities.'

Siddha. We have seen that a Tīrthaṅkara has still four karma left which bind him, and until these four do actually snap, the jīva which began its upward journey, perhaps from a clod of earth, has not yet reached its final goal. When by

[1] i. e. *Bhavya jīva*, those souls who will eventually obtain mokṣa.

austerities these last karma are destroyed and break 'like a piece of burnt-up string', the soul loses its body and becomes a Siddha.

The Siddha has the following characteristics: absolute knowledge, faith, insight, righteousness, and prowess. He also has the power of becoming minute and gigantic at will, and of moving anywhere unhindered; he is unaffected by anything, so that neither death, disease, rebirth, nor sorrow can any longer touch him. He is also without a body; and this is the reason why Jaina feel they can never pray to a Siddha. A Siddha has, however, one hundred and eight attributes, and these the Jaina recite, telling their rosary of one hundred and eight beads. An ordinary Jaina tells his beads five times a day, but a very devout Jaina might tell the one hundred and eight beads one hundred and eight times a day. The Jaina say they do not worship or salute the Siddha when doing this, but tell their beads only with the object of stirring up their spiritual ambition and in order to remind themselves of the qualities a Siddha must possess, in the hope that some day they too may reach their desired goal, and rest in perfect bliss in the state of Nirvāṇa, doing nothing for ever and ever.

Thirty-five Rules of Conduct.

How even non-Jaina may reach Mokṣa.

One of the unique glories of Jainism is that it, unlike most Indian-born religions, believes in the possibility of aliens reaching its goal. Even Europeans and Americans,[1] although they may never have heard of Jainism, if they follow, though unconsciously, the thirty-five rules of conduct, of necessity destroy their karma and so are sped to mokṣa like an arrow from a bow.

It will therefore be well worth our while to study these

[1] Quite uncivilized races might reach mokṣa, but it would be easier for Europeans and other civilized people, provided they were vegetarians, to do so.

rules, for they contain the pith of the Jaina creed expressed in terms of conduct. The thirty-five rules are contained in ten Sanskrit śloka which describe the true Jaina, and which might be rendered thus:

1. He who gains his livelihood by honesty, and admires and follows excellence of conduct, and marries his sons and daughters to well-born and well-behaved folk.

2. He is known to be afraid of committing sins, he follows the customs of his country, never speaks evil of any man and especially not of his ruler.

3. He lives in neither too secluded nor too open a residence. It must be situated in a good locality and have good neighbours. The house must not have too many entrances.

4. He always associates with good men, worships his parents, and abandons an unprotected place of evil reputation.

5. He regulates his expenditure according to his income,[1] dresses according to his position, and being endowed with eight kinds of intelligence hears religious discourses every day.

6. If he suffers from indigestion, he does not eat. He eats only at fixed times. He should gain his three objects[2] in such a way that one does not interfere with the other.

7. He gives alms to him who comes unexpectedly, to the sādhu and to the poor, is free from obstinacy and has a partiality for good qualities.

8. Knowing his own strength and weakness, he avoids such actions as are not suited to the time and country [in which he lives]. He worships persons who are rigid in keeping their vows and far advanced in knowledge, and he feeds those who deserve feeding.

9. He is provident, has more than ordinary knowledge, is grateful for what is done for him, is loved by people, is modest, merciful, of a serene disposition and benevolent.

[1] The old Jaina rule with regard to the regulation of income was to divide it into four equal parts, of which they set one part aside as savings, invested another part in trade, paid all their household expenses with the third portion, and devoted the remaining quarter to charity. The rule is not strictly followed now, but it is still usual to divide the income up and apportion it, though not giving so largely to charity as in the old days.

[2] Every Indian, Jaina included, has four great objects in his life: dharma, artha, kāma, mokṣa (religion, wealth, pleasure and mokṣa). A devout Jaina householder is only supposed to give attention to the first three, for if he acquit himself well in gaining these, the last will follow naturally.

10. He is always intent on defeating the six interior enemies[1] and controls all his five senses. Such are the suggestions of a householder's duties.

The Three Jewels (*Ratna Traya*).

The Jaina sum up all their belief, as expressed in the Tattva, in their vows, and in their rules of conduct, under the heading of the Three Jewels: Right Knowledge (*Samyak Jñāna*), Right Faith (*Samyak Darśana*), Right Conduct (*Samyak Čāritrya*).

Right Knowledge.

The Sanskrit śloka that defines Right Knowledge runs:

> 'Wise men call that knowledge Right Knowledge which one gets, whether concisely or in detailed form, from the Tattva as they exist.'

Right Knowledge is in fact knowledge of the Jaina creed; and this jewel must be gained before any other can be obtained, for only when Right Knowledge is possessed can a man know what virtue is, and what vows he ought to keep. Mahāvīra himself said: 'First knowledge and then mercy', for unless a man know what a jīva is, how can he show mercy to it?

Right Faith.

Central among the Three Jewels is Right Faith; for unless one believes in what one knows, how will one follow it? Samyak Darśana stands for true faith and insight into the great Jaina doctrines and scriptures. The Jaina say that it is like the digit 1, which, standing before the ciphers that follow it, gives them value, for without faith all conduct is worthless.

> 'To hold the truth as truth, and untruth as untruth, this is true faith.'

Right Conduct.

The Jaina say that there may be Right Knowledge and Right Faith, but if these are not accompanied by Right Conduct all are worthless. To the monk Right Conduct

[1] Both Hindus and Jaina believe that there are six interior enemies: passion (*kāma*), anger (*krodha*), greed (*lobha*), pride (*māna*), excessive exultation (*harṣa*) and envy (*matsara*).

means the absolute keeping of the five great vows. His conduct, as we have seen, should be perfect, or Sarva-ćāritrya, for he must follow the conduct laid down for him in every particular; but the layman is only expected to possess Deśaćāritrya (partial conduct), for, so long as he is not a professed monk, he cannot be absolutely perfect in conduct.

Three Śalya that injure Ćāritrya.

Right Conduct, however, can be ruined by three evil darts, or śalya. The first of these is intrigue or fraud (*Māyā śalya*), since no one can gain a good character whose life, social or religious, is governed by deceit. Even in such holy matters as fasting, intrigue can make itself felt.

A second poisonous dart is false belief or *Mithyātva śalya*, which consists in holding a false god to be a true one, a false guru to be a true guru, and a false religion to be a true religion; by so doing one absolutely injures Right Knowledge and Right Faith which lead to Right Conduct; this is therefore a highly poisonous dart. The great evil wrong belief does shows how supremely important it is for men to know who is the true Tīrthaṅkara, and the definition, which the Jaina repeat every day at their devotions, runs as follows:

'He who is omniscient, free from all love of the world and from all failings; he who is worshipped by the three worlds and who explains the inner meaning [of religion] as it exists: this adorable deity is the great god.'[1]

The Jaina similarly define a false god:

'Those gods who retain women, weapons and rosaries, who are steeped in attachment and so stained, who are in the habit of giving and accepting favours, these can give no help towards deliverance.'

In the same way it is of great importance to recognize good gurus, especially in a land swarming with worthless ascetics. This is the Jaina definition, which is also repeated by them every day:

'They who keep the (five) great vows, are steadfast, live only on

[1] i.e. Tīrthaṅkara.

alms, are immersed in meditation, preach religion: these are to be considered gurus.'

And in contrast the Jaina say:

'They are not gurus who are slaves to all desires, eat everything, have worldly possessions, are unchaste and preach falsely.'

Still more interesting is their definition of true religion:

'That which holds beings from falling into an evil state [after death] is called religion. Self-control is the foremost of its ten divisions. The omniscient says that such a religion is the means of liberation.'

The Jaina definition of false religion runs:

'Religion which is full of false precepts, which is stained by killing, even if it is thoroughly known, is the cause of wandering through rebirths.

Covetousness (*Nidāna śalya*) is the third poisonous dart which destroys Right Conduct. If, for instance, when a man is performing austerities, he admits some such worldly thought into his mind as, 'Now after this austerity I may have gained sufficient merit to become a king or a rich merchant', that very reflection, being stained with covetousness and greed, has destroyed like a poisonous dart all the merit that he might have gained through the act. In the same way, if a man indulges vindictive or revengeful thoughts when he is performing austerities, the fruit of his action is lost, and no merit is acquired and no karma destroyed.

Three Jewels compared.

It is interesting to compare these Three Jewels with the Buddhist Tri-Ratna: Buddha, the Law and the Order; and with the Mohammedan Triad: Happiness (*Khera*), Mercy (*Mera*), Prayer (*Bandagī*); and again with the Parsī Trio: Holy Mind, Holy Speech and Holy Deeds.

Perhaps also in no more concise fashion could Jainism be compared with Christianity than through their three jewels; for whilst the Jaina believe in Right Knowledge, Right Faith and Right Conduct, referring to an impersonal system, each of the Christian jewels, Faith, Hope and Love, refers to a personal Redeemer.

Faith, Hope and Love.

The Jaina religion enshrines no Faith in a supreme Deity; but for the Christian the dark problems of sin and suffering are lit up by his faith in the character and power of God, which ensure the ultimate triumph of righteousness.

Hope to the Jaina is almost a meaningless word: he has hope neither for his own future, overcast as it is by the shadow of innumerable rebirths, nor for that of his religion, which will, he believes, in its due season perish from off the earth. To the Christian, on the other hand, his present circumstances and his future are alike bathed in the golden sunshine of hope, so that hopefulness may be said to be the very centre of the Christian creed and the foundation of its joy. No evil can befall the man in this life who with Dante has learnt that in God's will is our peace; and even in the presence of death he is sustained by the living hope[1] of a glorious future assured to him by the resurrection of Jesus Christ from the dead.

As to the future of his faith, he waits with unswerving confidence the fulfilment of the magnificent śloka:

> 'The earth shall be filled with the knowledge of the glory of the Lord as the waters cover the sea.'[2]

But it is the third jewel, Love, that most clearly distinguishes the Christian from the Jaina ideal. To the Jaina, love to a personal God would be an attachment that could only bind him faster to the cycle of rebirth. It is a thing that must be rooted out at all costs, even as Gautama tore the love for his master Mahāvīra out of his heart. But to Christians love is the fulfilling of the law, and it is in its light that they tread the upward path; for it is through love that they see the form of their guide, and 'with unveiled face reflecting as a mirror the glory of the Lord are transformed into the same image from glory to glory'.

Such is the greater Tri-ratna that Christ is holding in His pierced hands and which He offers to the Jaina to-day.

[1] 1 Peter i. 3 ff.

[2] Habakkuk ii. 14.

And the Jaina in their turn, when they are won to Him, will pour into His treasury their trained capacity for self-discipline and self-denial and their deliberate exaltation of the spiritual and eternal over the comfortable and material, which are so greatly needed in the Christian Church in all ages.

Then all the jewels, set together and no longer separated, shall adorn a glorious diadem for the thorn-crowned Man of Sorrows.

CHAPTER XIII

JAINA WORSHIP AND RELIGIOUS CUSTOMS

Temple worship.

The Jaina are most courteous in permitting outsiders to witness the ritual of their temples, only asking that the spectators should remove their shoes. In the Digambara temples the idols are nude, and the eyes are cast down as a sign that the saint represented is lost to all worldly thought. The Śvetāmbara, like the Digambara, have images of the Tīrthaṅkara sitting in meditation in the Kāusagga position with legs crossed and hands in the lap, but unlike the Digambara their idols are given loin-cloths, have staring glass eyes looking straight in front of them, and are adorned with necklaces, girdles and bracelets of gold. The writer has elsewhere fully described the worship in the temples:[1] here it may suffice to give only a short summary.

Digambara worship.

The officiant in a Digambara temple must himself be a Jaina (though this is not the rule among the Śvetāmbara), and he will never eat any of the offering made to the idol. In the course of the morning worship he washes the idol (*Jaḷa pūjā*) and dries it, being most careful that no drop of water falls to the ground, marks it with three auspicious marks of yellow powder (*Ċandana pūjā*), and offers rice (*Akṣata pūjā*) and dried (not fresh) fruit (*Naivedya pūjā*).

In the evening the worship consists of *Āratī pūjā*, when a five-fold lamp is solemnly waved from left to right for a few minutes in front of the idol.

Śvetāmbara worship.

The strange part of Śvetāmbara worship is that, if no Jaina be present, it can be performed by a non-Jaina, and the writer has at various times seen paid officiants who were Brāhmans, gardeners, or farmers by caste performing the ritual.

If, however, a devout Jaina be present, he will, after bathing and changing his clothes to the two pieces of cloth he keeps for

[1] *Notes on Modern Jainism*, pp. 86 ff.

the purpose in the little dressing-room outside the temple, often bid as much as five annas for the privilege of performing the *Jaḷa pūjā*, when he will carefully wash the idol with water, then with milk, and then again with water; the same worshipper might also perform *Aṅgaluñċhanā pūjā* and dry the idol with five or ten separate cloths, which are kept in the temple, and whose number seems to vary according to the wealth of the shrine. A worshipper may do the *Ċandana pūjā* and mark the idol with fourteen auspicious marks, but only the paid officiant is allowed to perform the *Aṅga pūjā*, since this involves the handling of the valuable jewellery belonging to the idol. If the worshipper for whose benefit it is performed has paid a large sum, such as fifty rupees, the best crown, necklace, ear-rings, bracelets, armlets and girdle, all wrought in pure gold, will be brought out and put on the idol; if he only offers, say, twenty-five rupees, the idol will only wear its second-best silver-gilt ornaments. Then flowers and garlands (*Puṣpa pūjā*)[1] are offered, and this completes that part of the ritual for which special dress must be worn, and the performance of which is restricted to men.

The remaining acts of worship can be done by women, or by men in their ordinary dress, since the inner shrine need not be entered. They consist of *Dhūpa pūjā*, the waving of a stick of incense before the shrine; *Dīpa pūjā*, the waving of a lamp; *Akṣata pūjā*, the offering of rice; *Naivedya pūjā*, the giving of sweetmeats; and *Phaḷa pūjā*, the offering of fruit. It is interesting to notice the way each different worshipper arranges the rice in the *Akṣata pūjā*; it is usually placed thus:

(*c*)
(*b*)
(*a*)

The Svastika sign (*a*) is intended to represent the *Gati* or state in which a jīva may be born as either a denizen of hell,

[1] The writer once saw flowers offered even in a Digambara temple at Borsad (Kaira district).

or of heaven, a man, or a beast. The three little heaps (*b*) symbolize the *Three Jewels* of right knowledge, right faith, and right conduct, which enable a man to reach *Mokṣa*, represented by the sign (*c*).

When fruit is offered it is noticeable that the Śvetāmbara have no scruple about including fresh fruit in their gift, a thing which the Digambara—the stricter sect—will not allow, considering that by so doing they take life. The evening temple worship of the Śvetāmbara, as of the Digambara, practically consists in *Āratī pūjā*—waving a lamp before the shrine.

Meritorious as it is to perform the worship in the temples in one's own town, far more merit is gained by doing so at places of pilgrimage, particularly at special seasons of the year. On great festival days at Ābu, Girnār, and above all Śatruñjaya the temple court is thronged with would-be worshippers, all out-bidding each other for the privilege of performing the various ritual acts, whilst the temple custodians, acting as auctioneers, employ the familiar wiles of the auction room to run up the price. The auctioning is carried on under the phraseology of bidding for ghī (melted butter), and the man who offers the most *seers* of ghī obtains the coveted privilege. No ghī of course changes hands, the *seers* being only a conventional phrase for a fixed number of annas.

The present writer saw a man at Śatruñjaya perform the cheapest service—the *Sanātana pūjā*—for which privilege he had paid only two annas, though at Ābu he would have paid at least five-and-a-quarter. After bathing and donning the two cloths, he marked the idol in fourteen places and filled up time by playing on a harmonium. He then took in one hand a tray containing roses, almonds, rice, saffron and sugar, and in the other a jug containing water and milk, and round the jug and round his wrist he tied a red thread. After performing Dīpa pūjā and Akṣata pūjā, he did what is called *Camarī pūjā*, i. e. gently waved a brush of cow's hair in front of the shrine, whilst the paid officiant was decking the big idol in its jewellery. He then placed a little image of a Tīrthaṅkara in front of the larger image in the inner shrine and bathed it and marked it with the auspićious marks. It was interesting to notice that whilst doing this he kept on showing the little idol its own reflection in a pocket looking-glass, as a thoughtful ladies' maid might have done to her mistress as she assisted at her toilette; he completed his service by offering the articles on the tray to the Tīrthaṅkara.

The next cheapest service to this, the *Pañćakalyāṇa pūjā*, costs the worshipper about five-and-a-quarter rupees.

The singing of the idol's praises, *Sàitavarṇana Stuti*, can be done at any time and without the worshipper requiring to bathe or change. A man walks into the temple, makes the signs we noticed before

(c) (b) (a)

on a board and sings the idol's praises out of a hymn-book.

At Śatruñjaya behind one of the main temples are housed several solid silver chariots, and for the sum of about thirty shillings a pilgrim can seat himself in a tiny silver barouche and be drawn round the temple accompanied by silver elephants and other delights, and so feel that he is doing his pilgrimage *de luxe*.

The pilgrimage of all others, however, to try and do at Śatruñjaya is the 'Ninety-nine'. It takes about three months to perform, for the pilgrim must toil up the thousands of steps that lead from the bottom of the hill to the summit, encircle the most famous temple, and tramp down to the bottom again ninety-nine separate times, and the last days he must observe as strict fasts from food and drink. When the last toilsome ascent has been made, the priests drag out a silver throne, and, placing it under a canopy erected in the court of the main temple, set the image of a Tīrthaṅkara thereon. The pilgrim does the eight-fold worship (*Jaḷa pūjā*, *Ċandana pūjā*, *Puṣpa pūjā*, *Dhūpa pūjā*, *Dīpa pūjā*, *Akṣata pūjā*, *Naivedya pūjā*, and *Phaḷa pūjā*) eleven times over, and in the intervals hymns are sung to the accompaniment of a harmonium; and when the writer witnessed it, boys dressed in shepherd-plaid trousers and bright pink-frilled jackets danced to the jingling accompaniment of bells round their ankles. The pilgrim was in this case a little girl, who seemed to be utterly exhausted by fasting, thirst and fatigue.

Private worship.

The Sthānakavāsī Jaina, being non-idolatrous and having no temple which they can attend, naturally pay more attention to meditation and private worship than the other sects, and if the reader would really learn to understand the heart of Jainism, it will repay him to study their private devotions with some minuteness, since after all a man's meditations are generally a true reflection of his creed.

The Digambara Jaina are said to use a good deal of Sanskrit in their devotions; the Śvetāmbara employ both Sanskrit and Māgadhī; but the Sthānakavāsī, who claim to hold closest of all the sects to primitive practice, confine themselves as far as possible to Māgadhī. Sanskrit would seem therefore to have come into use with idol worship under Hindu influence, and where reverence is refused to images, the sacred language of the Brāhmans is also neglected.

Every devout Sthānakavāsī ought to rise two hours before sunrise in winter and summer, and, taking in his hands his rosary, consisting of 108 beads, recite the *Navakāra mantra*, saluting Arihanta, Siddha, Āċārya, Upādhyāya and Sādhu, and also Knowledge, Faith, Character and Austerity, and, this done, should if possible repair to the monastery. Every Apāsaro, as also every temple, has a little room where the Jaina keep their clothes for worship, which usually consist of five articles: two long pieces of cloth, one of which they wear round the loins and the other over the shoulders, a little strip to cover the mouth, a piece of cloth to sit on, and also a brush. The devout layman, wearing only the two cloths, sits down on what is in fact his prayer carpet, and, after asking permission from his guru, begs forgiveness of any living thing he may have injured on his way from his house to the monastery.

He is then in a position to perform *Sāmāyika*, the most essential portion of which, *Karemi bhante*, consists in the repetition in Māgadhī of a vow which might be thus translated : Sāmāyika.

'I vow that I will not sin in regard to Dravya for the space of forty-eight minutes anywhere in the whole world. In right earnest I vow not to sin in any of the six ways. O adorable one, I take this vow, and I will keep it in this manner : I promise to keep it in thought, word and deed myself, and not to cause others to break it in thought, word, or deed. Again, O adorable one, I thus free myself from all sinful actions; I condemn them in the presence of my spirit and preceptor, and I vow to keep my spirit free from such actions.'

The worshipper then praises the twenty-four Tīrthaṅkara of the present age in Māgadhī verse (*Ċauvīsanttho*[1]), which might be rendered : Ċauvīsanttho.

'I sing the praise of the twenty-four Tīrthaṅkara and other Kevalī, who have shed the light of religion on this world, who formed communities and so became Tīrthaṅkara. I salute Ṛiṣabhadeva, Ajitanātha [here follows the list of the twenty-four]. I praise these and all others who have shaken off the dust of karma and have destroyed old age and death. May these twenty-four Tīrthaṅkara show mercy to me. May these Tīrthaṅkara, famed in this world, whose praises I have sung, whom I have worshipped in mind, and who are excellent in this world, grant me that religion in which meditation forms the chief part and which protects from all diseases.

Ye are brighter than the moon, more brilliant than the sun, more awe-inspiring than the ocean. Grant to me, O Siddha, to reach Siddha-hood.'

Next follows *Vandaṇā*, i.e. salutation and prayer for forgiveness to the guru, if he be present, or in his absence to the north-east corner of the building, that being the direc- Vandaṇā.

[1] Or *Ċaturviṁśatistava*.

tion in which Mahāvideha, the abode of the Tīrthaṅkara, is said to lie. All sects, even when they add special Vandaṇā referring to idol worship, seem to use a general form, which could be freely translated as follows :

'O forgiving Sādhu! I desire to bow to you and to salute you to the best of my bodily powers, forsaking all evil actions. Permit me to approach you, to touch your lotus-like feet. I touch them. Pardon me if the touch annoys you. O adorable! The day is passing away. O adorable, holy as a place of pilgrimage! I crave forgiveness from you for all the evil actions I may have done during the course of this day. If I have committed any of the thirty-three errors (*asātanā*), if I have done anything wrong through body, speech, or thought, or from anger, pride, deceit, or greed, and if during this day I have in any way or at any time violated any of the duties enjoined by religion, I would be free, O forgiving Sādhu, from all such sins, which I condemn and condemn again in your presence. I will keep my spirit free from such sins.'

Paḍīkamaṇuṁ.

Paḍīkamaṇuṁ[1] proper then follows, in which the Twelve Vows are repeated and any breach of them is confessed. This part of the devotions is most lengthy, as sins are confessed in all their subdivisions: for instance, if the worshipper has sinned against knowledge in any of fourteen ways, or against faith in five ways, or has uttered any of the twenty-five kinds of falsehood ; the eighteen classes of sin are also enumerated at this time, and the man confesses any sins he may have committed in respect of any of them, or against any of the Pañca Parameśvara (or Five Great Ones). Every sect and sub-sect practises Paḍīkamaṇuṁ, but of course with infinite variation in the forms of confession used. The Sthānakavāsī make their confession in a form in which Māgadhī and vernacular words are mingled.

Kāusagga.

The worshipper then seats himself cross-legged and repeats the salutation to the Five Great Ones (i. e. *Navakāra mantra*), says again the *Karemi bhante*, and then repeats the very interesting *Iććhamiṭhāmi Kāusagga*, which might be translated as follows :

[1] It should be noticed that the whole of their devotions is sometimes loosely called Paḍīkamaṇuṁ.

'I now wish to arrest all the functions of my body. Before doing so, however, I pray for forgiveness if I have committed any fault (Atičāra) in body, speech, or thought during this day, if I have acted contrary to the scriptures, or gone astray from the path of mokṣa, or done anything against the laws of religion, or unworthy of doing; I ask forgiveness if I have thought evil of others, entertained unworthy thoughts, acted in ways undesirable, longed for undesirable things, or if I have done anything unworthy of a Śrāvaka (devout Jaina layman) in respect of the three Jewels, the three Gupti, the four Kaṣāya, the five Aṇuvrata, the three Guṇavrata, the four Śikṣāvrata, or violated any of the twelve duties of a Śrāvaka. May all such faults be forgiven.'

The worshipper then performs the fourth part of Kāusagga by reciting the Tassottarī pāṭha, in which he says:

'Sitting in one place I will now arrest all my bodily functions in order to purify and sanctify my spirit and to remove all darts (Śalya), and other sins from it. My arresting of bodily functions (Kāusagga) must not be regarded as broken, however, by any of the thirteen actions of inhaling, exhaling, coughing, sighing, sneezing, yawning, hiccoughing, giddiness, sickness, swooning, slight external or internal involuntary movement, or winking. I will also hold my spirit immovable in Kāusagga and in meditation and silence, until I recite Namo arihantāṇuṁ; until then I will keep it free from sin.'

The sixth and last part of Paḍīkamaṇuṁ is called Pačakhāṇa and consists of vowing to abstain from four kinds of food, for an hour if it is said at the morning Paḍīkamaṇuṁ, or for the coming night when it is repeated in the evening. The promise runs as follows: Pača-khāṇa.

'I take a vow to abstain from the four following kinds of food: food, drink, fruits, spices, in thought, speech and deed. I promise to keep my soul away from those four, provided that they are not forced on me or given to me whilst I am in a state of unconsciousness or meditation.'

There are at least ten variations of this vow: a man may promise to eat only once a day, or not until three hours after sunrise, or to take only one sort of food, or to fast altogether; but every variation seems to show the stress the Jaina lay on the duty of fasting, an emphasis that is easily understood in a religion whose adherents hope eventually to die fasting, and which teaches that the greatest crimes are those committed for the sake of eating.

Some Digambara Jaina, instead of taking a vow to fast, apparently promise to abstain from their specially besetting sins. At the end of Paḍīkamaṇuṁ and at the end of Sāmāyika the worshipper performs *Namotthuṇaṁ* or general praise.

The different parts of Paḍīkamaṇuṁ need not be said in any exact order, but it should generally last about forty-eight minutes every morning, and, since it is a daily duty, it is also called *Āvaśyaka.*

At the end of it a devout layman would go to the Apāsaro and if possible hear a guru preach, and on returning to his house would give alms to a sādhu or to a poor man. He breakfasts about ten or eleven, then goes to business, returning in time to take his last meal about five o'clock in the afternoon, so that he may have his meal over before sunset, since no Jaina may eat after dark.

Evening worship.

In the evening, and if possible in the monastery, he makes confession of the sins of the day (*Devasīya Paḍīkamaṇuṁ*), sings praises (*Sajhāya Stavana*), and vows not to eat till sunrise, and before he sleeps he must tell his beads and do salutation to the Five three times over. If he is a very devout layman, he will repeat the Santhāro pāṭha, reflecting that he may never wake again, and so be prepared to make a meritorious death.

Scripture reading.

Some time during the day the layman should read one of the scriptures, unless hindered by any of the thirty-two reasons, such as having been near a dead body, or finding a bloodstain on his clothes, or being in any other way ceremonially impure. Again, he must not read the books if there is a mist, or a thunderstorm, the fall of a meteor, an eclipse, a full moon, no moon, or when a great king or even a great man dies, or if the sky has been red at sunrise or sunset, or if there has been a dust-storm. He must not read them on any of the first three days of the bright half of the moon, in a house where meat is eaten, near a funeral pyre, on a battle-field, or in the twilight of the early morning or late evening. In fact on any day that a Sthānakavāsī Jaina feels too lazy to read the scriptures, he can find some ceremonial reason to prevent his doing so, and hence the scriptures are not in actual fact much studied by them.

Jaina Holy Days.[1]

Pajjusaṇa.

The ordinary routine of daily worship of course alters on the great days of Fasts or Festivals; for instance, at *Pajjusaṇa*, the solemn season which closes the Jaina year, many devout laymen fast for eight days or even longer and attend special services at the Apāsarā. They also take this opportunity of doing poṣadha,[2] i.e. temporarily becoming a monk. We have seen how the whole teaching of Jainism tries to lead the laity along the path of asceticism towards deliverance, and during the fast of Pajjusaṇa householders are urged to live a monk's life for at least twenty-four hours. During the twenty-four hours that he is performing poṣadha a layman never leaves the monastery, but spends his time in meditation and fasting. As a matter of fact every householder is supposed to perform poṣadha twice a month, but the generality of Jaina content themselves with doing it at the end of the year. If poṣadha be too exacting, a layman may observe the partial fast of *dayā* or *saṁvara*, when, though he sit in the monastery for some fixed period, he may take food and boiled water at will.

Saṁvatsarī.

The closing day of the Jaina year and of Pajjusaṇa, Saṁvatsarī, is the most solemn fast of all. Every Jaina fasts throughout the day from food and water, and the Apāsarā are crowded with men and women making their confessions. No outsider can visit these gatherings without being deeply impressed with the determination of all present

[1] For a full account of these see article 'Festivals and Fasts (Jain)' by the present writer in *E.R.E.*, vol. v, pp. 875 ff.

[2] Or poṣaha.

to carry no grudge and no quarrel over into the next year. At the close of the meeting every one present asks forgiveness from his neighbours for any offence he may even unwittingly have given, and they all write letters to distant friends asking their forgiveness also. This determination to start the new year in love and charity with their neighbours they do not confine to their own community; for example, the writer used to be bewildered by receiving letters from Jaina friends and paṇḍits who had never offended her in any way asking her forgiveness in case they had unwittingly vexed her. One cannot help feeling that this beautiful custom of the Jaina is one of the many precious things they will bring as their special tribute to that City of God into which at last shall be gathered all the glory and wealth of devotion of the nations.

Some time during the Pajjusaṇa week the Śvetāmbara Jaina often arrange a special procession though the town in honour of their Kalpa Sūtra.

Another pageant the same sect arrange is a cradle procession on Mahāvīra's birthday, which is now conventionally fixed for the first day of Bhādrapada, the fourth day of Pajjusaṇa. Sthānakavāsī Jaina are not permitted to celebrate the day, lest it should lead to idolatry, but the other sects decorate their temples with flags on this and on the conventional birthdays of other Tīrthaṅkara.

Divālī. Curiously enough Divālī, the next great holy day of the Jaina, is really a Hindu festival in honour of Lakṣmī, the goddess of wealth. All through our studies, however, we have seen the great influence that Hinduism has exerted on Jainism, and here it pressed a mercantile community at its weakest point, its love of money; naturally enough such a community was not willing to omit anything that could propitiate one who might conceivably have the bestowal of wealth in her power. The festival has, however, been given a Jaina sanction by calling it the day on which Mahāvīra passed to mokṣa, when all the eighteen confederate kings made an illumination, saying: 'Since the light of intelligence is gone, let us make an illumination of material matter.' How thin this excuse is, is shown by the fact that the celebrations seem, despite the protests of the stricter Jaina, to be more concerned with the worship of money than with the passing of Mahāvīra. On the first day (*Dhanateraśa*) the Śvetāmbara women polish their jewellery and ornaments in honour of Lakṣmī, on the second (*Kālīċaudaśa*) they propitiate evil spirits by placing sweetmeats at cross-roads, and on the third (*Amāsa*) all Jaina worship their account-books—*Śāradā pūjā*. A Brāhman is called who writes *Śrī* (i. e. Lakṣmī) on the account-books over and over again in such a way as to form a pyramid. The priest then performs *Lakṣmī pūjā*, the oldest obtainable rupee and the leaf of a creeper being placed on an account-book, and also a little heap of rice, pān, betel-nut and turmeric, and in front of it a small lamp filled with burning camphor is waved, and the book is then marked with red powder. No one closes the account-book for several hours, and when they do so, they are careful to say: 'A hundred thousand profits.'

Full-moon fasts.

Perhaps the full-moon fasts also bear witness to Hindu influence; at any rate these days are carefully observed by the Jaina. The great religious excitement of the community is found in going on pilgrimages, and on the full-moon days that fall in October–November (*Kārttikī punema*), or in April–May (*Ċaitrī punema*), they try if possible to visit Śatruñjaya. On the other full-moon days, which fall in the spring and summer, they fast and hear special sermons, but the summer full-moon day (*Āṣāḍhī punema*) is one to which the ascetics pay special attention, for wherever they spend that day, there they must remain till the rainy season is over.

Jñāna pañċamī.

In connexion with the antiquity of the Jaina scriptures it is interesting to notice that once a year a fast is observed called Jñāna pañċamī, on which day all Jaina sacred books are not only worshipped but also dusted, freed from insects and rearranged. If only this custom had prevailed with regard to all English parish registers, how many of our records might have been saved!

Mauna-gyārasa.

We have studied the road through which a jīva passes by toilsome stages towards deliverance; to recall these steps to the popular mind, the Śvetāmbara (and a few Sthānakavāsī) once a year keep a solemn fast called *Maunagyārasa* on the eleventh day of some month, preferably the eleventh day of the bright half of Mārgaśirṣa (November–December). The worshipper fasts absolutely from food and water and meditates, as he tells his beads, on each of the five stages (Sādhu, Upādhyāya, Āčārya, Tīrthaṅkara and Siddha) of the upward path, and the next day he worships eleven sets of eleven different kinds of things connected with knowledge, such as eleven pens, eleven pieces of paper, eleven ink-bottles, &c.

Saint-wheel worship.

The worship of the *Siddha čakra*, or saint-wheel, which is kept in every temple, serves also to remind the worshipper of the stages he must pass, for on the little silver or brass tray are five tiny figures representing the Five Great Ones (Sādhu, Upādhyāya, Āčārya, Arihanta, Siddha), but between the figures are written the names of the three jewels (Right Knowledge, Right Faith, Right Conduct) and also the word *tapa*, austerity, which might almost be called the key-word of the whole Jaina system. This little tray seems to bear inscribed on it the Jaina Confession of Faith, and it is regarded as of so much importance that no Śvetāmbara temple is complete without it, and twice a year in the spring and autumn it is worshipped by having the eight-fold pūjā done to it every day for eight days. *Jaḷajātra*, or the water pilgrimage, is celebrated with much rejoicing once during each of these eight days, when the little tray is taken to some lake near the town and ceremonially bathed before being offered the eight-fold worship.

Days of absti-nence.

Fasting is considered so important by the Jaina, that the

more devout observe twelve days in every month as days of abstinence, but the less strict content themselves with fasting more or less strictly on five days.

Consecration of an idol.

Besides the regularly recurring holy days of the year, there are special occasions of rejoicing, such as *Añjanaśalākā* (the consecration of a new idol), which is celebrated with great pomp, but which rarely occurs now owing to the enormous expense it entails on the donor of the idol. In the case of a Śvetāmbara idol, mantras must be repeated, the glass eyes inserted, and the statue anointed with saffron, before the idol is regarded as sacred, but the expense lies in the payment, not so much for this consecration, as for the feasting and processions which accompany it.

The Bathing of Gomaṭeśvara.

Another rare act of Jaina worship is the bathing of colossal figures such as that of Gomateśvara at Śrāvaṇa Belgolā, which takes place every twenty-five years. The actual bathing is not unlike the ordinary Jaḷa pūjā, and the privilege of pouring cups of curd, milk and melted butter over the idol is put up to auction.

Oḷi.

There is one day, *Oḷi* or *Āmbela*, which is the fast *par excellence* of Jaina women. It occurs eight days before Ċaitrī punema, and all women who long for a happy wedded life (and every woman in India marries) fast from specially nice food for twenty-four hours, remembering that a princess once won health for her royal husband who was a leper by fasting and worshipping the saint wheel on this day.

Hindu festivals.

The ever-present influence of Hinduism is perhaps felt even more by Jaina women than by Jaina men, and it is they who insist on keeping the Hindu festival of *Śītalāsātama*, the festival of the goddess of small-pox, and the two feasts of *Vīrapasalī*, when brothers give presents to their sisters and the sisters bless them, and of *Bhāībīja*, when the sisters ask their brothers to their houses. Often also girls and women fast on the Hindu holy days of *Bolachotha* and *Molākata*. It is much to be regretted that many Jaina men and women, despite all the efforts of the reformers, still take part in the *Holī* celebrations—the detestably obscene festival of spring; thoughtful Jaina feel that it ill becomes a community who boast of their purity to share an alien festival of which all enlightened Hindus themselves are now ashamed. At *Daśerā*, the great Kṣatriya festival, the Jaina eat specially dainty food, and on *Makarasaṅkrānti* they fulfil the duty of charity by giving food to cows and clothing to the poor.

Jaina, of course, ought not to observe the Hindu death ceremonies or *Śrāddha*, and they have so far discontinued the custom, that they no longer throw food to the crows; but they still observe them to the extent of eating specially dainty food on those days.

Jaina Superstitions.

Neither in the regular routine of their daily worship nor in the pleasurable excitement of their frequent holy days do the Jaina (and especially the Jaina women) find all the emotional outlet they need; and so, besides these recognized acts of ritual, they perform many others which are frowned on by their leaders. The women believe in nearly all the Hindu superstitions, so that they have as it were a second cult, that of warding off evil spirits and demons, to whom all their lifetime they are in bondage through fear.

The evil eye. The ordinary people amongst the Jaina believe most strongly in the evil eye and are terrified of coming under its influence (*Najarāi javuṁ*), though it is quite contrary to the tenets of their creed. They fear perfect happiness, and whenever they see it, they believe that some person who is a favourite with some god or goddess, such as Meladī Mātā, Khoḍiyāra Mātā, Kālakā Mātā, or Bhairava Deva, will harm the happy one through jealousy. Anything dark or bitter will avert this, and so, if new jewellery is worn, a black thread is tied on to it; if a new house is built, a black earthen vessel is placed outside; and the writer was herself entreated to mark her only child with a black smear on the cheek-bone or at least behind the ear. In the same way at a wedding a lemon is tied in the turban of the bridegroom and in the dress of the bride, that something sour may safeguard the sweetness of their lot.

When illness occurs, it is put down to the influence of the evil eye. If a child has fever, or is sick after eating, the women at once say that its illness was caused by some person possessing the wicked power of the evil eye, and elaborate remedies are taken. A very usual method is to take a little cup and put in it smokeless burning embers, and over them mustard, salt and grain, till a fine smoke is made, and then to turn it upside down on to a brass plate, and, holding it firmly in position, to fix the two together with manure and water. They call this *Najara bandhī* and put it under the sick child's bed. After three or four days, when in the course of nature the fever has abated; they pull out the cup and plate and throw the contents away at a junction of three roads.

If a man is ill, one method of removing the influence of the evil eye from him is to wave a loaf of millet bread round his head and then give it to a black dog; if the animal eats it, they believe the influence of the evil eye passes into him.

Evil spirits.

The more enlightened Jaina declare that they have no fear of evil spirits (*bhūta*), but the women are very much afraid of them and, like all Indians, believe that Europeans share this fear and have their elaborate freemasonry ritual as a means of dealing with such spirits. Bhūta are specially active at Divālī time, and in order to prevent them coming to visit their homes, the women before Divālī go to some cross-roads where three or four ways meet, carrying water-pots. They make a circle in the dust with the water and in the centre of this place a small cake of grain. Indeed at any season when they are afraid of evil spirits visiting their house, they put vermilion, grain and something black into the bottom of a broken pot to guard against their coming.

Bhūta also live in pīpal trees, and during the last days

of the month Śrāvaṇa one often sees women watering those trees to keep the evil spirits that live there happy and so prevent their coming out.

Ancestors. Śrāvaṇa is in fact an anxious month, and on the fifth day of it many Jaina women worship serpents, apparently to propitiate the spirits of their ancestors. They draw a picture of a snake on the walls of the room where the water-vessels are kept, in order to pacify the spirit of any of their forefathers who may have died suddenly in battle or been murdered before he could fulfil some strong desire he might have possessed; for they fear that such ancestors may return to carry out their interrupted purpose. To cool these desires, they encircle the picture of the snake three times with water (just as the lamp is waved before the idol at ārati) and offer it little cakes to make it happy.

The spirits of ancestors are also appeased once a year on either the eighth or twenty-ninth of Āśvina, when an offering of naivedya is made to them. A lamp is lighted and placed in some corner facing the quarter in which the ancestor once lived; an offering of sweetmeats is then made to the lamp and subsequently eaten by the offerers themselves.

Plague. When frightened by the prevalence of plague or cholera, the Jaina have recourse to the Brāhmans to ask how they shall appease the *mela deva* (evil god) who is affecting them. The priests instruct them to light a fire in their own houses and circumambulate it. Near the flames they place an offering of naivedya and then walk round the fire three times carrying water. After this they themselves eat the actual naivedya that has been offered and give dry materials for naivedya and money to the Brāhmans.

Small-pox. In the same way, if a child actually has small-pox, or if there be an epidemic of it, a Jaina mother almost invariably goes to the shrine of Śītalā Mātā, the goddess of small-pox, whose shrine is to be found in almost every Indian village, and vows to make an offering of artificial glass eyes or money to the Mātā if her child recover or escape infection altogether.

It is pitiful to see Jaina women who are childless going to Hindu temples and promising to offer cradles or money if only a little son may be born to them. They even promise that for three or four years the child shall be treated as a beggar, and no name given to him; all they ask is that their reproach may be taken away. Children.

The orthodox Jaina declare that all these superstitions which their women folk have copied from the Hindus are contrary to their religion and indeed must even be accounted Mithyātva Śalya;[1] but they do not see that they are born of fear, and that they will only disappear when the timid ones begin to trust a personal God and learn that the All-Powerful is the All-Loving too.

[1] See pp. 130 ff.

CHAPTER XIV

JAINA MYTHOLOGY

THE Jaina declare that they do not worship their gods, but that they regard them as instruments for working out the fruits of karma. They say also that their gods differ from the members of the Hindu pantheon in being graded: indeed they might almost be considered as having caste amongst themselves. In spite of being gods, they are inferior to men, since before they can attain mokṣa they must be born again as human beings; yet, if they have accumulated good karma in previous births, they may now be enjoying greater bliss than men.

Gods in Hell. The lowest gods are in Hell, where their work is to torment jīva; these deities are divided into fifteen classes according to their different functions. Amongst them are the *Amba*, whose special task it is to destroy the nerves of their victims (as a mango is pinched and crushed in a man's hand to soften it, so do they wreck the nerves of the jīva they torture); the *Ambarasa*, who separate bones and flesh; the *Śāma*, who beat and belabour men; the *Sabala*, who tear the flesh; the *Rudra*, engaged in striking men with spears; the *Mahārudra*, occupied in chopping flesh into mince-meat; the *Kāla*, who are roasting the flesh of their victims; the *Mahākāla*, who are tearing it with pincers; the *Asipata*, engaged in cutting their victims with swords; the *Dhanu*, who are shooting them with arrows; the *Kumbha*, who are indulging in the pastime, so often employed in Indian native states, of torturing with chillies; the *Vālu*, who steep men in hot sand; the *Vetaraṇī*, who like devilish dhobīs dash their victims against stones in streams of boiling water; the *Kharasvara*, who force men to sit on thorny trees; and last in the fearsome list, the *Mahāghoṣa*, who shut men up in black holes.

Gods in Pātāla.

On the same level as Hell, but in a different direction, is Pātāla; there are, however, no human beings in Pātāla, and so the gods who dwell there are not torturers as they are in Hell. They are divided into two main classes, *Bhavanapati* and *Vyantara*. These are again subdivided, there being ten kinds of Bhavanapati: first, the dark god *Asura Kumāra*, whose body is all black, who loves to wear red garments, and in whose crown is a great crescent-shaped jewel; then *Nāga Kumāra*, whose body is white, whose favourite garments are green, and in whose crown is a serpent's hood for a symbol; the body of *Suvarṇa Kumāra* is as yellow as gold, his clothes are white, and his symbol is an eagle; *Vidyut Kumāra* is red in body, he wears green vestments, and has a thunderbolt in his crown; the body of *Agni Kumāra* is also red, but his dress is green, and his symbol is a jug; the next god, *Dvīpa Kumāra*, is red, with green clothes, but has a lion for his sign; *Udadhi Kumāra* is a white god with green clothes, whose symbol is a horse; an elephant is the sign of the red *Diśā Kumāra*, who is clad in white; the god *Vāyu Kumāra* has a green body and wears clothes as red as the sunset sky, and his token is the crocodile; and the last of the ten Bhavanapati is *Sthanita Kumāra*, with a body as yellow as gold, white clothes, and a shallow earthen pot as his symbol.

The other denizens of Pātāla, the Vyantara, are demons of various classes, and all have trees as their trade-marks. *Piśāća* are black-bodied, and have a Kadamba tree as a symbol; *Bhūta*, whose sign is the Sulasa tree, are also black-bodied; so are *Yakṣa*, who possess the Banyan tree as their sign; *Rākṣasa* are white and have the Khaṭamba tree; the green *Kiṇnara* have the Aśoka tree; the white *Kimpuruṣa* the Ćampaka tree; the Nāga or snake tree is the symbol of the black-bodied *Mahoraga*; and the last of the Vyantara demons, the black *Gāndharva*, have the Ṭīmbara tree for their sign.

Besides these there are lower demons called *Vāṇavyantara*, who are named respectively Āṇapannī, Pāṇapannī, Isīvāyī, Bhūtavāyī, Kandīye, Mahākandīye, Kohaṇḍa and Pahaṅga. All these live in the lower regions.

Gods in Svarga.

Then there are the gods of the upper regions. In Svarga there are two classes of gods, *Jyotiṣī* and *Vimānavāsī*.

Jyotiṣī gods inhabit Sūrya (the sun), Ċandra (the moon), Graha (the planets), Tārā (the stars) and Nakṣatra (the constellations). The Jaina believe that there is a sun that moves and another that stands still, and that the same is the case with the moon, planets and stars, and that each of these has its own gods.

The class of Vimānavāsī has three divisions: first, the gods of *Devaloka* (Sudharmā, Iśāna, Sanatkumāra, Māhendra, Brahma, Lāntaka, Mahāśukra, Sahasāra, Āṇata, Prāṇata, Āraṇa and Aċuya); then the gods in *Graiveyika* who rule over Bhadde, Subhadde, Sujāe, Sumāṇase, Priyadaṁsaṇe, Sudaṁsaṇe, Āmohe, Supaḍībhadde and Jasodhare; and lastly in *Anuttaravimāna* there are five places, each with a god called Indra to rule over it, viz.: Vijaya, Vijayanta, Jayanta, Aparājita and Sarvārthasiddha.

As on earth (or rather as in India) there are sweepers who act as scavengers for men and live apart from them, so in the heavens there are gods who do menial service for the other gods and live apart from them. The name of these gods is *Kilviṣiyā*, and they are practically the out-caste or sweeper gods. There are three divisions of them: those who live beneath the first and second Devaloka, those who live below the third, and those who dwell under the seventh; a little higher in the social scale come the servant gods—the *Tiryak jāmbṛik*—who each live in a separate mountain in a different continent; and above these again are the *Lokāntika* gods, who are higher servants, and who live in the fifth Devaloka. Altogether there are in heaven and hell ninety-nine kinds of gods who are regarded as menial because they serve.

Could anything show more clearly the terrible way in which caste has fettered not only the lives and customs of the Jaina but even their imagination, than this fact that the very gods who serve are regarded as polluted and contaminated by that service? It is this belief that hinders Jaina from taking their share in the social uplift of India; and it is only the revelation of a Son of God who was amongst us as one that serveth that can set them free.

Over all the Devaloka there is a place called Siddhaśīlā, in which the Siddha live.

All the gods are in a state of happiness, eating, drinking and singing; the good gods (*Samakitī*) make a point of being present and listening whenever the Tīrthaṅkara preach, but the false gods (*Mithyātvī*) do not attend. Even the Samakitī will have to be born as men before they can attain mokṣa, but they will soon arrive there, whereas the Mithyātvī will have to undergo numberless rebirths.

Indra is the supreme god, ruling over all the gods, and his commands they must all obey.

The Jaina illustrate their ideas of heaven and hell by the diagram of a man's figure. The legs of the figure, they say, represent *Adholoka*, wherein are situated the seven hells or Naraka. *Ratna Prabhā*, the first hell, is paved with sharp stones; *Śarkara Prabhā*, the second, with pointed stones of sugar-loaf shape; *Vālu Prabhā* with sand; *Paṅka Prabhā* with mud; *Dhumra Prabhā* is filled with smoke; *Tama Prabhā* is dark enough; but *Tamatama Prabhā* is filled with thick darkness. The hideous torments inflicted in these terrible hells by the evil gods we have already studied, but in all these hells the jīva have the hope that they will eventually escape from thence when their karma is exhausted. A Śvetāmbara sādhu, however, told the writer of a still worse place, *Nigoḍa*, situated below the feet of the figure in our diagram, in which are thrown evil jīva who have committed specially heinous sins like murder, and who have no hope of ever coming out. They suffer excruciating tortures, such as having millions of red-hot needles thrust into them, and know that their pain is unending. So many jīva are condemned to Nigoḍa that there is an endless procession of them passing thither like a long, long train of black ants, of which we can see neither the end nor the beginning.

To return to our diagram, the waist of the figure is our world, *Tiryakloka*, which is made up of two-and-a-half islands, each containing a secret district called Mahāvideha, whose inhabitants alone can attain mokṣa; above comes Svarga or *Urdhvaloka*, where the gods of the upper world live; the breast of the figure represents *Devaloka*; the neck *Graiveyika*; and the face *Anuttaravimāna*, all of whose gods we have studied; while the crown of the figure is *Mokṣa*, where dwell those jīva who, after being born as men, have at length attained deliverance.

Jaina Divisions of Time.

In common with so many oriental faiths the Jaina think of time as a wheel which rotates ceaselessly downwards and upwards—the falling of the wheel being known as *Avasarpiṇī* and the rising as *Utsarpiṇī*. The former is under the influence of a bad serpent, and the latter of a good one.

Avasarpiṇī.

Avasarpiṇī, the era in which we are now living, began with a period known as *Suṣama Suṣama*, the happiest time of all, which lasted for four crores of crores of sāgaropama,[1]

[1] Jaina technical words for time:

Samaya, the smallest unit of time. Countless samaya pass whilst one is winking an eye, tearing a rotten piece of cloth, snapping the finger, or whilst the spear of a young man is piercing a lotus leaf.

Āvalikā, the next smallest division of time, is made up of innumerable divisions of samaya.

Then comes *Muhūrta*, which is composed of 16,777,216 āvalikā and is equivalent to forty-eight minutes of English time.

Ahorātra consists of thirty muhūrta, or a night and a day.

After Ahorātra the Jaina count like Hindus by fortnights, months, and years, till they come to *Palya*, composed of countless years, and *Sāgaropama*, which consist of one hundred millions of palya multiplied by one hundred millions.

and when every man's height was six miles, and the number of his ribs two hundred and fifty-six.

The children born in this happy period were always twins, a boy and a girl, and ten Kalpavṛikṣa (desire-fulfilling trees) supplied all their need; for one tree gave them sweet fruits, another bore leaves that formed pots and pans, the leaves of a third murmured sweet music, a fourth gave bright light even at night, a fifth shed radiance like little lamps, the flowers of a sixth were exquisite in form and scent, the seventh bore food which was perfect both to sight and taste, the leaves of the eighth served as jewellery, the ninth was like a many-storied palace to live in, and the bark of the tenth provided beautiful clothes. (In many of the Jaina temples representations of the happy twins are carved, standing beneath these desire-fulfilling trees.) The parents of the children died as soon as the twins were forty-nine days old, but that did not so much matter, since the children on the fourth day after their birth had been able to eat as much food as was equal to a grain of corn in size, and they never increased the size of this meal, which they only ate every fourth day. The children never committed the sin of killing, for during their whole lives they never saw a cooking-vessel or touched cooked food, and on their deaths they passed straight to Devaloka, without ever having heard of religion.

In the next period, *Suṣama,* which, as its name indicates, was only half as happy as the first, the twins born into the world were only four miles high, had only one hundred and twenty-eight ribs, and only lived for two palya of time, but the ten desire-fulfilling trees still continued their kind offices. The parents of the children lived longer now (the Jaina, according to this, would seem not to consider the long life of their parents essential to their own happiness!) and did not die till the children were sixty-four days old; and meanwhile human appetite had so far increased that twins ate a meal equal to a jujube fruit three days after their birth, and continued to do so every third day throughout their lives.

In *Suṣama Duṣama* the happiness has become mixed with sorrow; the twins are now only two miles in height, have only sixty-four ribs, and live only for one palya, but on their death they still go to Devaloka. It was during this period that Ṛiṣabhadeva, the first Tīrthaṅkara, was born. He taught the twins seventy-two useful arts, such as cooking, sewing, &c.; for he knew that the desire-fulfilling trees would disappear, and that human beings would then have only themselves to depend on. Ṛiṣabhadeva is also credited with having introduced politics and established a kingdom, but his daughter Brāhmī, the Jaina patron of learning, is even more interesting than her father. This learned lady invented eighteen different alphabets (oh, misdirected energy!) including Turkish, Nāgarī, all the Dravidian dialects, Canarese, Persian, and the character used in Orissa. From these, the Jaina say, were derived Gujarātī and Marāṭhī. It is strange that a people who believe the patron of letters to have been a woman should so long have refused to educate their own daughters: surely in this particular they might safely follow the example of so illustrious a being as their first Tīrthaṅkara.

In the period of *Duṣama Suṣama*, which lasted for one crore of crores of sāgaropama less forty-two thousand years, the height of man was five hundred span, the number of his ribs thirty-two, and his age one crore of pūrva. The women born in this age ate twenty-eight morsels of food, the men thirty-two, and they both dined once during the day. During this time the Jaina religion was fully developed, and there were born the remaining twenty-three Tīrthaṅkara, eleven Ċakravartī, nine Baḷadeva, nine Vāsudeva, and nine Prativāsudeva. People born during this epoch did not all pass to Devaloka, but might be reborn in any of the four Gati (hell, heaven, man, or beast), or might become Siddha.

Duṣama, the period in which we are now living, is entirely evil. No one can hope to live longer than one hundred and twenty-five years, to have more than sixteen ribs or a greater stature than seven cubits. The era began three years after Mahāvīra reached mokṣa, and will last for twenty-one thousand years. No Tīrthaṅkara can be born during Duṣama; nor can any one, lay or ascetic, however good, reach mokṣa without undergoing at least one rebirth (so that there would not seem to be much use in becoming an ascetic nowadays !). Bad as things are now, they must become yet worse, and Jainism itself is doomed to disappear during our present era; the last Jaina monk will be called Duppasahasūri, the last nun Phalguśrī, the last layman Nāgila, and the last laywoman Satyaśrī.

It is this belief that Jainism must disappear that is paralysing so much effort at the present time; for the younger Jaina feel that anything they may do to spread their faith, for instance, is only building castles in the sand that must be swept away by the incoming tide of destruction. It seems, in fact, impossible for any religion which is not illuminated and irradiated by Hope to become a really missionary faith.

Our present era, will be followed by a still more evil one, *Duṣama Duṣama*, which will also endure for twenty-one thousand years. A man's life will then only last sixteen or, according to some sects, twenty years at most, his height will only be one cubit, and he will never possess more than eight ribs. The days will be hot and the nights cold, disease will be rampant, and chastity, even between brothers and sisters, will be non-existent. At the end of the period terrific tempests will sweep over the earth, and but for the fact that the Jaina know their uncreated world can never be destroyed, they would fear that the earth itself would perish in the storms. Men and birds, beasts and seeds, will seek everywhere for refuge, and find it in the river Ganges, in caves and in the ocean.

Utsarpiṇī.

At last during *Duṣama Duṣama*, in some month of Śrāvana, and in the dark half of it, the era of Utsarpiṇī will begin, and the wheel of time start its upward revolution. It will rain for seven days seven different kinds of rain, and this will so nourish the ground that the seeds will grow.

Duṣama will bring slight improvement.

In *Duṣama Suṣama* the first of the new twenty-four Tīrthaṅkara will come.

The twenty-four coming Tīrthaṅkara.

The name of this first Tīrthaṅkara will be *Padmanābha.* In Mahāvīra's time this Padmanābha was a king in Magadha, and at present he is expiating his bad karma in the first hell. When in the upward revolution of the wheel *Suṣama* has been reached, the other twenty-three coming Tīrthaṅkara will be born.

Supārśva, the uncle of Mahāvīra, who at the present moment is in the second Devaloka, will be the second Tīrthaṅkara, and will be known as *Suradeva.*

The third will be Udāījī, who was the son of Kuṇika and so grandson of King Śreṇika; he is at present in the third Devaloka, but will be called the Tīrthaṅkara *Supārśva.*

The fourth, a certain Poṭila, now in the fourth Devaloka, will rule as *Svayamprabhu.*

Dṛiḍhaketu, the uncle of the husband of Mallinātha (the only woman Tīrthaṅkara), now in the second Devaloka, will be the fifth Tīrthaṅkara, *Sarvānubhūti.*

Kārttikaśeṭha, the father of the most famous of all Jaina laymen, Ānanda, who is at present in the first Devaloka, will be the sixth, *Devaśruta.*

Śaṅkhaśrāvaka, a man in the twelfth Devaloka, will be reborn as the seventh coming Tīrthaṅkara, *Udayaprabhu.*

The eighth will be Ānandaśrāvaka, now in the first Devaloka, who is to be called *Peḍhāla.*

Sunandāśrāvikā, in the first Devaloka, is to be reborn as the ninth Tīrthaṅkara, *Poṭila.*

A man called Śatakaśrāvaka, in the third hell, is to be re-incarnate as the tenth, *Śatakīrti.*

The eleventh is more interesting, for it is Devakī, the mother of Kṛiṣṇa, at present working out her karma in the eighth Devaloka, who will be incarnate as *Munisuvrata.*

The dark god Kṛiṣṇa himself, now in the third hell, is to become the twelfth Tīrthaṅkara, *Amama.*

Harasatyakī, the guru of Rāvaṇa of Hindu mythology, when he leaves the fifth Devaloka, is to be incarnate as the thirteenth Tīrthaṅkara, *Nikaṣāya.*

Kṛiṣṇa's brother Baladeva, now in the sixth Devaloka, will become *Niṣpulāka*, the fourteenth Tīrthaṅkara.

Sulasā, a man now in the fifth Devaloka, is to be the fifteenth, *Nirmama.*

We have not even yet come to the end of Hindu influence, for the stepmother of Kṛiṣṇa, Rohiṇī (the mother of Baḷadeva), who is in the second Devaloka, will be incarnate as *Ċitragupta*, the sixteenth Tīrthaṅkara.

Revatī, a woman now in the twelfth Devaloka, who in her past life was married to Mahāśutaka, a famous Jaina layman, will become *Sumādhi*, the seventeenth Tīrthaṅkara.

The eighteenth was in her past life Subhala, and later a very chaste woman (if not an actual satī), Magavatī, and is at the present time in the eighth Devaloka, from whence she will issue eventually as *Saṁvaranātha.*

The Hindu ascetic Dvaipāyana, who set fire to Dvārakā, and is now a god, Agni Kumāra, will at last be incarnate as the nineteenth Tīrthaṅkara, *Yaśodhara.*

The twentieth shows again the enormous popularity of the Kṛiṣṇa cult and the influence it wields over Jaina as well as Hindu thought, for it is that of Kuṇika, who in his past life was Javakumāra, a relative of Kṛiṣṇa's. At present he is in the twelfth Devaloka, but eventually he will issue forth to be born as *Vijaya.*

Nārada, who was a layman in the time of Rāvaṇa, and who is in the fifth Devaloka, will be the twenty-first Tīrthaṅkara, Mallinātha or Malyadeva.

Ambaḍa, a former ascetic (or, according to other traditions, a famous layman), now in the twelfth Devaloka, will become the twenty-second Tīrthaṅkara as *Devajina.*

The twenty-third is Amara, now in the ninth Graiveyaka, and will be called *Anantavīrya.*

The twenty-fourth and last of all the coming Tīrthaṅkara is Svayambuddha, now in the highest of all the Devaloka, who is to be incarnate as *Bhadrajina.*

The first of the new series of Tīrthaṅkara, Padmanābha, will much resemble Mahāvīra, and will accomplish as much as he did in spreading the faith. After him each succeeding Tīrthaṅkara will carry on the work, and the world will grow steadily happier, passing through every stage till the happiest of all is reached, when the decline of the wheel must once more begin that leads at last to the destruction of Jainism, and so on in endless succession.

CHAPTER XV

JAINA ARCHITECTURE AND LITERATURE

Jaina Architecture.

THE earliest Jaina architects seem to have used wood as their chief building material: it was easily obtained and very suitable for use in a tropical country; but one quality it conspicuously lacked, that of durability, and the earliest Jaina buildings have all disappeared as completely as the early wooden churches in Ireland.

The habit of using wood, however, left to subsequent Jaina architecture some notable legacies, one of which can be seen in the exquisite fineness of the carvings in the interior of Jaina temples, tracery so delicate that it seems almost incredible it can have been carried out in so stubborn a medium as stone; whilst another legacy is to be found in the many-curved strut that sustains Jaina arches and seems to have taken its origin from the wooden support of a timber arch.

But if the hand of time robbed Jainism of its wooden **Stūpa.** treasures, the lack of knowledge on the part of early scholars, which accredited all stūpa and all cave-temples to Buddhists, robbed Jainism for a time also of its earliest surviving monuments. It is only recently, only in fact since students of the past have realized how many symbols, such as the wheel, the rail, the rosary, the Svastika, &c., the Jaina had in common with the Buddhists and Brāhmans, that its early sites and shrines have been handed back to Jainism. The importance of accuracy in this respect is enhanced by the fact that in its architecture we have an almost perfect record of Jaina history enshrined in loveliness.

Jaina and Buddhist art must have followed much the

same course, and the former like the latter erected stūpa with railings round them in which to place the bones of their saints. But such has been the avidity with which everything possible has been claimed as Buddhist, that as yet only two stūpa[1] are positively admitted to be of Jaina origin. One of these was discovered by Dr. Führer on the Kaṅkāli mound near Mathurā, that centre of Jaina influence, and dates from the Satrap period, and another at Rāmnagar near Bareilly.

Dr. Burgess[2] gives the following account of the construction of a stūpa built on the Aśoka pattern about 200 B.C.:

'On a low circular drum, a hemispherical dome was constructed, with a procession path round the latter, and over the dome a box-like structure surmounted by an umbrella and surrounded by a stone railing. Round the drum was an open passage for circumambulation, and the whole was enclosed by a massive rail with gates on four sides.'

It is interesting to notice that even now after the passage of twenty-one hundred years, circumambulation (*pradakṣiṇā*) plays an important part in Jaina temple worship, and to sit for ever under an umbrella is the highest privilege of their Tīrthaṅkara.

Cave-temples. Of about the same date as the stūpa were the Jaina cave excavations containing ċaitya caves for worship and also caves for the monks to live and sleep in. The Jaina ċaitya were not as big as the Buddhist, for their religion did not necessitate the calling of such large assemblies; but in other respects the resemblance between them was so strong that like the stūpa they were all placed to the credit of the Buddhists. The wonderful caves in Junāgaḍh, for instance, with their traces of beautiful carving, are certainly Jaina, and now that the State is for the time under British administration, it is to be hoped that such thorough excavations may be carried out as will throw light on many disputed points.

Dr. Fergusson[3] also numbers amongst Jaina caves of the

[1] *Imperial Gazetteer*, ii. 111.
[2] Ibid., ii. 159.
[3] J. Fergusson, *History of Indian and Eastern Architecture*, London, 1910, vol. ii, p. 9.

second century B. C. those in Orissa, and as of later date those at Bādāmi, Patna, Elūrā and elsewhere.

If only we could trace the development from the earlier wooden structures to the exquisite eleventh-century temples, we should have solved one of the great problems of Jaina history; but we have as yet no material to do so. The blossoming period of Jaina architecture is like the sudden flowering of Flemish art under the Van Eycks: in both cases all the intermediate stages have been swept away by the ravages of time and the devastation of war, and we are abruptly confronted with the perfection of loveliness, whilst the toilsome steps that led up to it are hidden from us.

1. The Golden Age.

From this time the story of Jaina architecture is clear, and it seems to fall into four main divisions, the first of which, the golden age, almost corresponds with the Gothic movement on the continent of Europe.

The plan of the temples of this period is somewhat similar: each has an open porch (*maṇḍapa*), a closed hall of assembly (*sabhā maṇḍapa*), and an inner shrine or cell (*gabhāro*) in which the idol is kept. The whole is surrounded by a closed courtyard carrying on its inner wall numerous separate cells, each with its own small image of a Tīrthaṅkara. The temple is surmounted by a pyramidal roof, often ending in the representation of a water-pot, and only the carving on this pyramid (or *Śikhara*) as it appears over the temple wall gives any hint of the rich beauty enclosed within the courtyard. The inner shrine is usually guarded by richly carved doorways; the idol itself (nude and blind in the case of Digambara and with loin-cloth and staring glass eyes in the case of Śvetāmbara temples) is of no artistic merit; the sabhā maṇḍapa has very little carving, and is only too often defaced by vulgar decorations and hideous glass globes, but the outer portico (the maṇḍapa) is a very fairyland of beauty, the fineness of whose carving is only equalled by the white tracery of hoar-frost. From the dome of this porch hang pendants of marble, whose workmanship dims the memory of the stairway of Christ Church and the roof of the Divinity School in Oxford, and gives the spectator a new standard of beauty. The many pillars that support the dome are all so perfectly carved, that the element of 'control' is never lost, and the many curved struts between the pillars recall the days when the Jaina wrought their dreams in wood. No description can give the reader any idea of the dainty elaboration of the carving in white marble: indeed the learner needs to pass many times from the blinding glare of a dusty Indian day into the cool whiteness of these shrines and surrender himself to the beauty and stillness of the place, ere he can hope to unravel half their wealth of legends in stone.

We know that the eleventh, twelfth and thirteenth centuries saw the zenith of Jaina prosperity. Not only were kings reckoned amongst the most ardent disciples of this faith, but great wealth poured into the community; and as this acquisition of power and wealth coincided with a time of real religious fervour, it is not surprising that there followed a marvellous epoch of temple-building, in spite of occasional outbursts of fierce persecution. Mount Ābu, bearing on its bosom shrines that are marvels of fretted loveliness, the frowning rock of Girnār crowned with its diadem of temples, and Śatruñjaya in its surpassing holiness, half fortress and half temple-city, bear witness to the fervour of those days, when, for example, even the masons after completing the work for which they were paid on Mount Ābu voluntarily erected another temple as a free-will offering, which is called to this day the Temple of the Artificers.

It has already been pointed out that this the golden age of Jaina temple-building in India is also the period of the great Gothic cathedrals of Lincoln, Salisbury and Wells in England, and of Amiens, Rheims and Chartres in France. Both styles show a complete control of the principle of vaulting and a marvellous inventiveness in the wealth of detail with which the interiors are decorated.

2. Under the shadow of Islam.

The Mohammedans found in the Jaina temples not only quarries from which to steal ready-made the pillars for their mosques, but as it were garments for the expression of religion that could be 'made over' for their use. As easily as an elder sister's clothes are cut up and altered for the use of the younger, so conveniently were Jaina temples transformed for the appropriation of this newest arrival on the Indian scene. All that the victorious Mohammedans had to do was to make slight structural alterations.

'By removing the principal cell and its porch from the centre of the court, and building up the entrances of the cells that surround it, a courtyard was at once obtained, surrounded by a double colonnade, which always was the typical form of a mosque. Still one essential feature was wanting—a more important side towards Mecca; this they easily obtained by removing the smaller pillars from that side, and re-erecting in their place the larger pillars of the porch, with their dome in the centre; and, if there were two smaller domes, by placing one of them at each end.'[1]

No original mosque the Mohammedans ever erected rivalled these 'made-over' temples for beauty. In the zenith of their prosperity Jaina architects had taught Hindu builders much; now in adversity they still influenced their persecutors, and the still too-little-known mosques of Aḥmadābād owe more of their unrivalled beauty to Jaina inspiration than to any other source.

But the Jaina did not only teach; like true scholars, they also learnt even from their opponents, and it is to the blending of the pure Jaina style with Mughal features that we owe modern Jaina architecture. The present writer was shown both at Ābu and Śatruñjaya on the interior of the roof of the temple courtyard miniature representations of Mohammedan tombs, which she was assured had been placed there to guard the shrines from the iconoclastic zeal of the conquerors. This, however, was only a small

[1] Fergusson, loc. cit., ii. 69.

matter compared to the other modifications due to Mohammedan influence that were to follow.

3. Modern Jaina architecture. When the Mohammedan tyranny was overpast, the natural outcome of Jaina belief in the merit of building temples again showed itself in the erection of new shrines on the old sites, in additions to the temple cities, and also in the buildings that may still be seen in such places as Sonāgarh and Mukhtagiri. The peace and prosperity that have followed the establishment of British rule in India have led to an unprecedented outburst of temple-building; and all these shrines, whether erected in the sixteenth or in the nineteenth century, have so many characteristics in common, that they may be grouped together as modern. The pointed pyramidical roof is seldom seen, and the true Jaina dome is superseded by the Mughal, and the openings are now usually the foliated pointed arch which the Mohammedans introduced. The style, too, though rich and ornate, has lost much of its original eleventh-century purity.

Perhaps one distinct gain may be chronicled that is seen at its best in a Jaina temple in Delhi, namely, the filling in of the space behind the strut with beautiful pierced work, that makes the whole resemble a bracket supporting the arch.

On the debit side, however, there must be recorded the terrible vulgarity that often disfigures modern Jaina temples and is seen at its worst in places like the temple city of Pālitāṇā, where the older buildings throw the modern craze for crude colour washing and paintings into terrible relief. Perhaps the most famous of the modern temples is that erected by Śeṭha Haṭṭhisiṁha in Aḥmadābād in 1848, where despite all the beauty of its carving one still longs for the more austere loveliness of the earlier fanes. The old 'Gothic' days seem to have passed now into an over-elaborated period of mixed styles.

The Jaina architecture of the south forms a class apart; it has three chief divisions. First, temples (*Bastī*) that possess shrine, assembly hall and porch, like similar buildings in the north of India, but with more ornate outer walls. Secondly, open-air courtyards (*Betta*) containing images not of any of the orthodox Tīrthaṅkara of the north, but of Gōmata or Gomateśvara, a Digambara saint unknown in northern India. (It is to this saint that the famous colossi of the south are dedicated. The best known of these is that at Śrāvaṇa Belgolā in Mysore, which, cut from a single block of gneiss, stands some fifty-seven feet high; others are to be found at Yenūr and Kārkala in South Kanara.) The third class of temples is found in Kanara, and with their Venetian blinds they curiously recall the house of some European official, but their general style and especially their reversed eaves resemble the buildings of Nepāl. 4. Southern India.

Another feature of note in Southern Jaina architecture is the *stambha* or pillar. In Ābu the custodian of a temple drew the writer's attention to a stambha within the enclosure and explained that no temple was complete without one. But the Ābu pillar was plain indeed compared to the lavishly carved stambha that are to be found in the south. At Mūdabidri a most interesting question is raised by the presence on the bottom of these pillars of the curious interlaced basket-work pattern familiar in Irish manuscripts and on Irish crosses.

'It is equally common in Armenia, and can be traced up the valley of the Danube into central Europe; but how it got to the west coast of India we do not know, nor have we, so far as I know, any indication on which we can rely for its introduction. There was at all times for the last fifteen centuries a large body of Christians established on this coast who were in connection with Persia and Syria, and are so now. It would be strange, indeed, if it were from them the Jains obtained this device.'[1]

May not this symbol from the ancient crosses now so

[1] Fergusson, ii. 82.

strangely found in the very centre of a Jaina temple be a prophecy of the coming of the spring?

Jaina Writers.

Jainism has produced so vast and varied a literature, that we can mention here only the leading periods of activity and the languages used.

All the books of the Canon are in Ardha-Māgadhī, the vernacular spoken by Mahāvīra and his monks, which thus became the sacred language of Jainism.

All early commentaries on the Jaina Canon and a good deal of the secular poetry composed by Jaina are in what is known as Jaina-Mahārāṣṭrī, a vernacular closely allied to early Marāṭhī.

After the Christian era Sanskrit gradually won its way to the place of *lingua franca* in North India. It was generally used in inscriptions and in royal proclamations; and literary men of all the religions employed it in preference to other tongues, because it alone was understood by cultured men everywhere. This explains the existence of a great body of Buddhist literature in Sanskrit. The Jaina were rather later than others in substituting Sanskrit for their accustomed vernacular, but finally most of their sects also yielded, though in varying degrees. A large part of Jaina Sanskrit literature consists of scholastic and philosophic works connected with the exposition and defence of the faith; but the Jaina also hold a notable place in ordinary literature. They specially distinguished themselves in grammar, lexicography and moral tales. The two northern recensions of the *Pañćatantra*, for example, show considerable Jaina influence. The work of this period culminates in the activity of Hemaćandra, with whose writings we deal briefly below.

In South India the earliest literary movement was predominately Jaina. In Tamil literature from the earliest times for many centuries Jaina poets held a great place. The *Jīvaka Ćintāmaṇi*, perhaps the finest of all Tamil poems, is a Jaina work. Eight thousand Jaina, it is said, each wrote a couplet, and the whole when joined together formed the famous *Nāladiyār*. To-day this consists of only four hundred verses, but the discrepancy is accounted for by the action of a hostile monarch who flung the whole multitude of poems into a stream and destroyed all but four hundred particularly good ones! Each of the verses is quite unconnected with the other, but has a most unimpeachable moral, and so they are taught in Tamil schools to this day.

More famous still is the *Kurraḷ* of Tiruvaḷḷuvar, the masterpiece of Tamil literature. Its author, an outcaste by birth, is claimed by every sect as belonging to their faith, but Bishop Caldwell 'considers its tone more Jaina than anything else'.[1] In any case it must come from the earliest period. Another name that adds lustre to these times is that of a Jaina lady Avvaiyār 'the Venerable Matron', one of the most admired amongst Tamil poets, who is said to have been a sister of Tiruvaḷḷuvar. Nor was it only amongst the fields of poesy that the Jaina gained renown; a famous old dictionary and the great Tamil grammar are also accredited to them.

Jaina writers also laid the foundations of Telugu literature, and classical Kanarese literature begins with a great succession of Jaina poets and scholars. The period of their greatest activity runs from the eighth to the twelfth century.

But the greatest of all Jaina writers was undoubtedly Hemaćandra. He was born in Dhandukā near Aḥmadābād in A. D. 1088 of Jaina parents, his real name being probably Ćāṅgadeva. His mother dedicated him to the religious life under the care of a monk named Devaćandra, who took him to Cambay, where he was eventually ordained, receiving the new name of Somaćandra. In Cambay he studied logic, dialectics, grammar and poetry, and proved himself a past master in every branch of study he took up.

[1] *Imperial Gazetteer*, ii. 435

Hemaċandra's chance came when he was appointed spokesman of the Jaina community at Aṇhilvāḍa Pāṭaṇa to welcome the great Ċaulukya king, Jayasiṁha Siddharāja, on his return from a famous victory in Mālwā. His poem won the king's heart, and he was appointed court paṇḍit and court annalist in the royal capital. There he compiled two lexicons and wrote his famous Prākṛit grammar, with which the learned king was so delighted, that he engaged three hundred copyists for three years to transcribe it, and sent copies all over India. Hemaċandra was just as popular with Jayasiṁha's successor, Kumārapāla, whom, if he did not actually convert to Jainism, he at least persuaded to follow the Jaina rule of non-killing, and to build many temples. During this reign Hemaċandra continued to write a number of science hand-books, lives of Jaina saints, and other works, including a History of Gujarāt and the famous Yoga Śāstra and commentary thereon; and he also found time to instruct many scholars who carried on the literary tradition. (In Aṇhilvāḍa Pāṭaṇa one may still see the ink-stained stone on which Hemaċandra's cushion was placed, and where he dictated his works to his pupils.) About A. D. 1172 Hemaċandra died of self-starvation, in the approved Jaina fashion, shortly before his friend and patron Kumārapāla.

It is astonishing that with such a magnificent record of early writers the Jaina of to-day, despite their educational advantages, should number so few authors of note amongst them; their literary activity seems at present to find its chief outlet in journalism and pamphleteering.[1]

Modern Jaina literature is mostly in Gujarātī, but books in Hindī and in English are also numerous.

[1] It is interesting and encouraging to notice that out of every possible way of spreading their faith the Jaina have deliberately chosen as the best adapted for Oriental use the now classic methods selected by the great old Christian missionaries (true Tīrthaṅkara) of the past. Thus they have Jaina tracts, Jaina newspapers, Jaina schools and Jaina hostels; each sect has also its own Conference, with its Ladies' Day, and there are even Jaina Young Men's Associations.

CHAPTER XVI

THE EMPTY HEART OF JAINISM

THE more one studies Jainism, the more one is struck with the pathos of its empty heart. The Jaina believe strongly in the duty of forgiving others, and yet have no hope of forgiveness from a Higher Power for themselves. They shrink from sin and take vows to guard against it, but know of no dynamic force outside themselves that could enable them to keep those vows. They see before them an austere upward path of righteousness, but know of no Guide to encourage and help them along that difficult way.

A scholar-saint once summed up the Christian faith by saying that the personal friendship of Jesus Christ our Lord was that gift which God became incarnate to bestow on every man who sought it. It is this personal friendship with the Incarnate Son of God which is the great gift that Christianity has to offer to the Jaina. Already, with their power of hero-worship and their intense love of all that is gentle, long-suffering and loving, the Jaina cannot but be attracted to Him. It is perhaps easier for a Jaina than it is for us to appreciate the wonderful portrait of Himself which Christ drew in those rules for happiness which we call the Beatitudes; for, while approving of the Ten Commandments, to which in many respects their own rules bear a strong resemblance, it is to the Beatitudes that they are specially attracted, since these meet their faith at its highest and yet point out a still higher way.

The younger Jaina are worried by the old ascetic ideal that is placed before them. They feel, even when they can hardly express it, that the ideal needed for modern life is the development, not the negation, of personality; they are also increasingly bewildered by the conflict between modern science and their own faith. The appeal of Christianity may come to them through their realizing that the true way to ensure the growth of one's own character is by gaining the noblest of friendships, that of the man Christ Jesus.

But it is when talking to the older men and women that one realizes most how restless and dissatisfied they are at heart, since the ideal their religion offers them is a ritual rather than a personal holiness. A Jaina magistrate once said to the writer: 'I call Jainism a dummy religion. Even if I took bribes and gave false judgements, I should still be considered a holy man, so long as I was careful never to eat after dark.' And an older man made this pathetic confession: 'It is a terrible thing to a Jaina to grow old: we may have tried all our lives to keep our innumerable laws, but we know the awful doom that awaits us if we have broken even one of them, and for us there is no forgiveness.' His pitiful fear seemed wonderfully to enhance the glory of the old Evangel: 'I came not to call the righteous but sinners to repentance'; but the man could hardly grasp the fact that, while the Redeemer of the World never uttered one word of hope or forgiveness to strong, self-sufficient, self-righteous folk, He freely offered the riches of His grace to the sinful and fallen, to the weak and helpless, to women and to little children.

A short time ago the writer was talking to a student, who had himself left Jainism, but was explaining to her how many beautiful things there were in the Jaina creed. At length she asked him why he was no longer a Jaina. He turned to her and said: 'Because in all our creed there is no such word as "grace".'

The problem of suffering.

In a book such as this one can only throw out a few suggestions for a comparison between Jainism and Christianity, and one of the chief points on which they differ is in the value they give to sorrow. To Christian thought sorrow is not necessarily an evil: to the Jaina it is either a calamity to be avoided at all costs, or a punishment from which there is no escape. One can easily understand how Jainism arose: how sensitive souls, finding the pain of the world intolerable, would resolve to free themselves from every tie that might be the means of bringing sorrow upon them, and to give no more hostages to fortune. But they forgot that by shutting themselves off from pain they closed the gates for ever against development, not realizing that, as all advance in knowledge can be gained only at the price of weary drudgery, and even the supreme joy of motherhood is not won without danger and pain, so character can only be completely developed by the discipline of sorrow: the only result of shirking suffering is for scholars, ignorance; for women, barrenness; and for all, even the highest, moral atrophy.

The more one comes to know the Jaina, the more sure one feels that they will not for ever remain satisfied with the thought of a divinity which, by avoiding emotion, has become a characterless being, taking no interest in the lives of his followers and powerless to help them. Already many are attracted by the idea of a God who, becoming incarnate for us men and for our salvation, not only promulgated a law of self-denial and of loving-kindness to every living being more stringent and far-reaching than the Jaina rule, but also Himself suffered in His life and death more loneliness, more insults and more pain than ever Mahāvīra endured, and whose suffering only increased His love and power to help men in their sorrows. Alone amongst the religions of the world the faith of Christ Jesus opens to its followers conquest through pain and mystic joy in sorrow.

Despite the differences between Jainism and Christianity, the resemblance between them is striking. Both religions arose in the East, and both are to this day thoroughly Oriental in their character and spirit. The founders of the two faiths were each the son of a king, and each left his high estate for a life of poverty and insult. Each wandered homeless through sunny lands, followed by a band of twelve disciples, proclaiming the beauty of poverty of spirit, of meekness, of righteousness, of mercy, of purity, of peace, and of patient suffering. Alike they illustrated their teaching from the every-day life of the countryside, showing how much greater a thing it was 'to be' than 'to do', and how perilous 'to have'; but each teacher gave his followers a different motive to rule their lives, for the command of the one was to love and of the other to escape.

No supreme God.

The Jaina do not believe in one supreme God. Innumerable men of like passions with themselves have, by steadily eradicating all that belongs to personality, passed to take their places amongst the Siddha in a still land of endless inactivity; but none of these are first and none second: all are equal; and none take any interest in the human toilers who are climbing the steep ascent leading to the goal which they themselves have reached.

Forgiveness.

The loss suffered by those who have relinquished their belief in a supreme God it is impossible adequately to gauge. For instance, the Jaina can have no conception of the forgiveness of sin, for to them there is no God against whom they have sinned, but whose property it is to show mercy, and who, by pardoning past failure, can give an opportunity for future conquest. The Jaina, when they do wrong, only feel that they sin against themselves, injure their own characters, and so lose ground on the upward way, and that such lost progress can only be made up after countless ages of useless (because unremembered) suffering.

Prayer.

Again, a system without a God has no room for prayer, for it knows of no almighty and most merciful Father to whose love and wisdom His children can confide their secret desires; and to this day the Jaina count it a sin if a mother, watching beside her suffering child, should appeal to some higher power to save the little life.

There is no question that the Jaina feel to be more critical than the intricate problem of caste in modern India. The one solvent that can ever weaken the grip of those iron fetters is the thought that, despite all barriers and all differences, we have been created by the same Father and are therefore all children of one family; but a philosophy that denies the Fatherhood of God is able to deny the brotherhood of man; and the notices on their temple gates show that there are no people in India more caste-bound than the Jaina.[1] Caste.

The negation of a personal God affects also the Jaina idea of heaven. The Jaina, as we have seen, think of mokṣa as a bare place of inaction reached by those who through suffering and austerity have completely killed all their individuality and character and have finally snapped the fetters of rebirth. The Christian, like the Jaina, believes in a state whose bliss we shall never leave, but to the Christian heaven is also that sphere where the Lord God Omnipotent reigneth, and over which His will has absolute sway. There, in a golden atmosphere of happiness, the redeemed from all nations, with every power disciplined and developed, move without let or hindrance to accomplish the Divine will. There His servants serve Him, for they see His face. It is a land full of joy and singing, from which all sorrow has vanished, not because the character of its citizens has become so stultified that they can no more feel grief, but because the promise has been fulfilled that 'God Himself shall be with them, and be their God: and He shall wipe away every tear from their eyes; and death shall be no more; neither shall there be mourning, nor crying, nor pain, any more. . . . He that overcometh [the jina] shall inherit these things; and I will be his God, and he shall be my son.'[2] Mokṣa.

[1] The notice on Haṭṭhisimha's temple in Aḥmadābād runs: 'Low-caste servants in attendance on visitors and dogs cannot be allowed to enter the temple.'

[2] Rev. xxi. 3-4; 7.

Karma and transmigration.

Instead of a God delighting in mercy, who rules and judges the fair world that He has made, the Jaina have set in His place a hideous thing, the accumulated energy of past actions, karma, which can no more be affected by love or prayer than a runaway locomotive. On and on it goes, remorselessly dealing out mutilation and suffering, till the energy it has amassed is at last exhausted and a merciful silence follows. The belief in karma and transmigration kills all sympathy and human kindness for sufferers, since any pain a man endures is only the wages he has earned in a previous birth. It is this belief that is responsible amongst other things for the suffering of the thousands of child widows in India, who are taught that they are now reaping the fruit of their unchastity in a former life. There is no conscious justice in this solution, for how can a man possibly accept a sentence as righteous, when he does not even know for what he is being tried and has no recollection of ever committing the crime?

Ahiṁsā.

Much, however, as the Jaina find to admire in Christianity, one of their tenets, that of Ahiṁsā, casts for them a great shadow across the Christian faith: they feel that the followers of Christ are stained with the sin of animal murder, and until this feeling is removed, they will never really understand the beauty of our religion.

One would like to remind them first of the quite elementary fact that a great many Christians are actually vegetarians, and that no Christian is under any obligation to eat meat; in fact the great missionary apostle expressly said, 'If meat maketh my brother to stumble, I will eat no flesh for evermore'.[1] Not as though there were any sin in eating or in not eating meat. Jesus Christ, realizing that there were enough real sins already in the world, created no artificial ones by laying down ritual regulations for His followers to govern the details of their daily lives. But though He gave them no narrow code of rules, as though they had been

[1] 1 Cor. viii. 13.

slaves, He did lay down for them certain great principles on which they might fashion their lives in absolute freedom, and one of these was the principle of self-sacrificing service.

Science has taught us that the physical world is governed by the law of sacrifice: that all existence is maintained through the death of others, and that every living organism is built up through the silent and invisible work of the minute bacteria of decay, which release from the dead the material needed by the living. It is this same law of sacrifice, of life through another's death, which governs also the spiritual world. When animals and insects are killed that a Jaina may have light to study, material for clothing, shoes to wear, bread to eat, water with which to wash, or air to breathe, it seems to him that the sin of murder has been committed (for the Jaina have not yet learnt clearly to distinguish between human and animal life); but to the Christian it seems that he has accepted strength from others, which he is therefore bound to expend in service. And this is the reason that at every meal he thanks God for the food given and asks that the strength gained may be used in God's service.[1] For the follower of Christ has realized that his very entrance into the world was purchased by another's pain (perhaps death), and that throughout life his food, his clothing, and even his leisure for study or for art is earned by the toil of others. He cannot therefore count himself his own, but as a 'debtor' he is bound to use his life and his leisure in the service of others, that they in their turn may by his work be helped to labour more happily.

Following this thought, we seem to catch a glimpse of what is perhaps one great purpose of God, that all His creatures should be linked to one another by golden chains of self-sacrificing service. In the highest realm

[1] Compare the old College grace: 'Benignissime Domine, benedic nobis et hisce creaturis in usum nostrum; ut illae sanctificatae sint et nobis salutares, et nos inde corroborati magis apti reddamur ad omnia opera bona, in laudem tui nominis aeternam per Iesum Christum Dominum nostrum. Amen.'

of all the same law still holds: 'Surely He hath borne our griefs, and carried our sorrows. . . . He was wounded for our transgressions, He was bruised for our iniquities: the chastisement of our peace was upon Him; and with His stripes we are healed. All we like sheep have gone astray; we have turned every one to his own way; and the Lord hath laid on Him the iniquity of us all.'[1]

But the golden chain that binds us all into one loving whole is broken by cruelty, and it is here that the Jaina fail. Their belief in the duty of not killing is not in practice complemented by an equal fear of cruelty. It is surely happier for instance, for an animal to be well tended, well fed, and well cared for, and then to die swiftly and painlessly before old age and suffering come upon it, than to linger on, as one so often sees in India (even in a Jaina asylum for animals[2]), neglected, suffering, and even starving, once it has passed its prime.

Moreover, the logical outcome of the doctrine of Ahiṁsā is, as the Jaina themselves admit, a *reductio ad absurdum*. They must not move for fear of treading on and killing some minute insect; for the same reason they must not eat and they must not breathe. So that in order not to commit hiṁsā Jaina sometimes commit suicide, yet suicide they consider one of the wickedest of crimes.[3] It is scientifically impossible to take as a life's motto *Ahiṁsā parama dharma*, since it is contrary to the order of nature. To carry it out, a man ought not to be born, lest his birth should cost his mother her life; he must not continue to live when he is

[1] Isaiah liii. 4-6.

[2] These asylums or *Pāñjarāpoḷa* are peculiar to Jainism, and all sects of the Jaina unite in striving to acquire merit by supporting them. They are to be found in many of the large towns and villages throughout India, and house decrepit and suffering cattle, horses, donkeys, goats, &c.; even pāriah dogs are collected in special dog-carts (i.e. wheeled cages) by men armed with long iron pincers with which they can safely pick up the most savage and filthy curs. But, as far as any real kindness to animals is concerned, these institutions in their actual working leave much to be desired, however meritorious the intention of their founders may have been.

[3] The whole Jaina position in relation to suicide is, however, most puzzling. Apparently simple suicide is held to be a crime, but *santhāro*, or religious suicide, is a meritorious act.

born, since every instant he breathes he takes life; he must not commit suicide, for that is taking life; he must not even die a natural death, for in the burning of his corpse after death some life would be destroyed.

But though our Lord gave to His followers the law of self-sacrificing service, not that of Ahiṁsā, He was nevertheless careful to teach them how exceedingly precious in the sight of the Creator was the life of even the smallest of His creatures. 'Are not two sparrows sold for a farthing?' said Christ, 'and not one of them shall fall on the ground without your Father.'[1] And again in His great Sermon on the Mount: 'Behold the birds of the heaven, that they sow not, neither do they reap, nor gather into barns; and your heavenly Father feedeth them.'[2]

And so through all the history of Christendom it has been proved true that

'He prayeth well, who loveth well
Both man and bird and beast.
He prayeth best, who loveth best
All things both great and small;
For the dear God who loveth us,
He made and loveth all.'

System of ethics.

Another great difference between Christianity and Jainism lies in the fact that, while Jainism may fairly be regarded as a system of ethics rather than a religion, yet the intensely self-centred point of view of Jainism, in which all actions are judged by the profit (*puṇya*) that may accrue from them, differentiates it also from altruistic ethical systems; and this self-centred attitude, perhaps, it is which largely accounts for the failure of the Jaina as a whole to take their share in social reform.

Personality and life.

The supreme difference, however, between Jainism and Christianity we have already glanced at more than once; it lies in their treatment of personality and life. The object of Christianity is to educate every sense and to train the whole personality, till the highest development is reached, and we all attain 'unto a fullgrown man, unto the

[1] St. Matt. x. 29. [2] St. Matt. vi. 26.

measure of the stature of the fulness of Christ'.[1] The key-word of Jainism, on the other hand, is the elimination of personality. So long as a man has to live in this world, he should daily curtail his opportunities of development; and if he attains to the ascetic life, he should see to it that his personality withers the faster, for atrophy is his goal.

It will be remembered that before Mahāvīra's death nine out of his twelve disciples carried their Master's precepts to their logical conclusion and gained the goal of death through religious suicide by starvation; and we have seen how, through the long centuries right down to the present time, this has been the practice of his most devoted followers. What could be a greater contrast than the lives of the twelve men who followed Christ, and whose work after His death and resurrection turned the dead old world upside down; for the Master they served was one who had come to give Life, and to give it more abundantly.

The unknown God of Jainism. There is a strange mystery in Jainism; for though it acknowledges no personal God, knowing Him neither as Creator, Father, or Friend, yet it will never allow itself to be called an atheistic system. Indeed there is no more deadly insult that one could level at a Jaina than to call him a nāstika or atheist.

It is as if, though their king were yet unknown to them, they were nevertheless all unconsciously awaiting his advent amongst them, and proudly called themselves royalists.

The marks which they will ask to see in one who claims to be their king will be the proofs of Incarnation (*avatāra*), of Suffering (*tapa*), and of the Majesty of a Conqueror (*Jina*). But when once they recognize Him, they will pour out at His feet all the wealth of their trained powers of self-denial and renunciation. Then shall He, the Desire of all nations, whose right it is to reign, take His seat on the empty throne of their hearts, and He shall reign King of Kings and Lord of Lords for ever and ever.

[1] Eph. iv. 13.

APPENDIX

I. ANALYSIS OF THE NINE CATEGORIES

FIRST CATEGORY: JIVA.

It can be classified:

i. *In two divisions*: *a.* Siddha.
b. Saṁsārī.

ii. *In three divisions*: *a.* Male.
b. Female.
c. Neuter.

iii. *In four divisions*: *a.* Nārakī.
b. Tiryañċ.
c. Manuṣya.
d. Devatā.

iv. *In five divisions*: *a.* Ekendriya. (Pṛithvīkāya, Apakāya, Teukāya, Vāyukāya, Vanaspatikāya [Pratyeka, Sādhāraṇa].)
b. Be-indriya (Dvīndriya).
c. Tri-indriya (Trīndriya).
d. Ċorendriya (Ċaturindriya).
e. Pañċendriya [Saṁjñī and Asaṁjñī].

v. *In six divisions*: *a.* Pṛithvīkāya.
b. Apakāya.
c. Teukāya.
d. Vāyukāya.
e. Vanaspatikāya.
f. Trasakāya.

vi. *In seven somewhat artificial divisions for symmetry.*

vii. *In eight divisions*: *a.* Saleśī.
b. Those swayed by Kṛiṣṇaleśyā.
c. " " " Nīlaleśyā.
d. " " " Kapotaleśyā.
e. " " " Tejoleśyā.
f. " " " Padmaleśyā.
g. " " " Śuklaleśyā.
h. " " " Aleśī.

viii. *Artificial division into nine classes.*

ix. *In ten divisions*: Ekendriya { Paryāptā. / Aparyāptā.

Be-indriya { Paryāptā. / Aparyāptā.

Tri-indriya { Paryāptā. / Aparyāptā.

Corendriya { Paryāptā. / Aparyāptā.

Pañċendriya { Paryāptā. / Aparyāptā.

x. *In eleven divisions*: Ekendriya.
Be-indriya.
Tri-indriya.
Ċorendriya.
Nārakī.
Tiryañċ.
Manuṣya.
Bhavanapati deva.
Vyantara deva.
Jyotiṣī deva.
Vaimānika deva.

xi. *Artificial division into twelve classes.*

xii. *Artificial division into thirteen classes.*

xiii. *Artificial division into fourteen classes, two being new, viz.*:
Sūkṣma ekendriya.
Bādara ekendriya.

SECOND CATEGORY: AJIVA.

A. Arūpī Ajīva.

1. Dharmāstikāya (Dravya, Kṣetra, Kāḷa, Bhāva, Guṇa).
Skandha.
Deśa.
Pradeśa.

2. Adharmāstikāya (Dravya, Kṣetra, Kāḷa, Bhāva, Guṇa).
Skandha.
Deśa.
Pradeśa.

3. Ākāśāstikāya (Dravya, Kṣetra, Kāḷa, Bhāva, Guṇa).
Skandha.
Deśa.
Pradeśa.

4. Kāḷa (Dravya, Kṣetra, Kāḷa, Bhāva, Guṇa).

B. Rūpī Ajīva.

Pudgaḷāstikāya.

THIRD CATEGORY: PUṆYA.

Nine Kinds of Puṇya.

1. Anna puṇya.
2. Pāṇa puṇya.
3. Vastra puṇya.
4. Layaṇa puṇya.
5. Śayana puṇya.
6. Mana puṇya (Manas *or* Mānasa puṇya).
7. Śarīra or Kāya puṇya.
8. Vaċana puṇya.
9. Namaskāra puṇya.

Forty-two Fruits of Puṇya.

1. Śātavedanīya.
2. Ūñċagotra.
3. Manuṣya gati.
4. Manuṣya anupūrvī.
5. Devatā gati.
6. Devatā anupūrvī.
7. Pañċendriyapaṇuṁ.
8. Audārikaśarīra.
9. Vaikreyaśarīra.
10. Āhārakaśarīra.
11. Audārika aṅgopāṅga.
12. Vaikreya aṅgopāṅga.
13. Āhāraka aṅgopāṅga.
14. Taijasaśarīra.
15. Kārmaṇaśarīra.
16. Vrajraṛiṣabhanārāċa sanghayaṇa.
17. Samaċaturastra saṇṭhāṇa.
18. Śubha varṇa.
19. Śubha gandha.
20. Śubha rasa.
21. Śubha sparśa.
22. Agurulaghu nāmakarma.
23. Parāghāta nāmakarma.
24. Uċċhvāsa nāmakarma.
25. Ātapa nāmakarma.
26. Anuṣṇa nāmakarma.
27. Śubhavihāyogati.
28. Nirmāṇa nāmakarma.
29. Trasa nāmakarma.
30. Bādara nāmakarma.

31. Paryāpti nāmakarma.
32. Sthira nāmakarma.
33. Pratyeka nāmakarma.
34. Śubha nāmakarma.
35. Subhaga nāmakarma.
36. Susvara nāmakarma.
37. Ādeya nāmakarma.
38. Yaśokīrtti nāmakarma.
39. Devatā āyuṣya.
40. Manuṣya āyuṣya.
41. Tiryañċ āyuṣya.
42. Tīrthaṅkara nāmakarma.

Fourth Category: PĀPA.

Eighteen Kinds of Sin.

1. Jīva hiṁsā.
   a. Bhāva hiṁsā.
   b. Dravya hiṁsā.
2. Asatya or Mṛiṣāvāda.
3. Adattādāna.
4. Abrahmaċarya.
5. Parigraha.
6. Krodha.
7. Māna.
8. Māyā.
9. Lobha.
   (6–9: Kaṣāya or Caṇḍāla Ċokaḍī.)
   Kinds { a. Apraśasta. b. Praśasta.
   Length of time indulged in: Anantānubandhī, Apratyākhyānī, Pratyākhyānī, Sañjvalana.
10. Rāga or Āsakti.
11. Dveṣa or Īrṣyā.
12. Kleśa.
13. Abhyākhyāna.
14. Paiśunya.
15. Nindā.
16. Rati, Arati.
17. Māyāmṛiṣā.
18. Mithyādarśana Śalya.

Some of the twenty-five divisions of Mithyādarśana Śalya:

Laukika mithyātva.
Lokottara mithyātva.
Abhigrahika mithyātva.
Ajñāna mithyātva.

Avinaya mithyātva.
Aśātanā mithyātva.
Anabhigrahika mithyātva.

The Eighty-two Results of Sin :

Five Jñānāvaraṇīya.

1. 1. Matijñānāvaraṇīya.
2. 2. Śrutajñānāvaraṇīya.
3. 3. Avadhijñānāvaraṇīya.
4. 4. Manaḥparyāyajñānāvaraṇīya.
5. 5. Kevalajñānāvaraṇīya.

Five Antarāya.

6. 1. Dānāntarāya.
7. 2. Lābhāntarāya.
8. 3. Bhogāntarāya.
9. 4. Upabhogāntarāya.
10. 5. Vīryāntarāya.

The Four Darśanāvaraṇīya.

11. 1. Ċakṣudarśanāvaraṇīya.
12. 2. Aċakṣudarśanāvaraṇīya.
13. 3. Avadhidarśanāvaraṇīya.
14. 4. Kevaladarśanāvaraṇīya.

The Five Nidrā.

15. 1. Nidrā.
16. 2. Nidrānidrā.
17. 3. Praċalā.
18. 4. Praċalāpraċalā.
19. 5. Styānarddhi (*or* Thīṇarddhi).

Five Unclassified Results.

20. Nīċagotra.
21. Narakagati.
22. Aśātavedanīya.
23. Narakānupūrvī.
24. Narakāyu.

Twenty-five Kaṣāya.

25–40. *Sixteen* already discussed (Anger, Pride, Deceit, Envy, and their subdivisions)

and *Nine* Nokaṣāya, namely :—

41. Hāsya.
42. Rati.
43. Arati.

44. Bhaya.
45. Śoka.
46. Dugañċhā.
47. Puruṣaveda.
48. Strīveda.
49. Napuṁsakaveda.

Six Results affecting Class.

50. Tiryañċ anupūrvī.
51. Tiryañċ gati.
52. Ekendriya nāma.
53. Be-indriya nāma.
54. Tri-indriya nāma.
55. Ċorendriya nāma.

Six Physical Blemishes.

56. Aśubha vihāyogati.
57. Upaghāta nāma.
58. Aśubha varṇa.
59. Aśubha gandha.
60. Aśubha rasa.
61. Aśubha sparśa.

Five Saṅgheṇa.

62. Ṛiṣabhanārāċa saṅgheṇa.
63. Nārāċa (or Nārāya) saṅgheṇa.
64. Ardhanārāċa (-nārāya) saṅgheṇa.
65. Kīlikā saṅgheṇa.
66. Sevārtta saṅgheṇa.

Five Saṁsthāna.

67. Nyagrodhaparimaṇḍaḷa saṁsthāna.
68. Sādi saṁsthāna.
69. Kubjaka saṁsthāna.
70. Vāmana saṁsthāna.
71. Huṇḍa saṁsthāna.

Sthāvara Daśaka.

72. Sthāvara.
73. Sūkṣma.
74. Aparyāpti.
75. Sādhāraṇa.
76. Asthira.
77. Aśubha.
78. Durbhaga.
79. Dusvara.

80. Anādeya.
81. Ayaśa.
82. Mithyātva mohanīya.

FIFTH CATEGORY: ĀŚRAVA.

Forty-two Chief Channels by which Karma may enter.

Seventeen Major Āśrava.

1. Kāna (Karṇa). 2. Ānkha (Akṣa). 3. Nāka (Nās). 4. Jībha (Jihvā). 5. Sparśa.	Karma enters through the Five Senses.
6. Krodha. 7. Māna. 8. Māyā. 9. Lobha.	Karma enters through the Four Kaṣāya.
10. Killing. 11. Lying. 12. Thieving. 13. Coveting. 14. Unchastity.	Karma enters through not taking the five vows to avoid these sins.
15. Mind. 16. Body. 17. Speech.	Karma enters through not maintaining the Three Yoga (control).

Twenty-five Minor Āśrava.

1. Kāyikī.
2. Adhikaraṇikī.
3. Pradveṣikī.
4. Paritāpanikī.
5. Prāṇātipātikī.
6. Ārambhikī.
7. Pārigrahikī.
8. Māyāpratyayikī.
9. Mithyādarśanapratyayikī.
10. Apratyākhyānikī.
11. Dṛiṣṭikī.
12. Spṛiṣṭikī.
13. Prātityakī.
14. Sāmantopanipātikī.
15. Naiśastrikī.
16. Svahastikī.
17. Ājñāpanikī.

18. Vaidāraṇikī.
19. Anābhogikī.
20. Anavakāṅkṣāpratyayikī.
21. Prayogikī.
22. Sāmudāyikī.
23. Premikī.
24. Dveṣikī.
25. Īryāpathikī.

Sixth Category: SAṀVARA.

Fifty-seven Ways of Impeding Karma.

Five Samiti.

1. Īryā samiti.
2. Bhāṣā samiti.
3. Eṣaṇā samiti.
4. Ādānanikṣepaṇā samiti.
5. Parithāpaṇikā samiti (*or* Utsarga samiti).

Three Gupti.

6. Manogupti.
    - *a.* Asatkalpanāviyogī.
    - *b.* Samatābhāvinī.
    - *c.* Ātmārāmatā.
7. Vaċanagupti.
    - *a.* Maunāvalambi.
    - *b.* Vākniyami.
8. Kāyagupti.
    - *a.* Yathāsūtraċeṣṭāniyami.
    - *b.* Ċeṣṭānivṛitti.

Twenty-two Parīṣaha.

9. Kṣudhā parīṣaha.
10. Tṛiṣā "
11. Śīta "
12. Uṣṇa "
13. Daṁśa "
14. Vastra "
15. Arati "
16. Strī "
17. Ċaryā "
18. Naiṣidhikī (Naiṣedhikī) parīṣaha.
19. Śayyā parīṣaha.
20. Akrośa "

21. Vadha parīṣaha.
22. Yāñċā (Yāċanā) parīṣaha.
23. Alābha ,,
24. Roga ,,
25. Tṛiṇasparśa ,,
26. Mela ,,
27. Satkāra ,,
28. Prajñā ,,
29. Ajñāna ,,
30. Samyaktva ,,

Ten Duties of Monks (Daśa Yatidharma).

31. Kṣamā.
32. Mārdava.
33. Ārjava.
34. Nirlobhatā.
35. Tapa (Tapas).
36. Saṁyama.
37. Satya.
38. Śauċa.
39. Akiṁċinatva.
40. Brahmaċarya.

Five Ċāritra or Rules of Conduct.

41. Sāmāyika ċāritra.
42. Ċhedopasthāpanīya ċāritra.
43. Parihāraviśuddha ċāritra.
44. Sūkṣmasamparāya ċāritra.
45. Yathākhyāta ċāritra.

Twelve Bhāvanā (or *Anuprekṣā*).

46. Anitya bhāvanā.		Nine first Reflections.
47. Aśaraṇa	,,	
48. Saṁsāra	,,	
49. Ekatva	,,	
50. Anyatva	,,	
51. Aśauċa	,,	
52. Āśrava	,,	
53. Saṁvara	,,	
54. Nirjarā	,,	
55. Loka	,,	Three additional Reflections.
56. Bodhibīja	,,	
57. Dharma	,,	

SEVENTH CATEGORY: BANDHA.

Bondage to Karma is of four kinds:

1. Prakṛiti.
2. Sthiti.
3. Anubhāga.
4. Pradeśa.

EIGHTH CATEGORY: NIRJARĀ.

Karma can be destroyed by:—*Six Exterior* (Bāhya) *Austerities.*

1. Anaśana.
   - *a.* Itvara.
   - *b.* Yāvatkathika.
2. Uṇodarī.
3. Vṛittisaṅkṣepa.
   - *a.* Dravya.
   - *b.* Kṣetra.
   - *c.* Kāḷa.
   - *d.* Bhāva.
4. Rasatyāga.
5. Kāyakleśa.
6. Saṁlīnatā.
   - *a.* Indriya saṁlīnatā.
   - *b.* Kaṣāya saṁlīnatā.
   - *c.* Yoga saṁlīnatā.
   - *d.* Viviktaċaryā.

Six Interior (Ābhyantara) *Austerities.*

1. Prayaśćitta.
2. Vinaya.
   - *a.* Jñāna vinaya.
   - *b.* Darśana „
   - *c.* Ċāritra „
   - *d.* Mana „
   - *e.* Vaċana „
   - *f.* Kāya „
   - *g.* Kalpa „
3. Vaiyāvaċċa (Vaiyāvṛitya).
4. Svādhyāya.
5. Dhyāna.
   - Ārta dhyāna. } evil.
   - Raudra dhyāna. } evil.
   - Dharma dhyāna. } good.
   - Śukla dhyāna. } good.
6. Utsarga.

NINTH CATEGORY: MOKṢA.

Inhabited by Fifteen Kinds of Siddha.

1. Jina Siddha.
2. Ajina Siddha.
3. Tīrtha Siddha.
4. Atīrtha Siddha.
5. Gṛihaliṅga Siddha.
6. Anyaliṅga Siddha.
7. Svaliṅga Siddha.
8. Pūlliṅga Siddha.
9. Strīliṅga Siddha.
10. Napuṁsakaliṅga Siddha.
11. Buddhabohī Siddha.
12. Pratyekabuddha Siddha.
13. Svayambuddha Siddha.
14. Eka Siddha.
15. Aneka Siddha.

End of the Nine Categories.

ANALYSIS OF KARMA.

Four Sources of Karma.

Avirati.
Kaṣāya.
Yoga.
Mithyātva.

Eight Kinds of Karma.

A. Ghātin Karma.

1. Jñānāvaraṇīya karma.
   - *a.* Matijñānāvaraṇīya.
     - Utpātikī.
     - Vainayikī.
     - Pāriṇāmikī.
     - Kāmikī.
   - *b.* Śrutajñānāvaraṇīya.
   - *c.* Manaḥparyāyajñānāvaraṇīya.
   - *d.* Avadhijñānāvaraṇīya.
   - *e.* Kevalajñānāvaraṇīya.
   - *f.* Mati ajñāna.
   - *g.* Śruta ajñāna.
   - *h.* Vibhaṅga jñāna.

2. Darśanāvaraṇīya karma.
3. Mohanīya karma.
   Some of the twenty-eight divisions :
      Mithyātvamohanīya karma.
      Miśramohanīya karma.
      Samyaktvamohanīya karma.
      Darśanamohanīya karma.
      Ċāritramohanīya karma.
4. Antarāya karma.

B. Aghātin karma.

5. Vedanīya karma.
      Śātavedanīya.
      Aśātavedanīya.
6. Āyu karma.
   a. Deva āyu karma.
      Jyotiṣī āyu karma.
      Vyantara āyu karma.
      Vaimānika āyu karma.
      Bhavanapati āyu karma.
   b. Manuṣya āyu karma.
      Karmabhūmi { Asi, Masi, Kasi.
      Akarmabhūmi.
   c. Tiryañċ āyu karma.
   d. Naraka āyu karma.
7. Nāma karma.
8. Gotra karma.

Three Tenses of Karma.

Sattā karma.
Bandha karma.
Udaya karma.

Two types of Karma.

Nikāċita *and* Śithila karma.

Fourteen Steps of Liberation from Karma.

(Ċauda Guṇasthānaka.)

1. Mithyātva guṇasthānaka.
      Vyaktamithyātva guṇasthānaka.
      Avyaktamithyātva guṇasthānaka.
2. Sāśvāsadana guṇasthānaka.

3. Miśra guṇasthānaka.
4. Aviratisamyagdṛiṣṭi guṇasthānaka.
5. Deśavirati (*or* Saṁyatāsaṁyata) guṇasthānaka.
    a. Jaghanya deśavirati.
    b. Madhyama deśavirati.
    c. Utkṛiṣṭa deśavirati.
6. Pramatta guṇasthānaka.
7. Apramatta guṇasthānaka.
8. Niyatibādara (*or* Apūrvakaraṇa) guṇasthānaka.
9. Aniyatibādara guṇasthānaka.
10. Sūkṣmasamparāya guṇasthānaka.
11. Upaśāntamoha guṇasthānaka.
12. Kṣīṇamoha guṇasthānaka.
13. Sayogikevalī guṇasthānaka.
14. Ayogikevalī guṇasthānaka.

II. THE TWENTY-FOUR TĪRTHAṄKARA OF THE PRESENT AGE[1]

Name.	*Colour.*	*Cognizance.*	*Attendant Spirits.*	*Born at.*	*Died at.*
1. Ṛiṣabhadeva *or* Ādinātha	Yellow *or* Golden	Bull	Gomukha and Ċakreśvarī	Vinītānagara	Aṣṭāpada.
2. Ajitanātha	Yellow *or* Golden	Elephant	Mahāyakṣa and Ajitabalā	Ayodhyā	Sameta Śikhara.
3. Sambhavanātha	Yellow *or* Golden	Horse	Trimukha and Duritārī (*Digambara* Prajñaptī)	Śrāvastī	Sameta Śikhara.
4. Abhinandana	Yellow *or* Golden	Ape	Nāyaka and Kālikā (*Dig.* Yakṣeśvara and Vajraśṛiṅkhalā)	Ayodhyā	Sameta Śikhara.
5. Sumatinātha	Yellow *or* Golden	Red Goose *or* Partridge, *or* Curlew	Tumburu and Mahākālī (*Dig.* Puruṣadattā)	Ayodhyā	Sameta Śikhara.
6. Padmaprabhu	Red	Red Lotus flower	Kusuma and Śyāmā (*Dig.* Manovegā [Manoguptī])	Kauśambī	Sameta Śikhara.
7. Supārśvanātha	Yellow *or* Golden	Svastika	Mātaṅga and Śāntā (*Dig.* Varanandi and Kālī)	Benares	Sameta Śikhara.
8. Ċandraprabhu	White	Moon	Vijaya and Bhṛikuṭī (*Dig.* Jvālāmālinī)	Ċandrapura	Sameta Śikhara.
9. Suvidhinātha	White	Crocodile (? *Dig.* Crab)	Ajita and Sutārakā (*Dig.* Mahākālī)	Kānaṇḍīnagara	Sameta Śikhara.
10. Śītaḷanātha	Yellow *or* Golden	Śrīvatsa figure (? *Dig. Ficus religiosa*)	Brahmā and Aśokā (*Dig.* Mānavī)	Bhadrapura	Sameta Śikhara.
11. Śreyāṁsanātha	Yellow *or* Golden	Rhinoceros	Yakṣeta and Mānavī (*Dig.* Īśvara and Gaurī)	Siṁhapura	Sameta Śikhara.

12. Vāsupūjya	Red	Male Buffalo	Kumāra and Ċaṇḍā (*Dig.* Gāndhārī)	Ċampāpurī	Ċampāpurī.
13. Vimalanātha	Yellow *or* Golden	Boar	Ṣāṇmukha and Viditā (*Dig.* Vairoṭī)	Kampīlya-pura	Sameta Śikhara.
14. Anantanātha	Yellow *or* Golden	Hawk (? *Dig.* Bear)	Pātāla and Aṅkuśā (*Dig.* Anantamatī)	Ayodhyā	Sameta Śikhara.
15. Dharmanātha	Yellow *or* Golden	Thunderbolt	Kinnara and Kandarpā (*Dig.* Mānasī)	Ratnapurī	Sameta Śikhara.
16. Śāntinātha	Yellow *or* Golden	Deer [2]	Garuḍa and Nirvāṇī (*Dig.* Kimpuruṣa and Mahāmānasī)	Gajapura *or* Hastināpura	Sameta Śikhara.
17. Kunthunātha	Yellow *or* Golden	Goat	Gandharva and Balā (*Dig.* Vijayā)	Gajapura *or* Hastināpura	Sameta Śikhara.
18. Aranātha	Yellow *or* Golden	Nandāvartta Diagram	Yakṣeṭa and Dhaṇā (*Dig.* Kendra and Ajitā)	Gajapura *or* Hastināpura	Sameta Śikhara.
19. Mallinātha (acc. to the Śvetāmbara, a woman)	Blue	Water-jar	Kubera and Dharaṇapriyā (*Dig.* Aparājitā)	Mathurā	Sameta Śikhara.
20. Munisuvrata	Black	Tortoise	Varuṇa and Naradattā (*Dig.* Bahurūpiṇī)	Rājagṛiha	Sameta Śikhara.
21. Naminātha	Yellow *or* Golden	Blue Lotus (*Dig.* Aśoka tree)	Bhṛikuṭi and Gandhārī (*Dig.* Ċāmuṇḍī)	Mathurā	Sameta Śikhara.
22. Neminātha	Black	Conch Shell	Gomedha and Ambikā (*Dig.* Sarvāhṇa and Kūṣmāṇḍinī)	Saurīpura	Girnār.
23. Pārśvanātha	Blue	Snake	Pārśvayakṣa *or* Dharaṇendra and Padmāvatī	Benares	Sameta Śikhara.
24. Mahāvīra *or* Vardhamāna	Yellow *or* Golden	Lion	Mātaṅga and Siddhāyikā	Kuṇḍagrāma	Pāvāpurī.

[1] For fuller particulars see Dr. Burgess's Appendix to Bühler, *Indian Sect of the Jainas*, pp. 66 ff.
[2] According to Burgess, *Antelope*.

INDEX